CERTAIN LANGUAGE SKILLS IN CHILDREN

Their Development and Interrelationships

UNIVERSITY OF MINNESOTA
THE INSTITUTE OF CHILD WELFARE
MONOGRAPH SERIES NO. XXVI

Certain Language Skills in Children

THEIR DEVELOPMENT AND INTERRELATIONSHIPS

BY

MILDRED C. TEMPLIN

ASSOCIATE PROFESSOR, INSTITUTE OF CHILD WELFARE
UNIVERSITY OF MINNESOTA

1957

THE UNIVERSITY OF MINNESOTA PRESS

MINNEAPOLIS

PRINTED AT THE NORTH CENTRAL PUBLISHING COMPANY, ST. PAUL

Library of Congress Catalog Card Number: 57-8922

PUBLISHED IN GREAT BRITAIN, INDIA, AND PAKISTAN BY THE OXFORD UNIVERSITY PRESS, LONDON, BOMBAY, AND KARACHI

FOREWORD

Language is fundamental to the normal intellectual, social, and emotional development of children. Clinical evidence is overwhelming that children who, because of sensory defect, are unable to communicate do not grow normally in these respects. There is no question but that there is a reciprocal relation among these several areas, and that what we call healthy personality development requires intercommunication of children with children as well as of children with adults.

In order to conduct meaningful "dynamic" studies of social relations, personality growth, and the like, we must first have normative studies of children's developmental performances in articulation, vocabulary, and communication of meaning. The earlier monographs in this series by McCarthy and Davis established a groundwork of such studies, delineated areas of investigation, and supplied norms of fundamental significance. The present study goes well beyond these earlier efforts on two counts: (1) It collects in one study on one sample of children normative measures of articulation of speech sounds, sound discrimination, sentence structure, and vocabulary, thus allowing the study of interrelationships among these measures. (2) The design permits a comparison of contemporary norms with data established on similarly selected children in an earlier period. The monograph reports in considerable detail comparisons with existing studies.

Two important areas of findings can be mentioned: (1) New light is thrown on sex differences, and the often-assumed superiority of girls over boys is not entirely substantiated. (2) Attention is called to a possible effect of mass media and other sources of stimulation on children's verbal performance, since children now show greater loquacity. Thus, the study is not only of practical significance to those who wish to establish language, speech, or communication skills in children; it has implications for the theory of child development and for interpreting the impact of social change on children.

This monograph is a detailed, painstaking, workmanlike addition to the important contributions to language study which have already appeared in this series.

Dale B. Harris
Director, Institute of Child Welfare
University of Minnesota

ACKNOWLEDGMENTS

In the completion of this study I have received the cooperation of many. Although it is not possible to mention each person, I have appreciated each effort.

I wish to thank the children who were subjects in this study and all those who made it possible for me to locate them.

I wish to thank the principals and teachers in whose schools and the parents in whose homes the study was carried on.

I wish to thank Irene Andresen, Mary Ann Armstrong, Beverly Ayers, Albert Dreyer, Edith Holmes, Ronald Johnson, Anna Martorana and Richard Walker who as graduate assistants in the Institute of Child Welfare, and Lorna Mattson who as a senior in Education assisted in gathering data for this study.

I wish to thank Dr. Harriet E. Blodgett for obtaining needed intelligence tests.

I wish to thank Mrs. Evelyn Deno, Dr. Dale B. Harris, and Dr. Hildred Schuell for reading the manuscript.

I wish to thank my mother for her encouragement throughout the project.

This study was supported partially by grants-in-aid from the Parents' Institute Fund administered through the Graduate School of the University of Minnesota, and partially by the Institute of Child Welfare of the University of Minnesota. For this support I wish to thank Dr. Theodore C. Blegen, Dean of the Graduate School, and Dr. John E. Anderson, former Director, and Dr. Dale B. Harris, Director of the Institute of Child Welfare.

M. C. T.

CONTENTS

LIST OF TABLES

LIST OF TABLES IN APPENDIXES

LIST OF FIGURES

CERTAIN LANGUAGE SKILLS IN CHILDREN

I. INTRODUCTION

The development of language in children has long been an area of interest. The early biographers of babies reported their observations on the development of speech sounds, the use of the sentence, and the size and content of the young child's vocabulary. Since the beginnings of scientific study of child behavior, research studies have been concerned with many aspects of language. Evidence of the extent and variety of such interest is concretely provided in the 777 titles listed in the bibliography of a recent summary of language development in children (28). Many of these titles refer to investigations of children's language and speech. However, only a relatively small proportion of these have been carried on with substantial numbers of children carefully selected to meet a variety of sampling criteria. In only a few of these studies is more than one aspect of language investigated in the same children.

This monograph presents norms on the development of articulation of speech sounds, sound discrimination, sentence structure, and vocabulary as well as the interrelations of these language skills in children of preschool and elementary school age. It reports a normative and descriptive study of the development of these aspects of language over a five-year age range. The interrelations among these language skills are explored at the ages tested, since a measure of each language skill studied is available on every child in the sample. Despite the amount of research in language that has been going on for many years, data are often not available for many language skills on the range of performance which may be expected at any given age and the changes in performance which may be expected to occur with increasing age. The relationships among the expressions of language skills have been studied very little. This study presents some information in these areas which can be valuable both in studying and in handling children.

Factual materials which can serve as a basis for raising further questions and for formulating hypotheses are made available out of the descriptive study of children's performance on different aspects of language and out of the patterns of interrelations observed. Persons concerned with the growth and development of child behavior find detailed descriptions of changes with age in language performance as much a part of the total developmental picture as motor, social, or intellectual growth. Such information is needed to help ensure the most effective research with young children. Since verbal expression is frequently the medium through which social interaction, cognition, and other behavior is studied, knowledge of the probable verbal performance of children can often be vital in determining the most satisfactory design for an experimental study. This is particularly true when young preschool children are subjects of an experiment. Such information is valuable in setting up the most satisfactory procedures to be used in the study of young children as well as in interpreting the results of such study.

Anyone dealing with young children in a clinical or remedial setting has practical use for normative data and for data on the interrelationships among language skills. The clinical child psychologist, the school psychologist, the school nurse, and the pediatrician, among others, are becoming increasingly concerned with all aspects of the child and his behavior. Better understanding of a child can be gained if his language production as well as his intellectual, social, personality, and physical characteristics are included in an evaluation. Normative information on language production is needed to provide a standard against which the language status of any individual child may be evaluated. For those persons interested specifically in the development of language production or in the correction of deviations in it, detailed normative data in several language areas has a peculiar value.

The level of language production attained at any age is related, without doubt, to a variety of factors in the linguistic environment of the child. Earlier studies have shown that the number of adults in the child's immediate environment, the socioeconomic status of his home, and many other factors are associated with the level of language usage he attains. It is probable that if currently accurate norms of language production are to be always available, such studies need to be conducted periodically. The present study was begun after the introduction of television into many homes. Thus it is likely that more adult language was present in the environment of the children who were the subjects than would have been true even a few years earlier. On the other hand, it may be that the effect of such language stimulation in the child's environment would be even greater today than when the first data for this study were gathered just a few years ago.

Another reason why no present normative study of language can be really definitive is related to the units of measurement used in the analysis. In the study reported here, the traditional units — sounds, words, clauses, etc. — have been used in the measurement of growth in the language areas. Within a relatively few years different types of measurement may well be found more useful for such investigation. In the study of articulation of speech sounds, for example, the traditional vowel and consonant elements and blends have been used. It may be that a more functional unit, possibly a larger unit, will be found more useful in the future. This problem of units of measurement is not unique to language study. As the measuring techniques and procedures in any area are improved, it is possible to extend and refine information obtained in that area.

The study reported here is primarily concerned with the characteristics of the language produced by young children. Only sound discrimination is not measured in their overt language activity. There are many vital areas and relations in the linguistic process which do not come within the scope of the present investigation. It is not concerned with the function of language or the needs of the human being which may be met and satisfied through verbalization. Neither does it explore the role of language in personality development or in the social, emotional, and cognitive behavior of children. It is a descriptive study of the growth and interrelations of articulation of speech sounds, sound discrimination, vocabulary, and sentence structure in children from 3 to 8 years.

II. THE EXPERIMENT

The purpose of this study is twofold: (1) to describe the growth from 3 to 8 years of four aspects of language: articulation of speech sounds, speech sound discrimination, sentence structure, and vocabulary; and (2) to investigate the interrelations of these aspects of language over the age range studied.

The Subjects

Since the results of this study will provide normative data on language skills, rigid criteria were maintained in the selection of the sample. An attempt was made to control factors known to be related to language skills, such as age, sex, intelligence, family constellation, language spoken at home, bilingualism, twinning, impaired intelligence, and defective hearing. An equal number of boys and girls at discrete age levels are included. Intelligence was indirectly controlled through the selection of a representative sample according to father's occupation. The children were white, monolingual singletons, of normal intelligence, and with no gross evidence of hearing loss.

Age. The 480 children in this study range from 3 to 8 years. This age range covers a substantial part of the period of linguistic development: roughly from early use of language as communication until essential maturity in some aspects of language production has been achieved. Since early language growth is very rapid, it would have been desirable to include younger children. However, after a number of 2.5-year-old children had been tested, it was evident that the techniques used in this study were not satisfactory at this earlier age.

Since it was not possible to extend the upper age level until maturity was attained in all four aspects of language, an arbitrary cut-off had to be made. There is considerable experimental evidence that articulation is practically mature at 8 years of age (35), and all the grammatical constructions used by adults appear, at least in a rudimentary form, in the speech of 8-year-olds (5). Sound discrimination ability improves somewhat after 8 years of age (48). Size of vocabulary has been shown to increase into adulthood. Since a kind of maturity is likely to be attained in one area of language studied and is approached in two others by 8 years, this age was taken as the upper limit in the sample. Although language growth continues after 8, tremendous development has been accomplished by this age, and much future growth is in the perfection rather than in the introduction of new types of linguistic expression.

The total sample of 480 cases is made up of eight subsamples of 60 cases each at 3, 3.5, 4, 4.5, 5, 6, 7, and 8 years. The half-year intervals between 3 and 5 were selected since development is more rapid in this early period. More frequent measures at these earlier ages make the results more sensitive to growth changes. By 5, whole-year intervals between measurements were deemed satisfactory for the purpose of this study.

Each subsample is a discrete age sample since the children were tested within one month of their designated ages. Those in the 3-year subsample range in age from 2 years 11 months to 3 years 1 month; those in the 3.5 year subsample range from 3 years 5 months to 3 years 7 months; and so on. The exceptions to this standard, allowed when a child was within a day or two of the accepted age, are few and do not preclude the consideration of discrete age groups.

Sex. Of the 480 cases in the study, 240 were boys and 240 were girls. For each of the age subsamples, 30 boys and 30 girls were included to make up the 60 subjects.

Source of sample. Children 6 years and older were enrolled in the Minneapolis public schools. Of the 5-year-olds, 29 were in the public school kindergartens and 31 in the nursery schools of Minneapolis and St. Paul, Minnesota; of the children 4.5 years and younger, 202 were tested in various nursery schools and 38 in their homes. The preschool children were located in nursery schools, through registration cards of the Minneapolis public school system, or from survey data in the Hennepin County Welfare office. Sex and birthdate of younger siblings and occupation of father are listed on the public school registration cards. A list of the fourteen public schools and the twenty-one nursery schools from which children were selected is given in Appendix I.

Socioeconomic level. The total sample and each of the age subsamples were selected according to father's occupation to be representative of the United States urban population. The occupation of the father, as reported on school census records, enrolment blanks in the various nursery schools, or survey records at the Hennepin County Welfare office, was classified according to the Minnesota Occupational Scale (16). The proportion of cases to be included at each socioeconomic status (SES) level was calculated from the occupational distribution of the 1940 United States population classified according to this scale. Since the sample is an urban one, SES level IV, a rural category, was omitted in the calculation. As shown in Table 1, the number and per cent of subjects are identical at levels I, II, III, and V for both the theoretical and the actual samples. Twenty-five level VI subjects have been substituted in level VII. Occupational levels I, II, and III are combined into an upper socioeconomic status group (USES) and levels V, VI, and VII into a lower socioeconomic status group (LSES). Thirty per cent of the entire sample is in the USES and 70 per cent in the LSES group. The same proportions have been maintained for each of the age subsamples.

Table 1. Number and Percentage of Subjects in Theoretical Sample and in Actual Sample, by Socioeconomic Status *

Socioeconomic Status	Theoretical Sample		Actual Sample	
	No.	%	No.	%
Upper				
Class I. Professional	16	3.3	16	3.3
Class II. Semiprofessional and managerial	48	10.0	48	10.0
Class III. Clerical, skilled trades, and retail business	80	16.7	80	16.7
Total	144	30.0	144	30.0
Lower				
Class V. Semiskilled occupations, minor clerical, and minor business	128	26.7	128	26.7
Class VI. Slightly skilled trades and occupations requiring little training	80	16.6	105	21.9
Class VII. Day laborers	128	26.7	103	21.4
Total	336	70.0	336	70.0

* Category IV, a rural category, was not used in this study.

In each of the separate age subsamples the number of subjects is accurate for levels I through V: only at levels VI and VII are there any discrepancies. According to the theoretical distribution sixteen cases in each age subsample should be drawn from level VII. Substitutions for this level from level VI have been made as follows: two cases at 8 years, one at age 7, two at 6, three at 5, four at 4.5, four at 4, six at 3.5, and three cases at 3 years.

It should be pointed out that the distinction between classes VI and VII in this study may not always be clear-cut. Only those children whose fathers' occupations were listed as "laborer," "itinerant," "unemployed," or specific unskilled jobs were included in level VII. "Laborer" was by far the most frequent designation classified in level VII. Some of these probably were not unskilled but slightly skilled or even semi-skilled workers.

In selecting a child as a subject, his neighborhood as well as his father's occupation was considered. Children whose fathers' occupations were classified as SES level I or II were not included if they lived in the poorest sections of the cities, and those in SES level VI or VII were not selected from the better sections. In substituting level VI for level VII cases, children living in the poorest areas of the cities were selected.

Intelligence. Intelligence test measures were available on all but three of the children 6 years of age and older. These children had been given the Stanford-Binet in kindergarten by their teachers, by trained examiners at a later time, or by competent students in a testing class. The kindergarten tests are made up of items from a narrow age range of the Stanford-Binet and are administered by the teachers who have received training only on these particular items. The use of the IQ's obtained by kindergarten teachers and by students in training may be questioned, but they are probably at least as satisfactory as the results of group tests at these ages. The Stanford-Binet was not given children under 5 because it was thought that the time needed for the administration of 300 individual intelligence tests was too great for the value of the information to be gained. IQ-equivalents based on the Ammons Full-Range Picture Vocabulary Test scores were computed for these lower age groups (1).

Table 2. Mean IQ and IQ-Equivalents for 3-to-8-Year-Old Subsamples by Age, Sex, and Socioeconomic Status

	Boys (N = 30)		Girls (N = 30)		USES (N = 18)		LSES (N = 42)		Total Subsample (N = 60)	
CA	Mean	SD	Mean	SD	Mean	SD	Mean	SD	Mean	SD
					IQ-equivalents *					
3	126.5	21.2	119.6	18.4	127.1	22.8	121.3	18.7	123.0	20.0
3.5	121.0	17.8	115.7	15.7	125.1	17.2	115.5	16.0	118.4	16.8
4	113.9	17.4	114.2	17.5	118.9	19.2	112.0	15.8	114.1	17.4
4.5	107.9	16.4	112.7	17.4	117.6	15.4	107.1	16.8	110.0	17.0
5	103.3	15.8	113.6	16.2	109.7	15.2	107.9	17.3	108.4	16.0
					IQ's					
6	110.7	13.1	103.3	9.5	116.9	13.0	107.9	9.6	107.0	11.5
7	107.4	16.5	106.3	12.2	117.1	16.2	102.6	11.1	106.8	12.1
8	108.8	12.3	109.5	13.2	119.2	9.4	104.9	11.6	109.2	12.8

* Based on scores on the Ammons Full-Range Picture Vocabulary Test.

In Table 2 the mean IQ and IQ-equivalents for boys and girls and USES and LSES groups for each subsample are given. The IQ's for the 6-, 7-, and 8-year-olds are somewhat above average, but for an urban population the means are not exceptionally high. The mean reported IQ for all kindergarten children tested by teachers in the Minneapolis public schools in 1949–50 was comparable to these figures.*

The mean IQ for the combined 6-to-8-year-old subjects is 107.0, SD 13.1: that for the boys is 109.0, SD 14.1, for the girls 106.4, SD 11.9. This difference of 2.6 points in favor of the boys is not statistically significant ($t = 1.32$). The mean IQ for the USES group is 117.7, SD 13.1, and that for the LSES group is 105.1, SD 11.0. This difference is significant at the .01 level ($t = 6.16$). The range in IQ for the combined 6-to-8-year-olds is from 84 to 152.

With increasing age from 3 to 5 the mean IQ-equivalents decrease steadily until at the 4.5- and 5-year levels the IQ-equivalents are quite similar to the IQ's obtained on the Stanford-Binet for the 6-to-8 year subsamples which were similarly selected. The range in IQ-equivalents is from 74 to 172.

The mean IQ-equivalents at the early preschool ages are substantially higher than the IQ's at the primary ages. That the IQ-equivalents based on Ammons' tables are not satisfactory at these early ages is more probable than that the younger children are exceptionally bright, since the children at all ages are selected to meet the same SES criteria. Ammons' calculation of the IQ-equivalents is based on 30 cases at 3, 4, and 5 years, and the subjects at any designated age include a range of one year; i.e., "3-year-olds" range in age between 3 and 4 years. This sample is not so large numerically nor is it composed of as narrow an age range at any of the designated ages as the sample of the present study. The sample, however, was selected as representative of the occupational distribution of "husbands of white women with children under five" (1:8) based on the 1940 United States census data. This is a good sampling method. The Minnesota Occupational Scale and the census classification of occupations cannot be directly compared but, in general, the distribution by occupation of fathers of preschool children and the sample in the present study do not differ substantially.

The mean IQ-equivalents for all the subjects between 3 and 5 years is 114.8, SD 17.4: that for the boys is 114.5, SD 17.7, and that for the girls is 115.1, SD 17.0. This difference between the sexes is not statistically significant since $t = 1.36$. The mean IQ-equivalent for the USES

* IQ data were obtained from the records of the Child Study Department, Minneapolis Public Schools.

group over this age range is 119.7, SD 17.9; that for the LSES group is 112.8, SD 16.9. This difference is significant at the .01 level ($t = 2.93$). The range of IQ-equivalents for the combined 3-to-5-year-old group is from 74 to 172. Only two scores were below 80.

One 3.5-year-old child was rejected because of suspected intellectual inadequacy. This child was judged by the author to be like a 2-year-old from his physical and motor development. He was unable to cooperate on most of the tests. The two children receiving IQ-equivalents of 74 and 79 were not excluded since they responded to the language tests adequately.

Omitted cases. Although 480 children are included in the study, 58 subjects were excluded because they did not complete all the tests. The usual cause was inability to complete the testing within the one-month deviation from the designated age either because of absence from school or illness. In only three or four instances were the tests not completed because the child did not cooperate.

The Language Areas Measured

The four areas of linguistic skill considered in this study are the articulation of speech sounds, sound discrimination ability, the structure of the sentence, and vocabulary. All the data were gathered in controlled test and observational situations.

Articulation. Articulation of speech sounds is measured in tests especially constructed for this study by the author. These tests assess the ability of children to produce standard English sounds correctly in words, and not merely their ability to utter these sounds. The articulation tests consist of 176 sound elements measured in the child's production of selected words. These include 69 consonant sounds in the initial, medial, and final positions; 71 double-consonant blends; 19 triple-consonant blends; 12 vowels; and 5 diphthongs. The double- and triple-consonant blends are subdivided into initial, final, and final-reversed consonant blends. For example, "pl" forms an initial sound in "play," a final sound in "apple" and is reversed as "lp" in "help." The various sound elements tested are composed of 25 different consonant sounds, 12 vowels, and 5 diphthongs.

Although all children were tested on the same sound elements, different test words were used for children 3 to 5 and children 6 to 8. In Appendix II, A page 156, the test words used with each group are presented. A previous investigation has shown that the measured articulation of a child does not vary significantly with the particular word in which the sound is tested (49). Using different test words permitted some overlap of items in the preschool tests of articulation and sound discrimination, thus shortening the testing time.

Children 6 to 8 either read the test words or repeated them after the examiner. The preschool children repeated the words after the examiner or uttered them spontaneously in the identification of pictures. It has been previously demonstrated that similar results are obtained in the measurement of speech sound articulation of normal children whether a repeated or a spontaneous utterance is used (49). This flexible technique ensured a measure of each test sound on all children.

The following articulation scores were obtained: total articulation scores and subscores for each type of sound whether consonant, double-consonant blend, triple-consonant blend, vowel, or diphthong.* Since each correct utterance was counted as 1, the maximum total score was 176, and the maximum subscores were 69 for the consonant sounds, 71 for the double-consonant blends, 19 for the triple-consonant blends, 12 for the vowels, and 5 for the diphthongs. Counts were also made of the number and percentage of correct utterances of the consonant sounds according to the position of the sound in the test word and according to the type of consonant sound. The maximum scores according to position of the sound in a word were 23 for initial, 25 for medial, and 21 for final consonants. Eight nasals, 18 plosives, 23 fricatives, 12 semivowels, and 8 combinations were measured, and the maximum score for each sound type is the same as the number of sounds tested.

If any sound was not correctly produced, it was noted whether the error was an omission, a substitution of another standard English sound, or a defective sound. All substitutions of standard English sounds were transcribed using the International Phonetic Alphabet (IPA), and defective sounds were transcribed or described as adequately as possible. In the text, however, the sounds tested are presented using English letters and diacritical markings, since these are probably more familiar to

* Vowel sounds are all sounds produced with vibration of the vocal cords and without interference with the air stream sufficient to produce audible friction as it is emitted. Diphthongs are made up of two vowel sounds uttered in a continuous production of sound. Consonants are produced with or without the vibration of the vocal cords, and with some interference in the emission of the air stream. In this study, consonant sounds are classified in the following way. Nasals are those few sounds which are emitted through the nose. Plosives are sounds which result when the air stream is suddenly released after having been dammed up behind the lips, the tip of the tongue, or the back of the tongue. Fricatives are those sounds which are produced with some audible friction. Semivowels are sounds which are emitted with less interference than consonants but with more than vowels. Combinations are two consonants so consistently and intimately produced together that they are recognized as a single standard English sound. Consonant blends are two or more consonant sounds produced consecutively.

the majority of the readers. The specific vowels, dipthongs, and consonants tested are presented in Table 3.

Throughout the text the position of a sound in any test word is indicated by its relation to a dash (or dashes) representing the other letters. For example, "m–" indicates that the "m" is at the beginning of a word, "–m–" indicates that it is in the middle of a word, and "–m" that it is at the end of a word.

Table 3. Symbols Designating Each of the Consonants, Vowels, and Diphthongs Measured

Symbol	Illustrative Word	Symbol	Illustrative Word
Consonants		hw	*wh*en
m	*m*outh	ch	*ch*ip
n	*n*ail	j	a*g*e
ng	swi*ng*	*Vowels*	
p	*p*ie	ē	b*ee*t
t	*t*oe	ĭ	p*i*n
k	*c*ard	ĕ	*e*nd
b	*b*oy	ă	b*a*ck
d	*d*ish	ŏ	r*o*cks
g	*g*oat	ŭ	g*u*n
f	*f*eet	o͝o	b*oo*k
th	*th*in	o͞o	s*ou*p
s	*s*eat	ō	c*o*ne
sh	*sh*ip	ô	b*a*ll
v	*v*ery	ȧ	*a*mount
t͟h	*th*is	ûr	b*ir*d
z	*z*ipper		
zh	plea*s*ure	*Diphthongs*	
r	*r*ing	ū	m*u*sic
l	*l*amb	ā	s*ai*l
h	*h*ouse	ī	t*ie*
w	*w*et	ou	cl*ou*d
y	*y*ellow	oi	b*oi*l

Sound discrimination. A measure of sound discrimination was included in this study because of the possible relation between this ability and the accurate articulation of speech sounds in words. It was deemed particularly important to include this measure since articulation was assessed in words. Although motor and perceptual skills are involved in the production of all sounds, the importance of the perceptual skill is probably increased when the sound is uttered in the proper position in a standard English word. Different techniques of measurement of sound discrimination were used with the preschool and school-age children since differences in the developmental levels made the use of the same technique impracticable.

The technique used with the 6-to-8-year-old children is similiar to that used with older children and adults. Fifty pairs of nonsense syllables were uttered by the examiner, and each pair of syllables was to be judged as "same" or "different" by the child. Each item was made up of a pair of identical syllables, or a minimal pair which differed in only one phoneme. Examples of the two types of pairs are "le-le" and "esh-ech." The items used in the present study were the 50 most discriminating selected from an earlier investigation of sound discrimination by the author (48). These particular items have not been published previously, but are presented in Appendix II, B page 159. Since each correct response counted 1, the total possible score is 50.

A test of sound discrimination constructed especially for use with preschool children in this study is based on the identification of similarity and difference in the acoustic value of familiar words which can be pictured. Pairs of pictures of familiar objects whose names are words similar in pronunciation except for single sound elements (such as "box" and "blocks") were pasted on a single card and presented to the child. The child was asked to point to the picture of the thing denoted by the word the examiner said. Ninety-two words were used in fifty-nine pairs in the test. The child pointed out his choice of pictures in response to the stimulus word uttered by the examiner in at least two presentations of all the cards. If two identifications were correct, a third presentation of the cards was not made. If the stimulus word was both correctly and incorrectly identified, a third presentation of the pair of pictures was made. The limitations of young children's vocabularies and the necessity of picturing the words restricted the sound pairs that could be used to measure sound discrimination at this age. Some of the discriminations which at the older ages had been found most satisfactory could not be included since they did not occur in simple words which could be pictured. The preschool sound discrimination test used is in Appendix II, C page 159.

In order to feel more confident that sound discrimination rather than vocabulary or intelligence is being measured, it is necessary to ascertain whether or not the child is familiar with the words used. In an attempt to ensure that the test words used would likely be known by the children, test words were taken from those used in the vocabulary sections of preschool intelligence tests, in preschool word and story books, and in children's conversations. To determine whether each test word was in the child's vocabulary of recognition, duplicate or "reasonable facsimiles" of the pictures used in the sound discrimination test were mounted on separate cards and presented to each child for identification. By using twenty-nine of the same words, both in the preschool picture sound discrimination test and in the measurement of articulation, it was possible to reduce the number of words to be uttered or identified by each of the younger children. Since these tests were used with three hundred of the children, a substantial saving of time is represented.

It is likely that differences in the intrinsic interest of some pictures and variations in the familiarity of the test words affect the child's performance on this test. Various techniques of scoring were tried out and are discussed in Chapter IV.

Sentence development. Fifty verbal utterances were obtained from each child and then used as a basis for the study of the length of response, the different words, the parts of speech, and the grammatical structure used in a child-adult situation. These verbalizations were obtained by duplicating as nearly as possible the technique developed by McCarthy (27). McCarthy used picture books and toys. One book contained pictures of animals, another illustrated Mother Goose rhymes. The toys consisted of "a little red auto, a cat that squeaked, a telephone with a bell, a little tin mouse, a music box and a small ball." In the present study similar books and toys were used. Davis (5) modified McCarthy's technique somewhat by selecting materials that would likely have greater appeal to boys. This was not done in the present study.

Children were taken into a room with an adult examiner and, after rapport had been established, fifty remarks of the child, usually consecutive, were taken down. The adult wrote precisely what the child said. In the cases of a very few of the older, very verbal children, it was not possible to write down fifty consecutive verbalizations. Each of the remarks, however, was recorded in its entirety. The length of each response was determined by the natural break in verbalization of the child himself rather than on the basis of the complete adult sentence.

Vocabulary. The recognition vocabulary of all children was measured, although different vocabulary tests were used with the children above 6 and those from 3 to 5. With the older group the Seashore-Eckerson English Recognition Vocabulary Test was used (40). This test is based on a sample of one word taken from every eighth page in the Funk and Wagnall unabridged dictionary and permits an estimate of the child's total recognition vocabulary. It is a multiple-choice test, in which the choice words are of no greater difficulty than the word to be defined.

The test has been modified for use with primary-grade children by M. K. Smith (47). In this modification ninety to ninety-nine words are presented individually to the children, who are credited with knowing the word if they define it spontaneously or if they select the correct choice from the alternate choices which have been "translated" into child language. Correction for guessing is made in the suggested scoring. (See Chapter VI for scoring methods used in the present study.)

The Ammons Full-Range Picture Vocabulary Test, which is another measure of vocabulary of recognition, was selected for use with preschool children. The score is the number of words correctly identified. IQ-equivalents have also been obtained from this test. This test was decided upon after pilot work indicated that available modifications of the Seashore-Eckerson test could not be used satisfactorily with the younger preschool children.

Pilot trials indicated that the M. K. Smith modification was unsatisfactory for use with the 5-year-olds, since they tended to choose the first or last definition presented. It was assumed that this task involving four choices was too difficult or too uninteresting for them. As a master's thesis under the late Dr. Robert Seashore, an unpublished picture vocabulary test based on M. K. Smith's modification of the Seashore-Eckerson test was developed (24, 42). With the hope of using this test with the younger children, it was administered to children in the University of Minnesota Nursery School and Kindergarten. It was satisfactory with children at the 5-year-level, but was too difficult for bright 3-year-olds. The highest score obtained by any of the 3-year-old children tested was 7. This was not sufficiently high to allow for variation in vocabulary test scores. The development of a test for use with the preschool group based on the unused random lists drawn by Eckerson was considered. The idea was discarded for use in the present study since such a major task as developing the test would have delayed the total project too long.

A measure of the vocabulary of use in a controlled situation was obtained in the number of different words used in the fifty verbalizations of each child. A second, though limited, measure of vocabulary of use is available for the preschool children in the number of words included in the sound discrimination test which were correctly identified. This is referred to in the text as the sound discrimination vocabulary score.

Administration of the Tests

Each child was given all the language measures individually. The tests were administered in as many sessions as were necessary to maintain good rapport. For most of the subjects this meant two sessions, although in a few instances one or three sessions were used. The length of the sessions varied from fifteen minutes to nearly two hours although most sessions ranged from one half to one hour. In the longer sessions, breaks were taken if the child's interest waned.

For all but one of the children tested at home only one session was used. Although the length of time that the experimenter was in the home was often quite long, it was felt that if rapport with the child could be maintained, it was better to get all the necessary data during one visit than to go into a home a second time. The tasks were diverse and the testing procedures flexible enough to allow some variation in the order of presentation of the tasks. The identification of the sound discrimination test words, however, always preceded the administration of the sound discrimination test. In only a very few instances was it necessary to interrupt the testing because of fatigue or loss of rapport with the child. Then the testing was resumed after a chat with the mother which permitted a period of very different activity for the child.

All of the articulation testing was done by the author since training and experience in transcription of sounds into the International Phonetic Alphabet is essential. Graduate students and one undergraduate major in the Nursery School–Kindergarten–Primary curriculum aided in gathering the data on sentence development, sound discrimination, and vocabulary. All these students were given special training in the particular testing they were to do before they gathered the data that were included in the study.

The children were not tested in specific age groups, but according to their availability for testing. Most of the 5-to-8-year-olds were tested first, and those of the preschool age were tested later. However, they were not divided into specific ages within these general classifications. This has the advantage of preventing the examiners from building up standards of acceptable or typical performance at any specific age level during the testing procedure.

Analysis of the Data

Because this is a normative study, measures of central tendency and dispersion are presented for each of the four major language areas and for some of the subdivisions. Either the mean and standard deviation or the median and quartile deviation are used. When the distribution of scores is skewed as the maximum possible score is approached, the median is presented. This is true particularly for the measures of articulation and sound discrimination.

For comparisons of the development of the various language skills, correlational and terminal status techniques as well as the significance of differences between consecutively tested age levels are used. Correlations indicate the change in interrelationships at the different ages tested. Since the significance of differences between consecutively tested age levels has been used by other investigators, a more direct comparison of the present results with earlier findings is permitted. Through the use of terminal status measures, comparison of the growth curves of a variety of different language measures is possible.

In the terminal status analysis, the score of the oldest age group tested on a particular measure is taken as a terminal status measure and the percentage of this score which has been attained by each of the younger age groups tested is calculated (2). The score of the 8-year-old group is taken as a terminal status measure most frequently. For the picture sound discrimination test and the Ammons vocabulary test, which were used only with the preschool subjects, the scores of the 5-year-olds are taken as measures of terminal status.

The development of articulation, sound discrimination, sentence structure, and vocabulary are discussed separately. Studies pertinent to the procedure, results, and method of analysis of the data are presented at the beginning of the appropriate chapter. No attempt has been made to include an exhaustive review of the literature in the four areas of language studied. This has been done quite recently by McCarthy in the *Manual of Child Psychology* (28).

III. ARTICULATION OF SPEECH SOUNDS

Among the many investigations of language in children, only a few major ones study the development of the articulation of speech sounds. Until the last few decades much information has been based upon reports of observations of single children. These earlier reports contain various descriptions of the characteristics of the sounds produced by infants and young children. Particularly since the early 1930s the International Phonetic Alphabet (IPA) has been quite extensively used to transcribe and study speech sounds of substantial numbers of children. In recent years electronic devices have begun to be used in recording and analyzing infant speech sounds.

Current research in articulation is concerned with the use of speech sounds in meaningful words and conversation, and in the babbling and early utterances of infants. Since about 1940 Irwin has been using the IPA in the transcription of speech sounds of substantial numbers of infants from upper and lower socioeconomic families, in their own homes and in institutions, normal and deviate in intelligence, handicapped by cerebral palsy, etc. (17, 18, 19, 20, 21, 22, 23). In 1951 Lynip used the magnetic tape recorder and the Sound Spectograph, developed in the Bell Telephone Laboratories, to study speech sound patterns in the pre-word vocalizations of one infant (26). The present investigation is concerned only with the development of speech sounds in words, since at the youngest age studied communication by means of words is definitely established.

Undoubtedly future research in the articulation of speech sounds will increasingly use electronic devices. This study, however, used the IPA in the transcription of sounds. The use of recording equipment is not efficient when recording must be done in many different places under varying and often unsatisfactory acoustic conditions.

Pertinent Studies

The pioneering American investigation of the development of the articulation of speech sounds in words was published in 1931 by Wellman, Case, Mengert, and Bradbury (53). In their testing procedure, sounds were checked in words uttered spontaneously by the child in response to questions or stimulus pictures. The responses were transcribed in the symbols of the IPA. For each sound tested several possible test words were available. Questions asked were organized so that the word to be elicited was not used by the examiner immediately before the child responded. Testing was done in a room separate from the nursery playroom in as many six-to-ten-minute sessions as were needed to obtain the word responses desired. Total testing time varied between fourteen and eighty minutes.

The articulation test measured 133 sound units: 66 consonant elements, 48 consonant blends, 15 vowels, and 4 diphthongs. The consonant sounds were subdivided and studied as stops or plosives (p, b, t, d, k, g), nasals (m and n), and fricatives or sibilants (f, v, th, s, z, sh, ch, l, r). Reliability of the test, as determined by correlating halves composed of alternate sounds on the record blank, was $.96 \pm .01$. No test-retest or examiner reliability was reported.

The sample consisted of 204 children between the ages of 2 and 6 in the University of Iowa Laboratory Preschools. The mean IQ of the group was 115.9, SD 15.4. Articulation was analyzed in relation to age, sex, relative difficulty of sounds, position of the sound in a word, errors of speech sound production, and certain other developmental and ability factors. Since not all the children were tested on all the sounds, analyses were made for three different groups: (1) all 204 children whether completely or partially tested; (2) those children tested on every sound within a given sound group, excluding 10 sounds on which results for only a few children were recorded: 120 children were tested on all of the 61 consonant elements, 65 on the 47 consonant blends, 113 on the 11 vowels, and 113 on the 4 diphthongs; (3) those 57 children who were tested on 123 sounds. Since in the present study complete measures of articulation were obtained on all subjects, comparison of the results with the Wellman study are made with this last group.

Poole, in 1934, studied the articulation of 65 children between 2.5 and 8.5 years in the laboratory schools at the University of Michigan (35, 36). These children were from the USES groups; the fathers of most were on the staff of the university or the university hospital. Children were tested individually with pictures, objects, or actions to be identified in response to questions. Most test words were uttered spontaneously, but if they were not, the child was asked to repeat the desired words after the examiner. The measure included 23 consonant phonemes in all possible initial, medial, and final positions in words, making a total of 62 items. Poole's analysis of articulation is made by age, sex, position of sounds, and social adjustment as measured by the Haggerty-Olson-Wickman test.

In 1935 Henderson, at the University of Wisconsin, studied the development of speech sounds in 392 mentally retarded institutionalized children (13). The subjects ranged in age from 3 years 1 month to 18 years 7 months, and from preschool to the seventh grade. The mean IQ of the 66 children at 3, 4, and 5 years is reported as 75.82. The 193 children who could not read were tested with objects; those who could read were given a list of words containing the same test sounds. Most of the test words were spontaneously elicited, but some were occasionally and others always repeated. No vowel phonemes and the same 23 consonant phonemes measured by Poole were tested. However, since Henderson classified the final "l" as a vowel, there were 61 test items.

In 1937 H. M. Williams and his associates published several studies planned as preliminary to the construction of a scale of language development in preschool children (25, 54, 55, 56). These included studies of articulation of sounds in words, word usage, vocabulary, and the sentence as a unit of expression. Samples of subjects differed for the several studies, but the samples used in the investigation of speech sound production consists of "varying numbers . . . up to a maximum of 130 children" (55). Articulation was measured by a modification of the test and technique developed by Wellman *et al.* in which the 98 sounds were selected for measurement including those most frequently used in the International Kindergarten Union list and the first 2,500 words of the Thorndike list. If the test words were not spontaneously elicited, the examiner supplied them as a pattern. Although a phonetic transcription was made of 40 verbalizations of each child in play situations, the analysis of the types of errors offers most material for comparison with the present study.

As well as from developmental studies, information on the articulation of speech sounds is obtainable from reports of the many surveys of speech defects among public school children. For the most part these studies are oriented toward incorrect responses rather than toward correct responses. Whether the results of speech surveys can be compared with those of developmental studies depends upon the methods used in gathering, analyzing, and presenting the speech sound data.

Speech surveys carried on by trained persons and presenting results in detail permit some comparison even though the emphasis is on errors in production. Such a survey by Roe and Milisen, using the Detroit Articulation Picture Test, measured the articulation by 1,989 children in grades one through six of consonant sounds and consonant blends in 66 positions (38). The percentage of errors, reported for specific sounds measured in spontaneous utterances, are compared with results of the present study.

Comparison of Measuring Techniques Used in Pertinent Studies

Similarities and differences exist in the methods of investigation in the present study and the pertinent related studies mentioned above. There is substantial overlap in the ages of the samples in all these studies. Differences exist in the specific sounds tested, the way in which the sounds are classified, the use of spontaneous or repeated utterances of the children, the completeness of the testing, and the selection of the sample.

Transcription of speech sounds. In all the studies incorrect sound productions were transcribed using a relatively broad transcription of the IPA. In the present report, however, although the IPA was used in recording errors, the diacritical markings of the Webster unabridged dictionary are used in presenting all results.

Specific sounds tested. The various studies measure the articulation of different numbers of sound elements. Since the present study is most similar to that of Wellman *et al.* in the number and classification of sounds tested, more comparisons are made with it. Both Poole and Henderson tested p, b, m, w, hw, f, v, t, d, n, th, t̶h̶, s, z, sh, zh, l, r, j, g, k, ng, h in the initial, medial, and final positions for a total of 62 and 61 sound elements respectively. (Difference in classification of the final "l" accounts for the discrepancy in the number of tested sound elements.) Although Wellman included 133 sound elements in her test, those children whose articulation evaluation was considered complete were tested on 123 of these. Williams variously reports 98 and 104 most frequently used sound elements by children as being tested. The present study measures 176 sound elements. Despite the difference in the number of sounds tested, comparisons of specific sounds and certain types of sounds are possible between the current study and those of Wellman, Poole, and Henderson since they described precisely the sounds tested. Williams presents no complete list of the measured sounds, but only the 48 sounds for which substitutions were most frequent.

The vowels and diphthongs measured can be compared only with the Wellman study since the other investigators either did not measure vowels or did not report them separately. Three fewer vowels and one more diphthong are tested in the present study. Part of the discrepancy is the result of difference in classification. The "ā" as in *sail* was termed a vowel by Wellman and a diphthong by the author. Wellman tested the "ĕ" as in *end*, the "â" as in *there*, the "ô" as in *ball*, and the "ŏ with circumflex" as in *long*. The author did not discriminate between "ĕ" and "â" or between "ŏ" and "ŏ with circumflex" and only the vowels as in *end* and *law* were measured. As vowels and diphthongs are at a high level of accuracy of articulation at the early ages tested, these differences in classification are not too important in the comparisons.

Consonant sounds were tested in all studies, but the number of consonant elements measured varies. Williams did not report the precise number tested; Poole tested 62; Henderson 61; Wellman 66; and the present study 69. The following specific differences are found: Poole did not test the medial "hw," or the "sh" and "ch" in any position; Henderson did not test these same sounds and the final "l", which she considered as a vowel sound; Wellman did not test the medial "h," the medial "hw," and the final "zh." Among these consonant sounds not tested are some used infrequently in the free conversation of children.

Only slight differences in the classification of consonant sounds exist between the Wellman study and the current one. The six consonants p, b, t, d, k, and g were classified by Wellman as stops and by the author as plosives. Since all were tested in the initial, medial, and final positions, in both studies there are totals of 18 plosive or stop consonants. Only the nasals "m" and "n" were tested by Wellman for a total of six nasal elements. In this study, the "ng" sound is tested in the medial and final positions for a total of eight sound elements. Wellman tested f, v, th, ~~th~~, s, z, sh, ch, l, and r as sibilant sounds. The present study excludes "ch," "l," and "r," as fricatives or sibilants and adds "zh," in the medial and final positions. Although Wellman made no further breakdown of consonant sounds, combinations and semivowels are classified in the present study.

The greatest difference between the studies of Wellman and the author occurs in the number of consonant blends measured. Wellman tested 48 consonant blends, the author 71. The difference is not merely one of number, however. Ten of the blends included in Wellman's measurement were final blends ending with "s" and "z," the kind of blend occurring in the formation of the plural. These were not included in the present study since it was felt that the inclusion of all possible plural combinations would increase the length of the test beyond a usable length with the younger children and add many double-consonant blend items in which one element was frequently repeated. An attempt was made, however, to include most other double- and triple-consonant blends, whether or not they were frequent in the speech of young children.

Spontaneous or repeated utterances. Speech sounds in this study have been tested in either a spontaneous or a repeated utterance, whichever was obtained with the least loss of rapport with the child. Measures obtained in either way have been combined in the analysis. This was done with confidence since a preliminary study had shown that for total articulation scores the difference in measurement of spontaneous and repeated utterances was not statistically significant (49). Through the use of both the spontaneous and repeated utterance a complete measure of the articulation of each child was made possible within a feasible period of time.

In all the earlier studies some attempt was made to obtain spontaneous responses, but only Wellman kept the spontaneous and repeated utterances separated in the analyses. In order to do this several test sessions were necessary with most subjects and the number of children completely tested was reduced from a possible 204 to an actual 57. Thus with the exception of the sample of children "completely tested" by Wellman, the method of obtaining the responses was similar for all studies.

Position of consonant sound tested. Although the relation between the accuracy of sound production and the position of the sound in words has been studied previously, it is debatable whether or not the medial position may legitimately be considered. If the position of a sound in a word is considered, three positions are classified: (1) initial if the sound begins a word; (2) medial if it is used in the middle of a word; and (3) final if it ends a word. If the position of the sound in a syllable is considered, only initial and final sounds are used since the consonant must either begin or end the syllable. Among the investigations of children's articulation, Williams considers only initial and final sounds while Poole, Henderson, and Wellman *et al.* classify sounds into all three positions. Although it is a moot question whether the medial position for a consonant sound actually exists, the consonant elements tested in the present study were classified in three positions since this permitted comparisons with the most extensive studies of children's articulation. The consonant blends were tested in the initial and final positions only. This was done since comparisons were to be made with other studies; thus an arbitrary way of limiting the length of the articulation test was provided. In the present study 23 consonant elements were tested in the initial, 25 in the medial, and 21 in the final positions. Of the double-consonant blends 23 were tested in the initial, 18 in the final, and 30 reversed in the final positions. Of the triple-consonant blends 5 were tested in the initial, 2 in the final, and 12 in the final-reversed position.

Completeness of testing. Each child in the studies by Poole, Henderson, and the author was tested on all sounds in the test. This is also true for that part of the Wellman sample used for comparison. In Williams' study the number of children tested on each sound is not reported precisely and this number seems to vary from sound to sound.

Wellman explains lack of complete testing of a large proportion of the sample on the basis of a variety of factors, such as the greater difficulty of some sounds, the less frequent appearance of some in the words commonly found in children's vocabularies, insufficient time on the part of the examiner, and the faulty technique of the test in attempting to elicit words not in the child's vocabulary.

Age of sample. There is substantial overlap in the ages of the subjects used in the developmental studies, although in none is the age range identical with that of the present study. Children from 3 to 8 are tested in the present study. Wellman and Poole tested children at 2 and 2.5 years respectively. Poole and Davis tested children at 8.5 and 9.5 years respectively. The upper age limit in the Henderson sample is 18 years.

Selection of sample. Some of the earlier developmental studies were carried on with extremes of the population. The Wellman, Williams, and Poole samples were drawn from university nursery school, kindergarten, and elementary schools, and Henderson's sample from retarded institutionalized children. The present study uses a representative sample selected according to father's occupation in which age, sex, and, indirectly, intelligence were controlled.

Reliability of measurement. No reliability of the articulation test data nor of the examiner has been calculated in the present study. Other investigations found reliability of odd-even items on a similar test substantial: Wellman reported a reliability coefficient of .96, and Williams of .91. Henderson has reported the most extensive study of agreement of three trained judges in transcribing speech sounds of children under different conditions. Two third graders were tested in the same room with the judges; the responses of a 5-year-old child were broadcast to judges in another room; and electrically recorded responses were transcribed phonetically. The agreement among the three judges was 69 per cent when the judges were in the same room with the child being tested, 80 per cent when the child's responses were broadcast, and 90 per cent when the responses were recorded and then judged (14).

The data in the present study were gathered in a situation comparable to that in which Henderson obtained the lowest agreement among her judges. This held even though the children tested were third graders and agreement among the judges was greater when the proportion of correct items in a test was larger. Among children selected as those were in the current investigation, the proportion of incorrect sound utterances expected would be much greater among preschool children and not extensive among school-age youngsters. It is at the preschool level that establishing the examiner's reliability would be most important.

Henderson has pointed out that although all her participating judges were experienced, the one who had the most extensive recent experience in testing children showed 95 per cent constancy in judging correctness and incorrectness of sounds and 90 per cent constancy in judging specific error. This was the highest among the three judges. She has emphasized the importance, in attempting to establish reliability, of having persons with similar training and experience in testing young children. In the present study no one was available to act as a second judge who had had experience comparable with that of the author in testing the articulation of preschool children.

There is great practical difficulty in placing a second person in a position where he has the same opportunity to see and hear a young child as the examiner, and still not interfere with the good rapport necessary for testing. Henderson states that one "condition that tended to lower the extent of agreement was the variability of loudness of the respective sounds relative to the various situations of the three judges . . . They [the children] often spoke rather softly, which made for influential differences in comprehensibility at the various locations in which the respective judges sat. Moreover, since it was necessary for the subjects to sit close to the examiner, who gave the test, and since they often directed their responses to her, she had the advantage on the other judges. Such differences as loudness and visibility often affect the evaluation of the voiceless consonants and even of the voiced-voiceless pairs, since, lacking adequate auditory and visual audience, the judges may unwittingly be influenced by the context of the word in which the sound appears" (14:356). These comments refer to third-grade children and the problems mentioned would be magnified at the preschool level.

Since the author has had a substantial amount of training and experience in the use of phonetics and a good deal of experience in the testing of speech of young children, and because of the difficulties in introducing a third person into the test situation with preschool children, no reliability check was made. Repeated tests in the same child would not provide several judgments of the same utterance.

Results

The results of this study are compared with other investigations of the articulation of various types of speech sounds, types of consonant sounds, position of consonant sounds, voiced or unvoiced consonant sounds, specific consonant sounds, and errors in articulation. The total articulation score based on all 176 speech sound items is not useful for specific comparisons with other studies since the number and type of speech sounds tested differ. Means and standard deviations are presented in the text. Since for several of the distributions the measure of skewness exceeds 1.0, medians and Q's (quartile deviations) for the major measures are presented in Appendix V.*

Total Articulation Score

Table 4 indicates that the mean total articulation scores by age for boys and girls, USES and LSES groups, and total subsamples increase with age, and that the variance decreases with age for all groups.

Table 4. Mean Total Articulation Scores for Boys and Girls, Upper and Lower Socioeconomic Status Groups, and Total Subsamples by Age

CA	Boys (N = 30)		Girls (N = 30)		USES (N = 18)		LSES (N = 42)		Total Subsamples (N = 60)	
	Mean	SD	Mean	SD	Mean	SD	Mean	SD	Mean	SD
3	98.3	35.0	88.2	31.8	97.6	33.1	91.5	34.0	93.3	33.8
3.5	105.5	37.6	118.2	31.0	115.9	31.1	110.1	36.5	111.9	35.0
4	127.2	31.6	125.5	26.7	136.1	18.9	122.2	31.8	126.4	29.3
4.5	127.2	32.2	131.2	29.5	141.7	29.8	123.8	29.9	129.2	31.0
5	128.8	38.1	141.8	33.9	146.9	26.8	130.3	39.1	135.3	36.7
6	143.7	33.8	156.9	21.8	154.5	28.6	140.4	42.7	150.3	29.2
7	157.3	21.7	166.4	10.8	167.8	11.4	151.4	38.9	161.9	17.7
8	167.6	8.6	166.6	13.2	169.7	7.3	166.0	12.3	167.1	11.1

The increments in scores for the subsamples are significant at the .01 level between 3 and 3.5 years ($t = 2.96$) and between 6 and 7 years ($t = 2.63$), and at the .05 level between 3.5 and 4 years ($t = 2.46$) and between 5 and 6 years ($t = 2.48$). The differences in the scores between the other consecutive age levels are not statistically significant (t values range from 0.51 to 1.93). At 3 years of age the mean percentage of the total possible score is 53.3 and at 8 years it is 94.9. Thus, a substantial amount of articulation growth has taken place by 3 years, and essentially adult articulation is apparent by 8. The maximum increment occurs between 3 and 3.5 years, the two earliest ages tested, and a

* Skewness has been calculated using the formula

$$Sk = \frac{3\ (M - Mdn)}{SD}$$

sharp deceleration is evident after 7 years. Study of the articulation of sounds by younger children would add much to our knowledge of articulation development, but it is likely that the scores at 7 and 8 years are nearly representative of adult speakers.

Most of the distributions of total articulation scores of the subsamples are skewed. At 3 years the distribution is normal ($Sk = 0.12$), but at all other ages tested it is more skewed (Sk's range from 0.73 to 1.63).

The difference between the mean total articulation score of 136.8, SD 24.8, for the 240 girls over the entire age range and 132.0, SD 29.8, for boys does not reach the .05 level of confidence ($t = 1.92$). When differences between the scores of boys and girls at each age level are compared, only at 7 years does the difference reach the .05 level ($t = 2.07$), and at all other ages the differences are not significant (t values range from 0.23 to 1.67). Girls produced more sounds correctly than boys between 4.5 and 7 years. The magnitude of the difference increases until at 7 years it is significant at the .05 level of confidence. By 8 years of age, when boys have attained the mature articulation which girls reached a year earlier, differences between scores are no longer significant.

After about 4.5 years the scores of the girls are quite consistently about equal to those of the boys one test interval older. Girls attain mature articulation at about 7 years, while boys reach a similar level only after another year of growth. Essentially the same pattern of growth holds for boys or girls separately as for the sexes combined. The slightly earlier growth in articulation for girls, however, is apparent in the significant difference in articulation scores occurring between 3 and 3.5 years for girls ($t = 3.70$) and between 3.5 and 4 years for boys ($t = 2.42$). As mature articulation is approached, the differences in the articulation scores of girls are statistically significant at the .05 level between 5 and 6 years ($t = 2.05$) and 6 and 7 years ($t = 2.14$). Between 7 and 8 years the difference is significant for boys ($t = 2.42$).

The difference between the mean score of 141.2, SD 23.4, for the USES subjects over the entire age range combined, and 129.5, SD 33.2, for the LSES subjects is statistically significant at the .01 level of confidence ($t = 4.47$). The USES group receives a higher articulation score than the LSES group at the age levels tested. At 3 and 3.5 years the slight differences are not statistically significant ($t = 0.65$ and 0.63). Between 4 and 8 years the differences are somewhat greater but they reach significance at the .05 level only at 4, 4.5, and 7 years ($t = 2.09$, 2.13, and 2.50) while at 5, 6, and 8 years the differences are not significant ($t = 1.89$, 1.50, and 1.46).

For either SES group the differences between scores at consecutively tested ages never reach the .01 level of confidence. The .05 level is reached by the USES group between 3.5 and 4 years ($t = 2.48$) and by the LSES group between 5 and 6 years ($t = 2.05$). Between the other ages the range in t is 0.21 to 1.99 for the USES group and between 0.11 and 1.84 for the LSES group.

Consonant Elements, Consonant Blends, Vowels, and Diphthongs

The total articulation measure is subdivided into consonant element, double-consonant blend, triple-consonant blend, vowel, and diphthong subscores. Each subscore is the number of correctly produced sounds in that classification.

For the entire sample of 480 subjects, the mean score on diphthongs is 4.9, SD 0.2; on vowels it is 11.6, SD 0.5; on consonant elements 55.1, SD 11.8; on double-consonant blends, 50.8, SD 19.7; and on triple-consonant blends 11.8, SD 5.9. For the entire sample the following mean percentages of possible scores are attained in the production of these consonant sound types: 8.4 per cent on the diphthongs, 97.0 on the vowels, 79.8 on the consonants, 71.5 on the double-consonant blends, and 63.2 on the triple-consonant blends. Except for the difference between the percentages of correct utterance of the vowels and of the diphthongs, all differences among the consonant elements and consonant elements or blends and the vowels or dipthongs are statistically significant at the .01 level. The t between the consonant element and double-consonant blend percentage scores is 3.92; that between the consonant element and triple-consonant blend is 7.33; and between the double- and triple-consonant blend is 3.15.

In Table 5 the mean consonant element, consonant blend, vowel, and diphthong scores for the subsamples at each age are presented.

The significance of the differences in the speech sound subscores obtained between consecutively tested age levels is presented in Table 6. Although none of the differences for the vowels and diphthongs is significant, the increments in the consonant element and consonant blend subscores show some significant differences at the early ages tested and between 5 and 7 years of age. Wellman also found no significant differences in vowel and diphthong scores between consecutively tested levels. However, she reports critical ratios for the scores on consonant elements of 4.68 between 2 and 3 years, 2.01 between 3 and 4 years, and 3.38 between 4 and 5 years; critical ratios for scores on consonant blends are 4.31, 3.13, and 2.84 between the same age groups (53:36).

Table 5. Mean Scores and Standard Deviations on Consonant Elements, Consonant Blends, Vowels, and Diphthongs for Total Subsamples (N = 60) by Age

CA	Consonant Elements (69) *		Double Blends (71) *		Triple Blends (19) *		Vowels (12) *		Diph-thongs (5) *	
	Mean	SD	Mean	SD	Mean	SD	Mean	SD	Mean	SD
3	42.3	12.1	29.7	17.7	5.4	4.4	11.2	0.6	4.7	0.5
3.5 ...	47.4	10.9	39.6	19.1	8.6	5.5	11.4	0.7	4.9	0.3
4	52.6	9.0	46.8	16.1	10.6	4.9	11.5	0.7	4.9	0.3
4.5 ...	54.2	8.9	47.8	17.4	10.8	5.6	11.5	0.6	4.9	0.3
5	55.1	12.0	51.6	19.0	12.1	6.1	11.6	0.6	5.0	0.2
6	60.3	8.6	58.7	15.9	14.4	5.4	11.9	0.3	5.0	0.0
7	63.6	5.4	64.8	9.1	16.6	3.8	12.0	0.2	5.0	0.0
8	65.1	3.1	67.5	6.0	17.5	2.9	12.0	0.1	5.0	0.0

* Number of this type of sound tested.

Table 6. Values Showing Significance of Differences in Articulation Subscores between Consecutively Tested Age Intervals for Total Subsamples (N = 60)

CA	Consonant Elements	Double Blends	Triple Blends	Vowels	Diphthongs	Total Articulation
3–3.5	2.43**	2.91*	3.56*	0.17	0.19	2.96*
3.5–4	2.84*	2.25**	2.22**	0.08	0.00	2.46*
4–4.5	0.98	0.32	0.20	0.00	0.00	0.51
4.5–5	0.47	1.15	1.18	0.09	0.19	0.98
5–6	2.72*	2.27**	2.09	0.33	0.00	2.48**
6–7	2.52**	2.42**	2.44**	0.17	0.00	2.63*
7–8	1.85	2.00**	1.50	0.00	0.00	1.93

* Significant at the .01 level.
** Significant at the .05 level.

Table 7. Percentages of Articulation Scores of the 8-Year-Old Subsample Attained by Total Subsamples by Age on Consonants, Consonant Blends, Vowels, and Diphthongs

CA *	Consonant Elements	Double Blends	Triple Blends	Vowels	Diphthongs
3	65.0	44.0	30.9	93.3	94.0
3.5	72.9	58.7	49.1	95.0	98.0
4	80.8	69.3	60.6	95.8	98.0
4.5	83.3	70.8	61.7	95.8	98.0
5	84.7	76.5	69.1	96.7	100.0
6	93.1	87.0	82.9	99.2	100.0
7	97.8	96.0	94.9	100.0	100.0
8	100.0	100.0	100.0	100.0	100.0

* N = 60 in each age group.

Although by 8 years of age all sounds are approaching accurate articulation, the curve of growth varies among the several sound types. In order to make comparisons, the performance of the 8-year-old subsample on each sound type was taken as a measure of terminal status. In Table 7 the great differences among the sound types in the rate of development is particularly evident at the early ages. The performance of the 3-year-old subjects ranges from about one third to nine tenths of that of the 8-year-olds. Over these five years of the developmental period, the correct articulation of vowels and diphthongs increases only about one tenth over the mean performance at 3 years. On the other hand, over this same period the accuracy of the articulation of consonant elements more than doubles, and that of consonant blends more than triples.

To compare the accuracy of articulation of the types of sounds found in this study with the findings of Wellman, the percentages of possible correct articulation obtained in the two studies are presented in Figure 1. There is substantial agreement when comparisons are made between the percentage of possible scores attained between 3 and 6 years, the ages included in both studies. At the earlier ages the Wellman sample is about one half year accelerated, but this is not unexpected since the

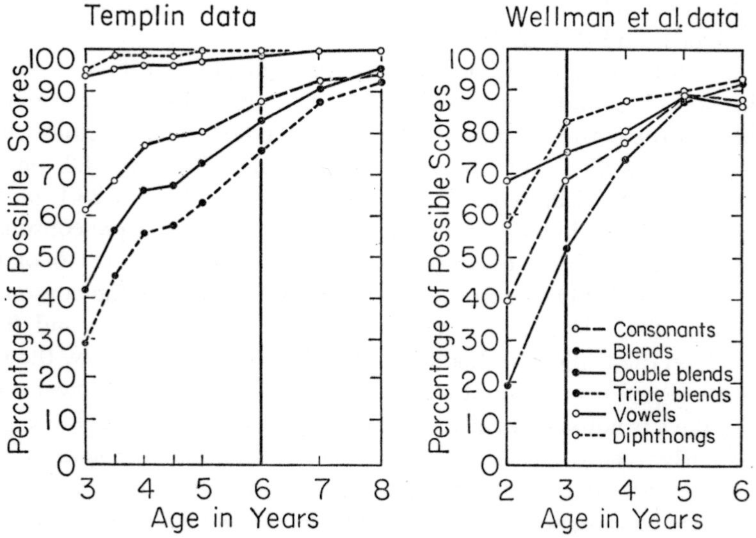

FIGURE 1. COMPARISON OF CORRECT ARTICULATION OF CONSONANT ELEMENTS AND BLENDS, VOWELS, AND DIPHTHONGS BY AGE AS REPORTED BY TEMPLIN AND WELLMAN

samples differ in intelligence and socioeconomic status levels. More of the consonant blends which are difficult to produce correctly are measured in the present study. The few vowels and diphthongs measured permit much fluctuation although the differences in actual mean scores are small.

In the present study, approximately the same level of accuracy is reached in the production of vowels and diphthongs by the 3-year-olds as in consonant elements by 7-year-olds and in the consonant blends by 8-year-olds. Over the age range included in this study, the increase in mean percentage of possible scores for vowels is 7 per cent; for diphthongs 6 per cent; for consonant elements 33 per cent; for double-consonant blends 53 per cent; and for triple-consonant blends 64 per cent. Although the increase in percentage scores varies substantially, the maximum increment for all sounds occurs between 3 and 4 years.

At the early ages particularly, the order of difficulty of the types of sounds is similar to that for the entire sample. At the older ages tested, no real order of difficulty exists since all types of sounds are produced with a relatively high degree of accuracy. The number of children producing the several types of sounds correctly at 3 years of age reflects the order of difficulty for the total samples. Of 60 subjects at 3 years, 46 to 60 articulated the various diphthongs correctly, 39 to 60 the various vowel sounds, 6 to 60 the consonant elements, 2 to 46 the double-consonant blends, and 0 to 29 the triple-consonant blends.

Scores obtained by boys or girls are not significantly different on any of the speech sound types tested when the age subsamples are combined over the entire age range. The mean percentage of possible scores for the boys is 98.4, SD 1.8, on the diphthongs, 97.3, SD 4.3, on the vowels, 78.3, SD 17.9, on the consonant elements, 70.1, SD 28.1, on the double-consonant blends and 61.1, SD 33.2, on the triple-consonant blends. For the girls the mean percentage scores are 98.4, SD 0.6, on the diphthongs, 96.7, SD 0.9, on the vowels, 81.3, SD 17.1, on the consonant elements, 73.0, SD 27.8, on the double-consonant blends, and 64.3, SD 31.2, on the triple-consonant blends. The scores obtained by the two sexes are equal on the diphthongs and the slightly higher vowel score for the boys is not statistically significant ($t = 0.02$). Although the girls consistently receive higher consonant element and consonant blend scores, the differences are not statistically significant: the t values are 1.31 on the consonant elements, 0.83 on the double-consonant, and 0.25 on the triple-consonant blends.

The similarity between the means for boys and girls on the various types of sounds at each age level is evident from Table 8. On the whole

Table 8. Mean Scores and Standard Deviations on Consonant Elements, Consonant Blends, Vowels, and Diphthongs for Boys and Girls by Age

CA	Consonant Elements (69) *		Double Blends (71) *		Triple Blends (19) *		Vowels (12) *		Diphthongs (5) *	
	Mean	SD	Mean	SD	Mean	SD	Mean	SD	Mean	SD
					Boys †					
3	43.5	12.5	32.7	17.7	6.1	4.7	11.4	0.5	4.7	0.4
3.5	45.3	12.0	36.3	20.2	7.8	5.6	11.3	0.8	4.8	0.4
4	52.5	10.0	47.3	17.0	11.0	5.3	11.6	0.7	4.9	0.2
4.5	52.9	9.3	47.1	18.1	10.6	5.7	11.6	0.5	4.9	0.3
5	52.6	13.0	48.8	19.4	10.9	6.4	11.6	0.6	5.0	0.2
6	58.2	10.4	55.3	18.1	13.3	6.0	11.9	0.4	5.0	0.0
7	62.4	6.4	62.5	11.4	15.5	4.4	11.9	0.3	5.0	0.0
8	64.9	3.3	68.0	3.2	17.6	2.6	12.0	0.0	5.0	0.0
					Girls †					
3	41.2	11.5	26.6	17.2	4.6	4.0	11.0	0.7	4.7	0.6
3.5	49.5	9.3	42.9	17.2	9.3	5.2	11.5	0.6	4.9	0.2
4	52.6	7.9	46.3	15.2	10.1	4.4	11.5	0.7	4.9	0.3
4.5	55.4	8.2	48.5	16.8	11.0	5.5	11.4	0.6	4.9	0.3
5	57.5	10.4	54.4	18.2	13.3	5.6	11.6	0.7	5.0	0.2
6	62.4	5.6	62.1	12.2	15.5	4.4	11.9	0.3	5.0	0.0
7	64.7	3.8	67.1	5.0	17.6	2.7	12.0	0.0	5.0	0.0
8	65.4	2.8	67.0	7.9	17.3	3.2	12.0	0.2	5.0	0.0

* Number of this type of sound tested.
† N = 30 in each age group.

Table 9. Percentage of Scores of 8-Year-Old-Girls Attained by Boys and Girls on Consonant Elements, Blends, Vowels, and Diphthongs, by Age

CA	Consonant Elements	Double Blends	Triple Blends	Vowels	Diphthongs
			Boys *		
3	66.5%	48.8%	35.2%	95.0%	94.0%
3.5	69.3	54.2	45.1	94.2	96.0
4	80.3	70.6	63.6	96.7	98.0
4.5	80.9	70.3	61.3	96.7	98.0
5	80.4	72.8	63.0	96.7	100.0
6	89.0	82.5	76.9	99.2	100.0
7	95.4	93.3	89.6	99.2	100.0
8	99.2	101.5	101.7	100.0	100.0
			Girls *		
3	63.0	39.7	26.6	91.7	94.0
3.5	75.7	64.0	53.7	95.8	96.0
4	80.4	69.1	58.4	95.8	98.0
4.5	84.7	72.4	63.6	95.0	98.0
5	87.9	81.2	76.9	96.7	100.0
6	95.4	92.7	89.6	99.2	100.0
7	98.9	100.1	101.7	100.0	100.0
8	100.0	100.0	100.0	100.0	100.0

* N = 30 in each age group.

the boys are slightly more variable, and somewhat slower to reach mature articulation. Between the ages of 3 and 4.5 either boys or girls may receive higher scores in any of the sound groups. After this age, the accuracy of the boys' articulation of consonant elements and consonant blends is quite similar to that of the girls one age interval older. This relation holds for the vowel and diphthong articulation scores to a somewhat lesser degree.

The vowel, diphthong, and consonant element subscores of boys and girls are not significantly different at any age (*t* ranges from 0.0 to 1.94). For the double- and triple-consonant blend subscores, only the scores of the 7-year-old girls approach or attain significance at the .05 level. The *t* for the difference in double-consonant subscores between the sexes is 2.03 at 7 years and ranges from 0.24 to 1.70 at the other ages. The *t* for the difference in the triple-consonant blend subscores between the sexes is 2.23 at 7 years and ranges between 0.13 and 1.72 at the other ages.

The greatest changes in scores occur between 3 and 3.5 years and between 6 and 7 years for the girls, and between 3.5 and 4 and 7 and 8 years for the boys. Between the younger age levels the differences are significant at the .05 level for all types of sounds. At the older ages they reach this level of confidence for the consonant blends but not for the consonant elements. None of the other differences is statistically significant.

In Table 9 the achievement of boys and girls throughout the age range tested is presented with the performance of 8-year-old girls on all sound types taken as a measure of terminal status. Since on all these speech sound types the achievement of the 8-year-old boys and girls is similar, the results would differ little had the performance of all 8-year-old subjects been taken as a measure of terminal status. Although the increases with age in accuracy of articulation vary considerably for the separate types of sounds, they are relatively similar for both sexes, except that they tend to occur slightly earlier for girls.

These results are in general agreement with Poole, who reports that boys and girls develop efficiency in the articulation of consonant elements at about the same rate from 2.5 to 5.5 years and that after this girls' scores increase more rapidly in accuracy, until mature articulation is attained by 6.5 years. The boys in Poole's study do not reach the same degree of accuracy of articulation until 7.5 years (35). Wellman reports girls somewhat superior in the production of consonant sounds. However, the differences are neither great nor consistent over the 2-to-6 year age range studied. Boys obtained higher consonant scores at 2 and 6 years, and girls at 3, 4, and 5 years. Although the differences were greater when the girls' scores were higher, the largest critical ratio reported is 2.56 with small samples. The girls at 3 obtained a mean consonant element score nearly equal to that of boys at 4, and girls at 4 nearly equaled the mean score of boys at 5. In agreement with the findings in the present study Wellman reported no consistent sex differences on vowel and diphthong scores.

When all ages are combined, the USES sample produces all sound groups more accurately than the LSES sample. The mean scores and standard deviations for the USES groups are 57.1, SD 10.58, on the consonant elements; 54.35, SD 18.03, on the double-consonant blends; 13.09, SD 5.90, on the triple-consonant blends; 11.74, SD 0.54, on the vowels; and 4.93, SD 0.28, on the diphthongs. Those for the LSES group are 54.17, SD 12.15, on the consonant elements; 48.46, SD 20.78, on the double-consonant blends; 11.49, SD 6.30, on the triple-consonant blends; 10.56, SD 0.34, on the vowels; and 4.92, SD 0.33, on the diphthongs. The differences between the scores are statistically significant at the .01 level for consonant elements ($t = 2.64$), double-consonant blends ($t =$

Table 10. Mean Scores and Standard Deviations on Consonant Elements, Blends, Vowels, and Diphthongs for Upper and Lower Socioeconomic Status Groups, by Age

CA	Consonant Elements (69) *		Double Blends (71) *		Triple Blends (19) *		Vowels (12) *		Diphthongs (5) *	
	Mean	SD	Mean	SD	Mean	SD	Mean	SD	Mean	SD
Upper Socioeconomic Status Groups (USES) †										
3	42.5	11.5	32.8	17.2	5.9	4.8	11.4	0.3	4.8	0.3
3.5	49.3	8.7	41.1	17.9	9.1	5.1	11.6	0.3	4.9	0.2
4	56.1	4.8	51.4	11.9	11.9	3.9	11.7	0.2	5.0	0.0
4.5	57.4	8.3	54.4	16.6	13.3	5.4	11.7	0.2	4.9	0.2
5	58.0	8.6	58.0	13.5	14.2	4.9	11.8	0.2	4.9	0.2
6	61.8	7.6	61.1	15.7	14.8	5.8	11.9	0.2	5.0	0.0
7	65.8	3.5	67.5	5.3	17.6	2.9	12.0	0.0	5.0	0.0
8	66.1	0.8	68.8	5.2	17.9	1.8	11.9	0.2	5.0	0.0
Lower Socioeconomic Status Groups (LSES) ‡										
3	42.3	12.3	28.3	17.8	5.1	4.2	11.1	0.3	4.7	0.3
3.5	46.6	11.7	39.0	19.5	8.3	5.6	11.4	0.3	4.9	0.2
4	51.0	9.9	44.8	17.3	9.9	3.2	11.5	0.2	4.9	0.2
4.5	52.7	8.7	45.0	17.0	9.7	5.3	11.5	0.2	4.9	0.2
5	53.8	13.0	48.8	20.3	11.2	6.4	11.6	0.2	4.9	0.2
6	59.7	8.9	54.4	19.8	14.2	5.1	11.9	0.3	5.0	0.0
7	62.6	5.7	60.4	16.8	16.2	4.0	11.9	0.3	5.0	0.0
8	64.7	3.5	67.0	6.3	17.3	3.2	12.0	0.0	5.0	0.0

* Number of sounds tested.
† N = 18 in each age group.
‡ N = 42 in each age group.

3.13), and triple-consonant blends ($t = 2.71$). While the difference in the correctness of articulation of diphthongs between the two groups is not statistically significant, that in the production of vowels is significant beyond the .01 level of confidence with a t of 23.88.

That the USES sample at nearly all age levels receives higher scores on the various sound groups is apparent from Table 10. For the consonant elements and blends, there is a tendency for the observed differences to be greater after 4 years of age than before. At 3 and 3.5 no t above 0.98 is obtained. At 4, 7, and 8 years the consonant element subscores differentiate between the USES and the LSES groups at the .05 level or above ($t = 2.69$, 2.67, and 2.45 respectively). The double-consonant blend subscores differentiate at the .05 level only at 5 and 7 years ($t = 2.05$ and 2.47). The triple-consonant blend subscores differentiate the SES groups only at 4.5 years ($t = 2.36$). None of the observed differences between the diphthong subscores of the USES and LSES age subsamples is significant. However, the vowel subscores differ significantly at six age levels, all except at 6 and 7 years (t values range from 2.00 to 3.00).

Table 11. Percentage of Scores of 8-Year-Old Upper Socioeconomic Status Groups Attained by Upper and Lower Socioeconomic Status Groups on Consonant Elements, Blends, Vowels, and Diphthongs, by Age

CA	Consonant Elements	Double Blends	Triple Blends	Vowels	Diphthongs
		USES *			
3	64.3%	47.7%	33.0%	95.0%	96.0%
3.5	74.6	59.7	50.9	96.7	98.0
4	77.3	74.7	66.5	97.4	100.0
4.5	82.3	79.1	74.3	97.4	98.0
5	87.8	84.3	79.4	98.3	98.0
6	93.5	88.8	82.7	99.2	100.0
7	99.6	98.1	98.4	99.2	100.0
8	100.0	100.0	100.0	100.0	100.0
		LSES †			
3	64.0	41.1	28.5	92.5	94.0
3.5	70.5	56.7	46.4	95.0	98.0
4	77.2	65.1	55.9	95.8	98.0
4.5	79.7	65.4	54.2	95.8	98.0
5	81.4	70.9	62.6	95.8	100.0
6	90.3	79.1	79.4	99.2	100.0
7	94.7	87.8	90.6	99.2	100.0
8	97.9	97.4	96.7	100.0	100.0

* N = 18 in each age group.
† N = 42 in each age group.

The increase in correct articulation of the several sound groups with age is more rapid for the USES than for the LSES sample. For the consonant elements and blends the higher score at 8 years is obtained by the USES group. The differences, while not statistically significant, are all in the same direction. Below 6 years the scores of the LSES samples are in general only slightly below those of the USES sample one test interval younger. After 6, however, the scores of the LSES groups are somewhat more than one test interval lower. This is a more substantial difference than that found between boys and girls. Since intelligence of the SES groups is not equalized, it may be that part of the difference observed is the result of differences in intelligence. While the difference between intelligence of the boys and girls in the study is not significant, that between the entire USES and LSES groups is significant at the .01 level of confidence.

The percentage score obtained on the several sound groups by the USES and LSES samples when the achievement of the 8-year-old USES sample is taken as a terminal status measure is presented in Table 11. Here as previously reported (Tables 7 and 9) for the combined and separate sex samples the correct articulation of vowels and diphthongs shows relatively little growth over the age range studied. The increase in accuracy of articulation of consonant elements over the age range is less than that of double blends which, in turn, is less than that of triple blends.

The differences observed between the USES and LSES groups are frequently not significant, while they are greater and more consistent than differences observed between the sexes. For all groups the order of difficulty of types of sounds remains constant, with diphthongs, vowels, consonants, double-consonant blends, and triple-consonant blends being the consistent order of difficulty.

Nasals, Plosives, Fricatives, Combinations, and Semivowels

The accuracy of production of the nasals, plosives, fricatives, combinations, and semivowels over the entire age range studied varies at the separate age levels. Considering the entire sample, the mean percentages of correct utterance are 96.4 for the nasals, 90.1 for the plosives, 87.7 for the semivowels, 69.0 for the fricatives, and 59.5 for the combinations. This rank order of correct production of types of consonant sounds is in agreement with that of earlier investigations. Templin and Steer (50) report the same order of correct utterance in a group of nursery school children studied at Purdue University. Wellman *et al.* report 95.5 per cent correct utterance for nasals, 85.8 for plosives, and

67.9 for fricatives by their selected sample of children from 2 through 6 years.

For the subsamples by age the mean number of the various types of consonant sounds produced correctly is presented in Table 12. So that comparisons may be made among these consonant sounds the percentage of total possible score and the percentage of the scores of the 8-year-old subsample taken as a measure of terminal status are presented in Figure 2. For all types of consonant sounds except the combinations at least 95 per cent of the total possible score is attained by 8 years of age. The proportionate increase of these several consonant sound types over the five-year period studied differs considerably. When the scores of the 8-year-old subsample are used for the basis of comparison, the fricatives show the greatest increment over the five-year period. By 7 years of age, however, there is practically no difference among the types of consonant sounds in the proportion of the terminal status scores achieved.

Table 12. Mean Scores and Standard Deviations on Nasals, Plosives, Fricatives, Combinations, and Semivowels for Total Subsamples, by Age

	Nasals (8) *		Plosives (18) *		Fricatives (23) *		Combinations (8) *		Semivowels (12) *	
CA †	Mean	SD	Mean	SD	Mean	SD	Mean	SD	Mean	SD
3	7.4	1.1	14.2	2.9	9.4	5.1	2.7	2.1	8.6	2.5
3.5	7.7	0.6	15.1	2.2	11.8	5.1	3.5	2.2	9.3	2.5
4	7.7	0.6	16.0	1.8	13.8	5.0	4.7	1.9	10.4	2.0
4.5	7.7	0.6	15.8	2.0	15.3	5.0	5.0	1.8	10.4	1.8
5	7.6	0.8	16.0	2.2	15.7	6.5	3.1	1.9	10.6	2.0
6	7.8	0.4	17.4	1.3	18.4	5.2	5.5	1.4	11.3	1.5
7	7.9	0.3	17.5	0.8	20.7	3.7	5.8	1.1	11.7	0.8
8	8.0	0.1	17.8	0.4	21.8	2.1	5.8	1.0	11.8	0.5

* Number of this type of sound tested.
† N = 60 in each age group.

When the percentage of possible score is taken as a basis for comparison, the order of difficulty of the consonant sound types which is found for the entire sample holds at each of the age intervals tested. When the comparison is made on the terminal status scores, however, the order of difficulty of the combinations and fricatives is reversed. This is due to the lower percentages of possible score attained by the 8-year-olds on the combinations.

The 8-year-olds attain at least 94.4 per cent of total possible scores on all types of consonants except the combinations, on which only 72.7 per cent of the total possible correct utterance of combinations has been

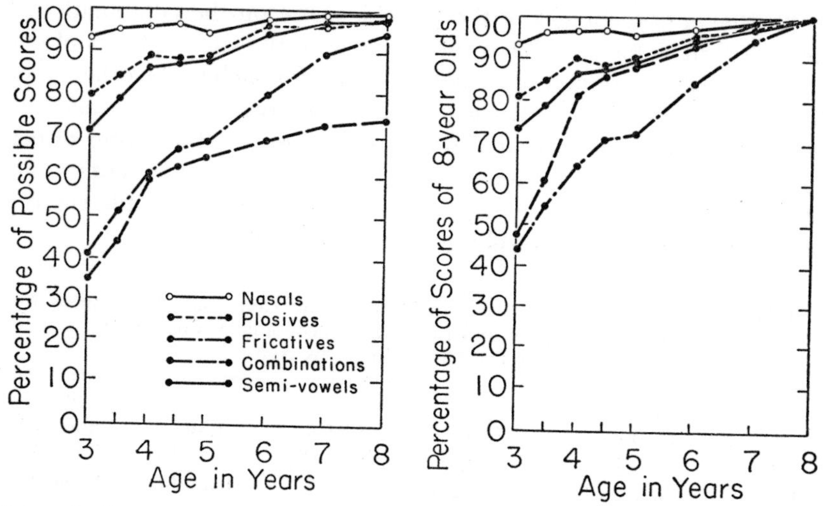

FIGURE 2. COMPARISON BY AGE OF THE PERCENTAGE OF SCORES OF THE 8-YEAR-OLD SUBSAMPLE TAKEN AS A MEASURE OF TERMINAL STATUS AND THE PERCENTAGE OF TOTAL POSSIBLE SCORES ON NASALS, PLOSIVES, FRICATIVES, COMBINATIONS, AND SEMIVOWELS

achieved. Since only eight elements are classified as combinations, the low percentage is largely accounted for by frequent substitution of "w" for the "hw" sound in both the initial and medial positions.

At each age from 3 to 6 the order of correct utterance of sounds according to percentage of total possible score in the Wellman study and that reported in the present study agree. The highest accuracy is on the nasals, next on the plosives, and lowest on the fricatives. The actual percentages, however, disagree somewhat. For all three types of consonant sounds the higher percentage of correct utterance is attained by the subjects in the present study at 3 years of age. The percentages of possible score at 3 years in the current study are 92.5 on the nasals, 79.1 on the plosives, and 41.0 on the fricatives. The percentages at this age on the same sounds in the Wellman study are 60.8, 52.6, and 33.9. At the other ages the percentage of possible score is very similar for the nasals and plosives. The fricatives, however, are less frequently correctly produced at comparable ages in the present study. The mean percentages of possible score for the present study at 4, 5, and 6 years are 60.1, 68.4, and 79.9 respectively. For the Wellman study at the same ages they are 70.3, 88.1, and 82.7. These differences in percentages of possible scores may be accounted for by the specific sounds tested, the differences in the SES levels, and the size and selection of the sample.

The mean percentages of the possible score on the combinations is presented in Table 13. This is the only one of the various types of consonant sounds presented separately, because for each of the others there is so little difference between percentage of possible score and percentage of 8-year-old terminal status score. For all other types of consonant sounds the achievement of the 8-year-olds is 95 per cent or more of the total possible score, thus percentages of total possible score or of the scores of the 8-year-old girls are very similar.

Table 13. Mean Percentages of Possible Score on Combinations Attained by Boys and Girls, Upper and Lower Socioeconomic Status Groups, and Total Subsamples, by Age

CA	Boys (N = 30)		Girls (N = 30)		USES (N = 18)		LSES (N = 42)		Total Subsamples (N = 60)	
	Mean	SD	Mean	SD	Mean	SD	Mean	SD	Mean	SD
3	35.9	28.5	32.1	24.3	34.8	29.3	33.6	25.3	34.0	26.5
3.5	43.8	29.5	43.8	26.1	46.5	26.6	42.6	28.4	43.8	27.9
4	58.4	22.0	58.8	24.1	72.3	12.9	52.6	24.0	58.6	23.1
4.5	59.6	26.5	65.4	18.5	68.0	24.8	60.1	21.9	62.5	23.0
5	60.4	27.8	67.1	17.3	66.0	19.5	62.8	24.8	63.8	23.4
6	65.4	23.0	71.6	9.6	67.4	24.8	69.0	14.0	68.5	17.9
7	70.0	16.0	74.6	11.9	77.3	7.5	70.3	15.9	72.3	14.3
8	71.6	15.1	73.8	8.1	75.8	8.9	71.4	13.1	72.7	12.3

Neither boys nor girls are markedly superior in the articulation of any of the various types of consonant sounds. At 3.5, 4.5, and 6 years girls tend to receive slightly higher scores, and at 3 years boys tend to receive the higher score; but at 8, 7, and 4 either sex may receive the higher score. Girls receive the higher score in 26 of 40 comparisons, but in only a few scattered instances are the differences significant at the .05 level (*t* ranges from 0.0 to 2.22).

In Table 14 the percentage of the achievement of boys and girls separately on the various consonant sounds is presented when the scores of the 8-year-old girls are taken as a measure of terminal status. The mean score of girls is used for both boys and girls so that a comparison between the sexes is possible. Had the mean percentage of possible scores attained by the two sexes differed to an appreciable extent, the mean scores of boys and girls separately would have been used for determining measures of terminal status so that the patterns of growth could have been seen for each sex. At each age the percentages of the terminal status scores of the 8-year-old girls attained in the separate

Table 14. Percentage of Scores of 8-Year-Old Girls Attained by Boys and Girls on Nasals, Plosives, Fricatives, Combinations, and Semivowels, by Age

CA	Nasals	Plosives	Fricatives	Combinations	Semivowels
			Boys *		
3	92.8%	79.8%	45.5%	48.6%	76.5%
3.5	94.5	82.0	48.7	59.3	76.5
4	94.5	89.4	64.1	79.2	87.2
4.5	96.2	86.8	67.6	80.8	86.4
5	96.2	87.7	64.1	81.9	88.7
6	97.0	95.4	78.3	88.6	94.4
7	100.0	97.8	91.0	94.9	97.8
8	100.4	98.2	99.4	97.1	101.5
			Girls *		
3	92.8	79.0	40.8	43.6	69.9
3.5	97.5	86.3	59.5	59.3	82.6
4	97.9	89.1	62.4	79.7	89.8
4.5	97.0	89.2	72.5	88.6	91.0
5	94.5	91.1	79.8	91.0	92.7
6	98.7	98.2	89.9	97.1	98.6
7	98.7	97.6	98.2	101.2	101.5
8	100.0	100.0	100.0	100.0	100.0

* N = 30 in each age group.

Table 15. Percentage of Scores of 8-Year-Old Upper Socioeconomic Status Group Attained by Upper and Lower Socioeconomic Status Groups on Nasals, Plosives, Fricatives, Combinations, and Semivowels, by Age

CA	Nasals	Plosives	Fricatives	Combinations	Semivowels
			USES *		
3	92.3%	85.0%	38.3%	45.8%	72.3%
3.5	96.5	88.4	56.5	61.5	80.3
4	97.9	90.6	65.4	78.8	90.6
4.5	98.6	93.1	74.3	89.3	92.0
5	97.2	94.1	75.3	92.7	95.8
6	99.2	99.1	86.1	88.9	97.2
7	99.2	99.7	98.0	101.8	101.4
8	100.0	100.0	100.0	100.0	100.0
			LSES †		
3	93.6	78.0	43.2	44.5	72.6
3.5	96.2	83.3	50.8	56.2	78.3
4	96.0	87.3	59.6	69.6	86.6
4.5	96.2	86.9	66.4	79.5	86.1
5	94.7	88.5	67.3	83.0	87.3
6	97.7	97.0	79.7	91.2	97.0
7	99.9	98.0	89.1	92.9	97.8
8	100.8	99.9	95.3	94.4	101.9

* N = 18 in each age group.
† N = 42 in each age group.

types of consonant sounds are similar except for the fricatives. Here the growth of the girls tends to be somewhat more rapid.

In Table 15 the percentages of the USES and LSES groups are presented for these consonant sounds when the scores of the 8-year-old USES group is taken as a measure of terminal status. Essentially the same relation is found here as between the sexes. The achievement of the 8-year-old LSES group is only slightly more retarded in relation to that of the USES.

Position of Consonant Sound Tested

The mean percentage of correct utterance of the consonant elements for the 480 subjects of all ages is 83.5, SD 15.5, on the initial sounds; 80.1, SD 16.6, on the medial sounds; and 74.6, SD 22.5, on the final sounds. The differences among all three of these positions is significant: the t between the initial and medial position is 3.11, and those between the final and the initial and the final and the medial positions are 7.06 and 4.14, respectively. Wellman, reporting on the articulation of 120 children, found a mean of 97.9 subjects producing initial consonants correctly, 94.8 the medial, and 87.1 the final. Differences significant at the .01 level are found between the final and initial positions ($t = 4.50$) and between the final and medial positions ($t = 3.44$). The difference between the initial and medial positions was not significant ($t = 1.42$).

When the age ranges used in the present study and in Wellman's are compared, the results attained are similar. Omitting the 6-year sample, since Wellman had only four cases at this age level, when the mean percentage scores for the initial, medial, and final positions of the 300 children 5 years of age and under are compared, the mean percentage initial score is 78.65, SD 18.26, the medial 76.04, SD 16.60, the final 67.24, SD 20.62. The difference between the initial and medial position is not statistically significant ($t = 1.83$). The differences between the final and both the initial and medial positions are significant at the .01 level. The t for the former is 7.18, that for the latter is 5.75.

The mean percentage of correct utterance of consonant sounds according to position in the word is presented in Table 16 for boys and girls, USES and LSES, and for the total subsample at each age tested.

Figure 3 presents for each age subsample the percentage of the correct articulation of initial, medial, and final sounds by the 8-year-olds as a measure of terminal status. Here the clear separation of sounds in the beginning or the middle of words from those at the end of words is evident for every age. Whether or not one admits a medial sound

Table 16. Mean Scores and Standard Deviations on Initial, Medial, and Final Consonant Elements for Boys and Girls, Upper and Lower Socioeconomic Status Groups, and Total Subsamples, by Age

	Boys (N = 30)		Girls (N = 30)		USES (N = 18)		LSES (N = 42)		Total Subsamples (N = 60)	
CA	Mean	SD	Mean	SD	Mean	SD	Mean	SD	Mean	SD
					Initial Consonants (23) *					
3	16.0	3.6	15.2	3.9	15.1	4.3	15.8	3.5	15.6	3.8
3.5	16.7	3.8	18.0	2.9	17.6	2.8	17.2	3.7	17.3	3.5
4	18.9	3.1	18.6	2.6	19.5	1.7	18.5	3.2	18.8	2.9
4.5	18.5	2.7	19.8	3.0	19.7	2.9	18.9	2.9	19.1	2.9
5	18.4	4.0	20.1	3.1	20.0	2.5	19.0	2.2	19.3	3.7
6	19.7	2.9	21.2	1.7	20.5	2.6	20.5	2.5	20.5	2.5
7	21.1	1.8	21.7	1.0	21.8	1.3	21.3	1.5	21.4	1.5
8	21.8	1.0	21.8	1.9	21.9	0.5	21.7	1.0	21.8	0.9
					Medial Consonants (25) *					
3	16.0	4.7	15.7	4.2	15.6	3.8	16.0	4.7	15.9	4.5
3.5	17.2	4.4	18.5	3.7	18.7	3.4	17.5	4.4	17.9	4.1
4	19.3	3.9	19.6	2.8	21.0	2.2	18.8	3.6	19.4	3.4
4.5	19.5	4.1	20.3	2.7	21.1	2.5	19.4	3.3	19.9	3.5
5	19.3	4.6	21.0	3.7	20.8	1.8	19.8	4.6	20.2	4.2
6	21.6	3.4	22.5	2.3	22.3	2.6	22.0	3.0	22.1	2.9
7	22.6	1.9	23.1	1.2	23.4	1.1	22.6	1.8	22.8	1.6
8	23.2	1.2	23.4	1.3	23.7	0.5	23.1	1.5	23.3	1.3
					Final Consonants (21) *					
3	11.5	4.6	10.2	4.3	11.8	3.4	10.5	4.6	10.9	4.5
3.5	11.5	4.5	12.9	3.4	13.1	3.2	11.9	4.3	12.2	4.0
4	14.2	3.8	14.4	3.1	15.6	2.1	13.8	3.8	14.3	3.5
4.5	14.9	3.6	15.4	3.4	16.7	2.9	14.5	3.5	15.2	3.5
5	14.8	4.9	16.4	4.1	17.1	3.5	15.0	4.9	15.6	4.6
6	16.9	4.7	18.7	2.2	19.1	2.7	17.3	4.0	17.8	3.8
7	18.7	3.0	19.9	2.1	20.6	1.4	18.8	2.9	19.3	2.7
8	20.0	1.4	20.2	1.1	20.5	1.2	19.9	1.4	20.1	1.3

* Number of this type of consonant element tested.

in theory, the substantial similarity found in the development of initial and medial sounds provides little basis for making a practical distinction according to these positions.

In Figure 4 the mean percentages of correct utterance of sounds in the initial, medial, and final positions for consonant elements and blends and for the various types of consonant sounds are presented. On the whole, final consonant elements are less correctly produced than initial or final sounds until about 90 per cent correct articulation is attained. Above this percentage, differences in articulation according to position tend to disappear. The differences between the final and both the initial

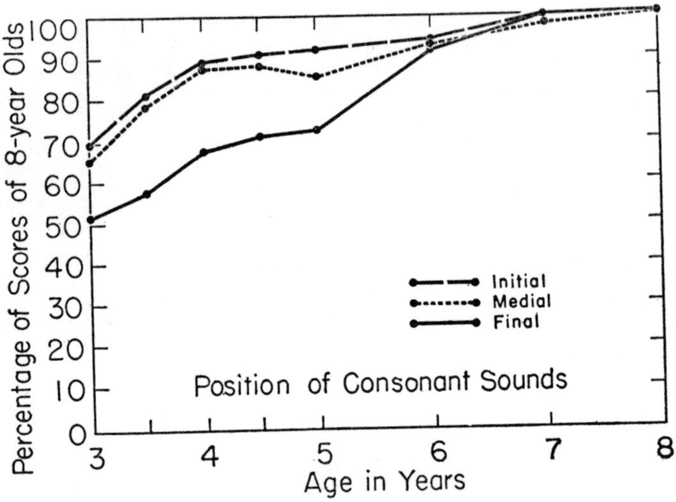

FIGURE 3. PERCENTAGE OF SCORES OF THE 8-YEAR-OLD SUBSAMPLE TAKEN AS A MEASURE OF TERMINAL STATUS ON INITIAL, MEDIAL, AND FINAL CONSONANT ELEMENTS BY AGE

and medial positions are greater at the earlier ages tested; after 7 they are minimal.

The type of sound tested is important in the age at which differences in accuracy of articulation according to test position tend to disappear. Differences in accuracy of articulation of nasals in the initial, medial, and final positions disappear by 4.5 years. Similar differences have disappeared at 7 years for the plosives and semivowels. At 8 years final fricative sounds are still produced less accurately. Since the mean percentage of correct utterance of final fricatives is 91.7, it is likely that the differences would have disappeared had older children been tested. The articulation of combinations, however, is atypical. At the early ages, when many of the sounds are produced inaccurately, the final position is more difficult, but at the later ages it is easiest. This occurs since the "hw," a difficult sound for most children, is not tested in the final position.

Consonant blends were tested in the initial and final positions. Of the 28 initial consonant blends, 23 were double and 5 were triple blends. Of the 62 final blends, in 20 the consonants appeared in the same order as in the initial blends, and in 42 the consonants appeared in reverse order. Table 17 presents the percentages of correct articulation of these double and triple initial, final, and final reversed blends with the performance of the 8-year-old subsample taken as a measure of terminal

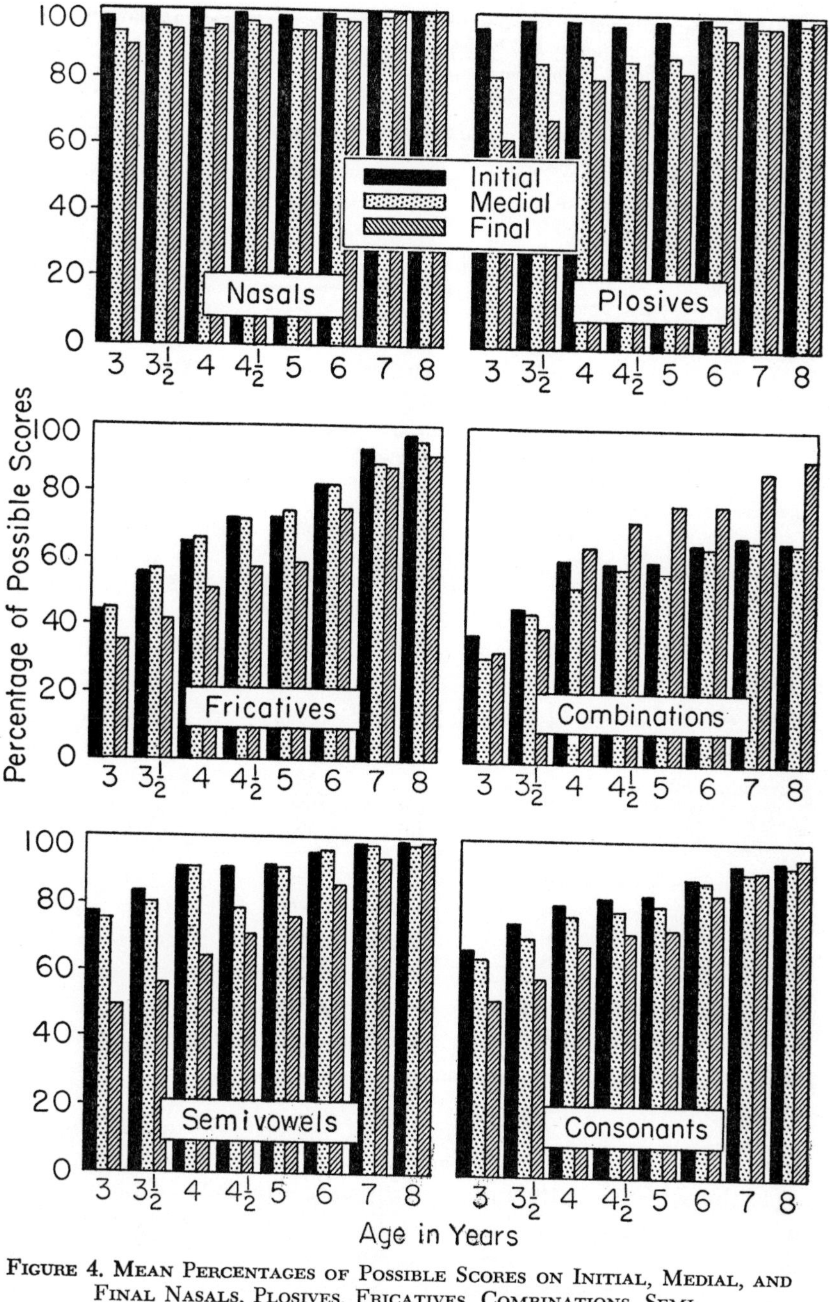

FIGURE 4. MEAN PERCENTAGES OF POSSIBLE SCORES ON INITIAL, MEDIAL, AND FINAL NASALS, PLOSIVES, FRICATIVES, COMBINATIONS, SEMIVOWELS, AND CONSONANT ELEMENTS BY AGE

Table 17. Percentages of Consonant Blend Scores of the 8-Year-Old Subsample Attained by Each Total Subsample from 3 to 8 Years

	Double Blends			Triple Blends		
CA	Initial (N = 23)	Final (N = 18)	Final-reversed (N = 30)	Initial (N = 5)	Final (N = 2)	Final-reversed (N = 12)
3	49.1	36.8	45.4	30.4	38.8	29.1
3.5	58.6	50.3	57.4	54.3	61.6	44.5
4	75.9	62.0	66.5	67.4	66.6	56.4
4.5	76.4	64.3	70.4	63.0	66.6	60.9
5	80.0	73.1	75.3	71.7	77.7	66.4
6	85.5	87.1	88.0	78.2	83.3	83.6
7	97.3	95.3	95.4	91.3	94.4	96.4
8	100.0	100.0	100.0	100.0	100.0	100.0

Table 18. Percentages of Consonant Blend Scores of 8-Year-Old Girls Attained by Boys and Girls from 3 to 8 Years

	Double Blends			Triple Blends		
CA	Initial (N = 23)	Final (N = 18)	Final-reversed (N = 30)	Initial (N = 5)	Final (N = 2)	Final-reversed (N = 12)
			Boys *			
3	49.5	41.9	50.3	34.0	43.7	32.4
3.5	55.9	50.0	53.5	46.8	57.9	40.5
4	76.8	61.5	68.5	72.3	68.4	56.7
4.5	73.2	61.0	71.3	59.6	63.1	59.5
5	74.5	67.2	72.0	63.8	68.4	58.6
6	92.3	90.0	91.3	85.1	84.2	88.3
7	101.4	96.6	97.9	100.0	100.0	100.0
8	100.0	96.6	98.6	97.9	89.4	99.1
			Girls *			
3	45.4	31.6	39.2	25.5	31.5	25.2
3.5	68.2	56.9	63.0	57.4	63.1	48.6
4	75.0	59.8	68.2	59.6	63.1	55.9
4.5	79.1	66.1	68.5	63.8	63.1	61.3
5	85.0	77.0	77.6	78.7	78.9	73.0
6	78.6	81.0	83.6	70.2	73.7	77.5
7	93.2	90.8	91.6	80.8	84.2	91.9
8	100.0	100.0	100.0	100.0	100.0	100.0

* N = 30 in each age group.

status. For the double-consonant blends, particularly at the younger ages, those blends in the initial position are articulated accurately somewhat more frequently. For the triple-consonant blends the percentage of correct articulation does not seem to be related to the position in which the blends were tested. The increments in the scores between the two youngest age levels tested reaches the .05 level for all blends except

Table 19. Percentages of Consonant Blend Scores of 8-Year-Old Upper Socioeconomic Status Groups Attained by Upper and Lower Socioeconomic Status Groups from 3 to 8 Years

	Double Blends			Triple Blends		
CA	Initial (N = 23)	Final (N = 18)	Final-reversed (N = 30)	Initial (N = 5)	Final (N = 2)	Final-reversed (N = 12)
	Upper Socioeconomic Status Groups (USES) *					
3	54.7	39.1	50.9	37.5	36.8	30.6
3.5	63.6	54.0	60.0	52.1	63.2	48.6
4	79.1	66.1	68.5	68.7	57.9	67.6
4.5	80.9	76.4	79.6	75.0	78.9	75.7
5	88.4	85.1	80.6	83.3	84.2	76.6
6	84.0	90.2	91.7	79.2	84.2	84.7
7	98.7	97.1	98.3	93.7	94.7	101.8
8	100.0	100.0	100.0	100.0	100.0	100.0
	Lower Socioeconomic Status Groups (LSES) †					
3	44.9	35.1	42.2	25.0	36.8	27.9
3.5	54.7	47.1	55.0	50.0	57.9	42.3
4	72.0	58.0	64.0	60.4	68.4	50.4
4.5	71.6	58.0	64.7	54.2	57.9	54.0
5	73.8	66.6	71.3	62.5	68.4	61.3
6	83.6	83.3	84.1	75.0	73.7	82.0
7	93.3	92.0	92.0	85.4	89.4	92.8
8	96.9	97.7	97.6	93.7	94.7	98.2

* N = 18 in each age group.
† N = 42 in each age group.

Table 20. Age at Which 75 Per Cent of Children First Uttered Various Types of Sounds Correctly

CA	Types of Sounds *
3......	Initial, medial, final nasals; initial, medial plosives; initial, medial semivowels; vowels; diphthongs.
4......	Final plosives.
5......	Final semivowels; final combinations; initial double-consonant blends.
6......	Initial, medial, final fricatives; final double-consonant blends; reversed triple-consonant blends; reversed double-consonant blends.
7......	Initial, final triple-consonant blends.

* Initial and medial combinations are not produced correctly by 75 per cent of children by 8 years.

the initial double-consonant blends. The t value for the latter is 1.45 and the t values for the other blends range from 2.41 to 3.43. For the initial double-consonant blends the increment between 3.5 and 4 years is statistically significant ($t = 2.61$).

Table 18 presents the percentage of the scores on consonant blends of the 8-year-old girls taken as a measure of terminal status which is attained by boys and girls at the younger ages. The achievement of the girls is not significantly superior to that of the boys on these consonant blends. In fact, the performance of the boys exceeds that of the girls on all the blends at 3, 4, 6, and 7 years of age and on the final reversed double-consonant blends at 4.5 years. Only two of these differences reach the .05 level of confidence: the initial double-consonant blends ($t = 2.50$) and the initial triple-consonant blends ($t = 2.51$) at 7 years. On none of the blends on which the girls receive the higher scores is the difference significant.

The percentage of the consonant blend scores of the 8-year-old USES group attained by all the younger SES groups is presented in Table 19. At each age the score of the USES group is higher on all of the consonant blends tested. Scattered among the various blends measured and throughout the age range tested eight of the differences reach the .05 level of confidence and three reach the .01 level.

Table 20 presents the ages at which 75 per cent of the subjects in any age subsample first produced the various consonant sound elements correctly in the initial, medial, and final positions. Only on the initial and medial combinations is this criterion not reached by 8 years of age. The final combinations reach this level at 5 years because the "hw" sound is not tested since it does not appear in English words in this position.

Unvoiced and Voiced Consonant Sounds

Consonant sounds are classified as "voiced" sounds if the vocal cords vibrate in their production and as "voiceless" or "unvoiced" sounds if they do not. The plosive and fricative sounds are made up of pairs of voiced and unvoiced sounds and one such pair is found in the combinations. The sound "t" is the unvoiced equivalent of the voiced sound "d" since the tongue position of both is the same, and the distinguishing characteristic is the vibration of the vocal cords on the latter sound. Similarly, the other pairs of unvoiced and voiced sounds are p and b, k and g, s and z, sh and zh, f and v, th and th, and ch and j.

Table 21 indicates a variable pattern of accuracy of production of voiced and unvoiced sounds. On the whole, more children produce the unvoiced consonant sounds correctly, but this does not hold consistently for all such sounds. For the specific pairs of sounds the voiceless element of each pair except the "t-d" pair is produced correctly by more children at each age. This is probably at least partially the result of the particular word used for testing the medial "t." The word "kitten" is frequently and commonly pronounced so that the medial "t" approaches a "d" sound. When this occurred it was considered an inaccurate production of the "t" sound.

For the plosive sounds considered as a group, the voiced plosives are articulated more accurately at all ages except 3 years. However, at no age level is the observed difference significant. The t values are all less than 1.23.

Table 21. Mean Number of Children Correctly Producing Voiced and Voiceless Items in Paired Consonant Sounds, by Age

CA	Consonant Pairs								Plosives	Fricatives	Consonants
	Voiced Sounds										
	b	d	g	v	~~th~~	z	zh	j			
3	48.0	47.7	43.3	18.7	12.0	20.3	9.0	21.0	46.3	15.5	28.3
3.5	51.3	51.3	50.7	23.7	14.0	33.0	13.5	24.7	51.1	21.8	33.7
4	54.7	56.7	54.3	30.7	25.0	35.0	20.0	41.7	55.2	28.4	40.6
4.5	54.3	55.3	52.7	32.7	28.3	39.3	23.0	43.3	54.1	31.5	41.9
5	56.7	54.7	54.7	37.0	33.7	38.7	25.5	48.3	55.3	34.5	44.4
6	59.0	58.7	58.0	49.0	44.0	38.7	40.5	52.0	58.6	43.3	50.4
7	58.0	59.7	58.7	53.3	50.0	51.7	48.5	55.0	58.8	51.1	54.6
8	60.0	59.7	60.0	59.0	56.0	53.0	51.5	56.3	59.9	55.2	57.2
	Voiceless Sounds										
	p	t	k	f	th	s	sh	ch			
3	54.3	40.3	51.0	50.7	15.3	38.7	26.7	28.0	48.6	32.0	37.7
3.5	55.7	39.0	53.7	52.7	19.3	47.0	37.7	36.3	49.4	39.2	42.7
4	56.7	41.7	56.0	55.0	29.7	45.3	42.3	43.0	51.4	43.1	46.2
4.5	57.0	40.7	55.7	58.3	35.3	46.3	50.7	50.0	51.1	47.7	49.3
5	56.7	41.7	56.3	54.7	37.7	46.7	49.3	50.7	51.6	47.1	49.2
6	59.0	54.7	58.0	59.0	52.3	45.3	52.0	52.0	57.2	52.2	54.0
7	59.7	55.3	59.0	60.0	55.0	53.7	57.0	57.3	58.0	56.4	57.1
8	60.0	55.7	60.0	60.0	58.0	57.0	58.0	57.7	58.6	58.2	58.3

Among the fricative sounds, however, the unvoiced fricatives are produced accurately by a larger number of children at each age level tested. These differences are all statistically significant. Only the difference at 8 years is significant at the .05 level ($t = 2.33$). At all other ages the differences are significant at the .01 level with t values ranging from 3.14 to 4.04.

Wellman reports differences in the accuracy of production of voiced and unvoiced sounds which are not statistically significant either at single age levels or over the age range 2 to 6 years. In the present study, when all consonant sounds in which voiced and unvoiced pairs occur are considered, the differences are not statistically significant at six of the age levels. Only at 4.5 and 7 years are the differences significant ($t = 3.52$ and 2.03 respectively). At both of these ages the unvoiced consonants are produced more accurately. In the Wellman study the pairs tested were p and b, t and d, k and g, th and ~~th~~, and s and z. The results from the two investigations do not contradict one another since the present study includes two additional fricative pairs and one combination pair, and the obtained differences vary with the specific pairs and the particular types of consonant sounds.

Specific Speech Sound Elements Tested

The relative difficulty of specific sounds is an important consideration in articulation development. The level of articulation development of any particular child is probably often ascertained on the basis of the misarticulation of a few sounds which are repeatedly used in his speech.

Eight-year-old children in this study produce nearly all sounds quite accurately. This finding agrees with previous investigations indicating essentially mature articulation at this age. Only 15 of the 176 specific sound elements tested are not produced correctly by 90 per cent of the children at 8 years. Of these sounds, 85 per cent correct articulation is achieved by 8 years on zh–, –sh, –j, thr–, shr–, sl–, skr–, and –sp; 75 per cent on –z–, –tr, and –kt; 73 per cent on –tl; 57 per cent on –lfth; and less than 10 per cent on hw– and –hw–.

The "hw" sounds do not increase in accuracy of production with age. For the initial "hw–" as in "white" the percentage of correct articulation is 10 per cent at 3 years, 25 at 4, and then decreases to 8.3 per cent at 8 years. In the medial position this sound is produced correctly by 16.7 per cent at 3 years, 26.7 per cent at 3.5, and then decreases to only 3.0 per cent at 8. Nearly all of the misarticulations of this sound were the omission of the "h" attack and the substitution of the "w." In the development of modern English the "h" attack on the "r" and "l" has disappeared and young children in a midwestern community, at least, usually omit this attack on the "w."

In Table 22 each tested sound is entered at the age at which 75 per cent of the subjects produced it correctly. The only four tested sounds which are not produced correctly by this percentage of subjects are hw–, –hw–, –tl, and –lfth. For some sounds the 75 per cent level of attainment does not continue consistently after the earliest age at which it is entered. This occurred for –t which was first entered at 3 years; for –rm, –kr, br–, sm–, –rt, –ft, –mpt, pl–, l–, sp–, sn–, which were first entered at 4 years, and for –sh–, first entered at 4.5 years.

The essential similarity of the articulation of boys and girls is seen in Table 23 where the comparison of the ages at which 75 per cent of boys and girls correctly articulated specific sounds is presented. Of the 176 sounds tested, only three, hw–, –hw–, and –lfth are not articulated adequately by at least 75 per cent of one of the sexes; 73 sounds are produced correctly at the same ages: 74 within one test interval; 26 within two test intervals; and only 6 sounds beyond this.

Only on six sounds did boys and girls achieve the criterion at age levels separated by more than two test intervals. In all instances one

Table 22. Earliest Age at Which 75 Per Cent of All Subjects Produced Each Tested Sound Element Correctly *

CA	Sound Elements
3	Vowels: ē, ĭ, ĕ, ă, ŏ, ŭ, o͝o, o͞o, ō, ô, ȧ, ûr
	Diphthongs: û, ā, ī, ou, oi
	Consonants: m–, –m–, –m, n–, –n–, –n, –ng–, –ng, p–, –p–, –p, t–, –t, k–, –k–, b–, –b–, d–, –d–, g–, –g–, f–, –f–, –f, h–, –h–, w–, –w–
	Double-consonant blends: –ngk
3.5	Consonants: –s–, –z–, –r, y–, –y–
	Double-consonant blends: –rk, –ks, –mp, –pt, –rm, –mr, –nr, –pr, –kr, –br, –dr, –gr, –sm
4	Consonants: –k, –b, –d, –g, s–, sh–, –sh, –v–, j–, r–, –r–, l–, –l–
	Double-consonant blends: pl–, pr–, tr–, tw–, kl–, kr–, kw–, bl–, br–, dr–, gl–, sk–, sm–, sn–, sp–, st–, –lp, –rt, –ft, –lt, –fr
	Triple-consonant blends: –mpt, –mps
4.5	Consonants: –s, –sh–, ch–, –ch–, –ch
	Double-consonant blends: gr–, fr–, –lf
5	Consonants: –j–
	Double-consonant blends: fl–, –rp, –lb, –rd, –rf, –rn, –shr
	Triple-consonant blends: str–, –mbr
6	Consonants: –t–, th–, –th–, –th, v–, –v, ~~th~~–, –l
	Double consonant blends: –lk, –rb, –rg, –rth, –nt, –nd, –~~thr~~, –pl, –kl, –bl, –gl, –fl, –sl
	Triple-consonant blends: skw–, –str, –rst, –ngkl, –nggl, –rj, –ntth, –rch
7	Consonants: –~~th~~–, –~~th~~, z–, –z, –zh–, –zh, –j
	Double-consonant blends: thr–, shr–, sl–, sw–, –lz, –zm, –lth, –sk, –st
	Triple-consonant blends: skr–, spl–, spr–, –skr, –kst, –jd
8	Double-consonant blends: –kt, –tr, –sp

* hw–, –hw–, –lfth, and –tl are not produced correctly by 75 per cent of the subjects by 8 years of age.

Table 23. Comparison of Earliest Ages at Which 75 Per Cent of Boys and Girls Produced Each Tested Sound Element Correctly *

CA	Sound Elements
	Produced Correctly by Boys and Girls at the Same Age
3	m–, –m–, –m, n–, –n–, –n, –ng–, –ng, p–, –p–, –p, t–, k–, –k–, b–, –b–, d–, g–, –g–, f–, –f–, –f, h–, –h–, w–, –w–, ē, ĭ, ĕ, ă, ŏ, ŭ, o͝o, o͞o, ō, ȧ, ûr, ā, ī, ou, oi
3.5	–s–, –br, –mp
4	j–, l–, –s, tr–, kl–, kr–, bl–, st–, –lp, –mpt, –fth
4.5	–sh–, –ch–, –ch
5	–lb, –rd
6	–t–, –th–, –rb, –rg, –rth, –nd, –~~th~~r, –ngkl
7	–zh, –st, –lz, –lth
8	–tr, –kt
	Produced Correctly by Boys and Girls within One Test Interval
3–3.5	Girls earlier: –d–, s–, –y–, ū, –ngk
	Boys earlier: –l–, –r, ûr, –fr, –pr, –gr, –nr
3.5–4	Girls earlier: sh–, –z, –r–, –kr, –dr, –sm, –lt, –rm, –mr, –mps, tw–, br–, –d
	Boys earlier: –ks
4–4.5	Girls earlier: –sh
	Boys earlier: r–, pl–, pr–, kw–, gl–, sp–
4.5–5	Girls earlier: ch–, gr–
	Boys earlier: sl–, –rp, –lf, –rf
5–6	Girls earlier: th–, –th–, ~~th~~–, –l, –pl, –kl, –bl, –gl, –fl, –lk, –nt, –nggl, –rch
6–7	Girls earlier: v–, –~~th~~–, z–, –zh–, thr–, sw–, –rst, –kst, –rj, –jd, –ntth, skr–, str–, skw–
	Boys earlier: –v, –j
7–8	Girls earlier: –z, shr–
	Boys earlier: –sp
	Produced Correctly by Boys and Girls within Two Test Intervals
3–4	Girls earlier: –k, y–
3.5–4.5	Girls earlier: –rt, –rk, –pt
4–5	Girls earlier: –j–, dr–, –shr, –mbr
	Boys earlier: –b, fl–, –sk, –rn, ô
4.5–6	Girls earlier: fr–
5–7	Girls earlier: –sk, –zm, –skr
6–8	Girls earlier: –~~th~~, –sl, –str
	Produced Correctly by Boys and Girls within More Than Two Test Intervals
3–6	Girls earlier: –t
4–6	Girls earlier: –g
	Boys earlier: spl–
4–7	Girls earlier: sm–, sn–
5–8	Girls earlier: spr–

* –tl attained by 75 per cent of girls at 8 years but not by boys at any age tested; hw–, –hw–, –lfth not attained by 75 per cent of boys or girls at any age tested.

or both of the following were noted. The sex attaining the criterion at the earlier age tended to show only slight increments in performance at the ages immediately following. The sex attaining the criterion at the later ages tended to approach the 75 per cent criterion at several preceding age levels.

A comparison of the ages at which 75 per cent of the subjects correctly produced the specific consonant elements with no regard to their position in a word in the present study, that of Wellman, *et al.*, and that of Poole is made in Table 24. There are, of course, some discrepancies, but the agreement is substantial, especially if the differences in the samples are taken into account. Both Wellman and Poole studied children from university laboratory schools. Both had fewer than 70 subjects completely tested covering the entire age range, and in both the subjects were grouped into whole-year intervals. Wellman's 3-year-olds and Poole's 3.5-year-olds range between 3 and 4 years. Considering Poole's 3.5-year-olds with the 3-year-olds of Wellman, there is substantial agreement among the three studies in the approximate order of

Table 24. Comparison of the Ages at Which 75 Per Cent of the Subjects Correctly Produced Specific Consonant Sounds in the Templin, the Wellman, and the Poole Studies

	Age Correctly Produced				Age Correctly Produced		
Sound	Templin	Wellman	Poole	Sound	Templin	Wellman	Poole
m	3	3	3.5	r	4	5	7.5
n	3	3	4.5	s	4.5	5	7.5†
ng	3	..*	4.5	sh	4.5	..‡	6.5
p	3	4	3.5	ch	4.5	5	..‡
f	3	3	5.5	t	6	5	4.5
h	3	3	3.5	th	6	..*	7.5†
w	3	3	3.5	v	6	5	6.5†
y	3.5	4	4.5	l	6	4	6.5
k	4	4	4.5	t̶h̶	7	..‡	6.5
b	4	3	3.5	z	7	5	7.5†
d	4	5	4.5	zh	7	..‡	6.5
g	4	4	4.5	j	7	6	..‡
				hw	*	..*	7.5

* Sound was tested but was not produced correctly by 75 per cent of the subjects at the oldest age tested. In the Wellman data the "hw" reached the percentage criterion at 5 but not at 6 years, the medial "ng" reached it at 3, and the initial and medial "th" and "t̶h̶" at 5 years.

† Poole, in an unpublished study of 20,000 preschool and school-age children reports the following shifts: "s" and "z" appear at 5.5 years, then disappear and return later at 7.5 years or above; "th" appears at 6.5 years and "v" at 5.5 years.

‡ Sound not tested or not reported.

appearance of correct articulation of consonant sounds. Poole did not test the "ch" and "j" sounds.

There is complete agreement in the age placement on five of the seventeen sounds reported in all three investigations, a spread of one year on six sounds, and a spread of two or more on six sounds. Where the discrepancy is greatest the present study more nearly agrees with Wellman if the sound is correctly produced at an early age and with Poole if it is correctly produced at a later age. Among the six sounds showing the greatest discrepancy, the present study agrees exactly with one or the other of the studies on the placement of the "f" sound, within one half year on that of the "s," "l," and "z" and within a year on the "r" and "t." The shifts reported in the more recent unpublished data obtained from Poole are in the direction of the results of the present study and of Wellman.

There is an essential similarity in the sequence of sounds reported in these three studies. Henderson in her study of institutionalized mentally retarded subjects reports 75 per cent of her subjects correctly articulating "w," "h," and "m" at 3 years, "p" at 4 and "n" at 5. These are among the earliest sounds to be produced correctly in the present study based on a representative sample and the Wellman and Poole studies on children above average in intelligence. In all but one instance they are placed at 3 or 3.5 years.

Roe and Milisen in a speech survey of nearly 2,000 children in grades one through six report the "z," "hw," "th," and "j" as most frequently misarticulated. In the present study one of these sounds is not correctly articulated by 75 per cent of the subjects at 8 years. Two reach this criterion at 7 years and one at 6 years. The "m," "n," and "h" were the only consonant elements measured in the present study which did not appear in the list of misarticulations. Using the twenty consonants about which information is available in both studies, the rank order correlation between frequency of error of articulation of sounds in the elementary grades, and the development of accurate articulation is —.62. This correlation is probably spuriously high because during the first three elementary school grades some development in speech sound articulation is still under way. If only those subjects above the third grade were considered, a measure would be available of the relation between sounds incorrectly articulated after essentially mature articulation should be achieved and the order of development of sounds in normally speaking children. This could not be done with the data in the present study nor with the data published by Roe and Milisen.

The articulation of specific speech sounds has been summarized in this section. For evaluating the articulatory performance of a child on any of the specific speech sounds tested, tables are presented in Appendix IV. Appendix Table 1 presents the number of children in each age subsample correctly articulating each sound element. Since 60 children have been tested on each, direct comparisons of the accuracy of production among the sounds can be made. Appendix Table 2 presents the percentages of correct utterance of each sound element by age with the articulation of the 8-year-old subsample taken as a measure of terminal status.

Inaccuracies in Articulation

Whenever a sound element was not produced correctly, the inaccuracy was classified into the following categories: omissions, defective sounds, and substitutions. Defective sounds were nonstandard English approximations of English sounds, the lateral "s," etc. Substitutions were the use of a different standard English sound. The substituted sound was transcribed using the IPA, but the specific substitutions are not discussed in this monograph.

For the sample as a whole, substitution errors were approximately 10 times as frequent as omissions, and about 4.5 times as frequent as the use of defective sounds. Table 25 shows that omission errors decrease with age from 13.3 per cent of the errors at 3 years to only 2.2 per cent at 8 years. There is no regular trend with age for either substitution of standard English sounds or defective sounds.

That frequency of occurrence of error in articulation varies with the position of the consonant is evident from Table 26: 27.1 per cent of all errors were on initial sounds; 34.6 per cent were on medial sounds; 38.3 per cent were on final sounds. The differences among all positions are statistically significant (t between initial and medial positions is 3.9; between initial and final 13.0; and between medial and final 15.7). For both boys and girls the trend in frequency of error is similar. The differences among all the interrelations are significant for the girls ($t =$ 5.2, 5.9, and 5.8) as well as for the boys ($t = 5.7$, 6.6, and 6.0). This is true despite the fact that there are fewer final consonant elements measured.

From 3 through 6 years there is little change in the proportion of error in the initial, medial, or final positions. At ages 7 and 8 proportionately more errors occur in the medial than in the final position. This may be partially a reflection of the number of errors at these older ages in the articulation of the "hw" sound, which is measured only in the initial and medial position.

Table 27 presents the shift with age in the frequency with which various types of errors occur in the initial, medial, and final positions in a word. In all positions errors of omission are least frequent, defective sound errors next, and substitution errors most frequent. However, the distribution of error shifts with the position of the sound produced. Omissions increase substantially from the initial to the medial to the final position; defective sound errors exhibit the same trend, but to a lesser degree; substitutions, however, decrease in occurrence from the initial to the medial to the final positions.

The frequency of error varies greatly for the different sound categories. From Table 28 it is apparent that the number of errors made in the production of fricative sounds is nearly twenty-five times as great

Table 25. Number and Percentage of Omitted Defective and Substituted Consonant Elements by Age

	Omitted		Defective		Substituted		Total	
CA	N	%	N	%	N	%	N	%
3	213	13.3	203	12.7	1,182	74.0	1,598	100.0
3.5	160	12.3	219	16.9	918	70.8	1,297	100.0
4	87	8.8	170	17.1	736	74.1	993	100.0
4.5	68	7.6	177	19.9	645	72.5	890	100.0
5	77	9.2	148	17.7	610	73.1	835	100.0
6	50	9.6	71	13.7	398	76.7	519	100.0
7	15	4.6	44	13.4	268	82.0	327	100.0
8	5	2.2	56	24.2	170	73.6	231	100.0
Total	675	10.1	1,088	16.3	4,927	73.6	6,690	100.0

Table 26. Number and Percentage of Consonant Errors in Initial, Medial, and Final Positions, by Age

	Position of Error							
	Initial		Medial		Final		Positions Combined	
CA	N	%	N	%	N	%	N	%
3	443	27.7	547	34.2	608	38.1	1,598	100.0
3.5	340	26.2	429	33.1	528	40.7	1,297	100.0
4	260	26.2	334	33.6	399	40.2	993	100.0
4.5	232	26.1	305	34.3	353	39.6	890	100.0
5	223	26.7	289	34.6	323	38.7	835	100.0
6	152	29.3	175	33.7	192	37.0	519	100.0
7	93	28.4	133	40.7	101	30.9	327	100.0
8	72	31.2	103	44.2	56	24.2	231	100.0
Total	1,815	27.1	2,315	34.6	2,560	38.3	6,690	100.0

Table 27. Shift in Number and Percentages of Types of Inaccuracies in the Production of Initial, Medial, and Final Consonant Sounds, by Age

CA	Initial				Medial				Final			
	Omitted	Defective	Substitution	Total Error	Omitted	Defective	Substitution	Total Error	Omitted	Defective	Substitution	Total Error
					Number							
3	19	37	387	443	53	59	435	547	141	107	360	608
3.5	21	35	284	340	34	62	333	429	105	122	301	528
4	5	39	216	260	11	50	273	334	71	81	247	399
4.5	2	30	200	232	12	54	239	305	54	93	206	353
5	5	38	180	223	7	37	245	289	65	73	185	323
6	4	13	135	152	9	20	146	175	37	38	117	192
7	0	5	88	93	2	18	113	133	13	21	67	101
8	0	11	61	72	2	18	83	103	3	27	26	56
Total	56	208	1,551	1,815	130	318	1,867	2,315	489	562	1,509	2,560
					Percentage							
3	4.3	8.4	87.3	100.0	9.7	10.8	79.5	100.0	23.2	17.6	59.2	100.0
3.5	6.1	10.3	83.6	100.0	7.9	14.5	77.6	100.0	19.9	23.1	57.0	100.0
4	1.9	15.0	83.1	100.0	3.3	15.0	81.7	100.0	17.8	20.3	61.9	100.0
4.5	0.9	12.9	86.2	100.0	3.9	17.7	78.4	100.0	15.3	26.3	58.4	100.0
5	2.2	17.0	80.8	100.0	2.4	12.8	84.8	100.0	20.1	22.6	57.3	100.0
6	2.6	8.6	88.8	100.0	5.1	11.4	83.5	100.0	19.3	19.8	60.9	100.0
7	0.0	5.4	94.6	100.0	1.5	13.5	85.0	100.0	12.9	20.8	66.3	100.0
8	0.0	15.3	84.7	100.0	1.9	17.5	80.6	100.0	5.4	48.2	46.4	100.0
3–8	3.1	11.5	85.4	100.0	5.7	13.7	80.6	100.0	19.1	22.0	58.9	100.0

Table 28. Number and Percentage of Errors for Various Categories of Sounds, by Age

CA	Nasals		Plosives		Fricatives		Semivowels		Combinations	
	N	%	N	%	N	%	N	%	N	%
3	35	2.2	226	14.2	815	51.0	205	12.8	317	19.8
3.5	21	1.6	175	13.5	671	51.8	160	12.3	270	20.8
4	20	2.0	120	12.1	551	55.5	97	9.9	205	20.5
4.5	18	2.0	134	15.3	462	51.6	96	10.8	180	20.3
5	25	3.0	118	14.1	436	52.2	82	9.8	174	20.9
6	12	2.3	39	7.5	278	53.6	39	7.5	151	29.1
7	5	1.2	29	8.9	141	43.3	19	5.8	133	40.8
8	1	0.5	14	6.0	74	32.0	11	4.7	131	56.8
Total ..	137	2.1	855	12.8	3,428	51.2	709	10.6	1,561	23.3

as the number of errors in the production of nasal sounds. The absolute number of errors by age decreases for all sound categories. The percentage frequency of errors by age is quite stable from 3 to 5 years. From 6 to 8 years, however, there is a decrease in the percentage of errors in the production of nasals, fricatives, and semivowels, an increase in errors in the combinations, and no trend for the plosives.

The distribution of types of error varies considerably by age among the several types of consonant sounds. Table 29 shows that although for all types of consonant sounds the proportion of omissions decreases with age, only rarely is the proportion of omissions at any age as high as at the older ages for the plosives and the semivowels. The proportion of errors due to the production of defective or nonstandard English speech sounds is highest for the plosives. While substitutions constitute the most frequent type of error for all groups of consonant sounds, they are most common for the combinations.

Summary

1. The general articulation score increases with age until essential maturity in articulation is reached by 8 years. Boys take about one year longer than girls, and lower socioeconomic status groups about one year longer than upper socioeconomic status groups, to attain essentially adult articulation.

2. In the early years, diphthongs, vowels, consonant elements, double-consonant blends, and triple-consonant blends are produced in that order from most to least accurate. This holds for both sexes and socioeconomic status groups, and other studies are in substantial agreement.

3. The order of accuracy of articulation of consonant elements, from

Table 29. Number and Percentages of Types of Errors on Nasals, Plosives, Fricatives, Combinations, and Semivowels

CA	No. of Errors	Percentage			
		Omitted	Defective	Substitution	Total
		Nasals			
3	35	31.4	17.1	51.5	100.0
3.5	21	19.0	19.0	62.0	100.0
4	20	0.0	5.0	95.0	100.0
4.5	18	0.0	5.6	94.4	100.0
5	25	8.0	16.0	76.0	100.0
6	12	8.4	0.0	91.6	100.0
7	5*	...	...	...	...
8	1*	...	...	...	...
		Plosives			
3	226	23.9	33.6	42.5	100.0
3.5	175	25.2	34.8	40.0	100.0
4	120	20.8	31.7	47.5	100.0
4.5	134	23.1	44.8	32.1	100.0
5	118	24.5	28.0	47.5	100.0
6	39	56.4	10.3	33.3	100.0
7	29	27.6	20.7	51.7	100.0
8	14	21.4	28.6	50.0	100.0
		Fricatives			
3	815	9.3	10.4	80.3	100.0
3.5	671	9.1	14.9	76.0	100.0
4	551	4.5	19.6	75.9	100.0
4.5	462	4.3	19.3	76.4	100.0
5	436	7.3	19.9	72.8	100.0
6	278	5.4	19.4	75.2	100.0
7	141	3.5	22.0	74.5	100.0
8	74	0.0	47.3	52.7	100.0
		Semivowels			
3	205	28.8	2.9	68.3	100.0
3.5	160	26.9	4.4	68.7	100.0
4	97	23.7	4.1	72.2	100.0
4.5	96	17.7	4.2	78.1	100.0
5	82	15.9	6.1	78.0	100.0
6	39	10.3	5.1	84.6	100.0
7	19	10.5	10.5	79.0	100.0
8	11	15.2	36.4	45.4	100.0
		Combinations			
3	317	4.1	9.5	86.4	100.0
3.5	270	3.0	17.4	79.6	100.0
4	205	6.8	9.3	83.9	100.0
4.5	180	0.0	12.8	87.2	100.0
5	174	0.6	10.9	88.5	100.0
6	151	5.3	7.3	87.4	100.0
7	133	0.0	3.0	97.0	100.0
8	131	0.0	9.9	90.1	100.0

* Percentages not calculated for fewer than 10 errors.

most to least accurate, is: nasals, plosives, fricatives, combinations, and semivowels.

4. The mean percentage of correct utterance is somewhat greater for the initial and medial than for the final position of the consonant elements.

5. There is a tendency for voiceless consonant elements to be produced somewhat more accurately than voiced ones, although this does not hold similarly for fricatives, plosives, and specific sound pairs. The unvoiced fricatives are produced significantly more accurately than the voiced fricatives at most age intervals. The voiced plosives, however, tend to be produced more accurately but not at a statistically significant level.

6. There is substantial agreement in the order of frequency of correct articulation of specific sounds among several studies.

7. In agreement with previous investigations, 8-year-old children produced nearly all sounds correctly, in all positions.

8. The percentage of errors of omission decreases with age, but there is little relation to age in errors of substitution or defective sounds.

9. Frequency and type of error in articulation varies with the type of sound and its position in the word.

IV. SPEECH SOUND DISCRIMINATION

By speech sound discrimination is meant the ability to make auditory distinctions among the different speech sounds. This is an auditory perceptual skill; and, unlike all other aspects of language considered in this study, is only indirectly observable in the language produced.

The correct articulation of speech sounds is a matter of both motor and perceptual skill. The motor component probably makes the greater contribution to the production of sounds in the babbling and verbal play of the infant. At this time vocalizations recognizable as standard English sounds are produced long before they appear in meaningful words. When such words appear, however, the perception of speech sounds becomes increasingly important in determining that the sound is used in the appropriate position in a word. Investigation of speech sound discrimination was included in this study since this ability is deemed important to the adequate articulation of sounds in words.

Pertinent Studies

The ability of children to discriminate between speech sounds has not been investigated extensively. Partly because of difficulties in obtaining such measures at very early ages, more work has been done with school-age than with preschool children. Most of the literature pertinent to the present study deals with techniques of measurement.

The sound discrimination test published by Travis and Rasmus in 1931 (52) has served as the prototype for the development of most other measures. This test is made up of 366 pairs of nonsense syllables which are identical or differ from one another in only one phoneme, for example "thā-fā" (see p. 14). In 300 pairs the discrimination is made between consonants and in 66 pairs it is made between vowels. The subject listens to the examiner utter each pair of syllables and indicates on a blank whether he perceives them as the "same" or "different." The test may be administered to individuals or to groups and requires at the very least 30 to 45 minutes.

Listening to 366 pairs of nonsense syllables and making judgments about each is not only a monotonous and fatiguing task, but demands considerable intellectual development. Unless the subject cooperates throughout the test, the results are not valid. Even if the discrimination pairs are administered during several sessions, the difficulty of making judgments between abstract nonsense syllables restricts the use of the test to the elementary grades and above. The test is useful for adolescent or adult subjects, but a shorter, more concrete, and more interesting test is needed for primary-grade children. For preschool children a technique of measurement using concrete rather than abstract items is imperative if a valid measure is to be obtained.

In 1942 the author published a study (48) of the sound discrimination ability of children in second through sixth grades. Sound discrimination was measured in 200 items similar to those in the Travis-Rasmus test. No discriminations among vowels were included. The number of discriminations to be made among nasals, plosives, fricatives, semivowels, and combinations was approximately proportional to the errors in articulation of these types of sounds as found in a previous study of the articulation of 130 preschool children (50). In half of the 200 items the phoneme to be discriminated was identical with the other half, but its position in the syllable differed. In 100 items the discrimination phoneme was in the initial position, and in the other 100 items it appeared in the final position. The item "sā-zā" in one group would appear as "ās-āz" in the other. The only exceptions were the use of the medial position for those sounds that do not appear in the initial or final positions in English. Since there is no initial "ng" in English, the medial "ng" was included with the initial items; since there is no final "hw" in English, the medial "hw" was included with the final items. Using a group technique of administration similar to that of Travis and Rasmus, a satisfactory measure of the sound discrimination ability of second-grade children was obtained. From the 200 items a short test of the 70 most discriminating items was selected. This short test correlated at 0.92 with the 200-item test. The sound discrimination measure used with the 5-to-8-year-olds in the present study consisted of the 50 most discriminating items of these same 200.

In reading readiness tests and work books speech sound discrimination is often sampled at the kindergarten level, but there are few carefully designed attempts to measure it. The author has located no systematic study of this ability in younger preschool children. Pronovost and his students at Boston University have been developing a picture technique to study sound discrimination ability in kindergarten and first-grade children (12, 30, 37). Their initial work was carried on at about the same time the earlier data for this study were gathered.

Mansur first constructed a picture sound discrimination test patterned after the Travis-Rasmus test in 1950 (30). Instead of nonsense syllables differing in only one sound element, the test was made up of pairs of such words which could be pictured. In the administration of the test, both words in the pair were uttered by the experimenter as an aural stimulus to the child. The child's task was to identify the stimulus pair of words from among the four pairs of pictures on a single sheet before him. For the word-pair "pole-bowl" the four pictures presented were of two poles, two bowls, a bowl and a pole, and a pole and a bowl (in reverse order). Thus for any stimulus word pair, *ab*, the four pictures were arranged as follows: *aa*, *bb*, *ab*, and *ba*. In subsequent revisions by Haroian (12) and Pronovost and Dumbleton (37) this presentation has been simplified so that the child indicates the pair of words uttered on a card bearing pictures of one like and one unlike pairing of the words, that is, either *aa* or *bb* and *ab* or *ba*. These revisions of Mansur's test have also increased the number of discriminations. The original test included 20 pictured word pairs. The revision by a group of students as reported by Pronovost and Dumbleton consists of 36 pairs of discrimination words presented in 72 items so that a recognition of similarity and difference is obtained for each pair (37).

This revised test has been used at the kindergarten and first-grade level. It might possibly be used with younger children, but this is doubtful because of the complexity of the administration and the likelihood that words such as "pole," "chain," "crown," and "pup" may not be readily identified by preschool children when they are pictured.

Sound Discrimination of Children from 3 to 5 Years

Because of the current status of information, any investigation of speech sound discrimination of preschool children must be exploratory. The test used with the 3-to-5-year-old children is a picture test especially constructed for this study. This test has been described in Chapter II and is presented in Appendix IIC.

Scoring the picture sound discrimination test. Three different methods of scoring the picture sound discrimination test result in three scores as follows:

Score A. The score is the number of items in which *two out of three* responses are correct and in which no attention is given to whether the test words were identified correctly.

Score B. The score is the number of items in which *two out of two* responses are correct and in which no attention is given to knowledge of the test words.

Score C. The score is the number of items in which *two out of either two or three* responses are correct and in which *both* discrimination words have been correctly identified previously.

Two factors were taken into account in determining the scoring techniques: (1) the number of trials needed to obtain two correct responses to any item; and (2) the correctness of the identification of the test words. Scores A and B separate out the accuracy of discrimination when no errors were made in the responses, and when an error did occur, but do not take into account whether or not the test words were correctly identified. Score C takes into account this latter factor. When both words were known, however, the distinction between the number of trials necessary to obtain two correct responses is not made because of the small difference in mean scores.

Results. Accurate identification of the test word by the child underlies the adequacy of the measure of sound discrimination. Table 30 shows that the mean number of sound discrimination vocabulary words correctly identified does not approach the maximum possible score at any age although it increases steadily with age. At the ages tested neither boys nor girls consistently identify more words. The USES groups identify more words correctly at each age level than the LSES groups. Only at 3 and 4.5 years, however, does the difference reach the .05 level of confidence ($t = 2.33$ and 2.29 respectively).

No child of 5 years identified all 92 test words accurately. The range in the number of correct identifications increased with age, but the increase in the minimum number of words identified is greater than the increase in the maximum number. The minimum numbers of words identified at consecutive age levels from 3 through 5 is 29, 44, 40, 44, and 54; maximum numbers are 80, 80, 89, 86, and 85. By 4 years of age correct identification of all the words is approached by some of the children. At 3 years, some children identify only one third of the words; between 3.5 and 4.5 some identify fewer than half of the words; and even at 5 years some identify considerably fewer than two thirds of the test words correctly. The attempt to select words simple enough to be known by all the children was only partially successful. The test words selected were more satisfactory in this respect at 4 years of age and above than at 3 and 3.5 years.

In Table 31 the mean sound discrimination scores obtained using each of the scoring techniques indicate that the increase in scores with age is considerably greater when Score C rather than either Score A or B is used. Although the maximum possible score is the same with all scoring techniques, from 3 to 5 years the mean scores increased 4.4 points for Score A, 6.8 for Score B, and 15.6 for Score C.

The significance of the differences between consecutively tested age levels varies considerably among the three scores obtained. The incre-

Table 30. Mean Sound Discrimination Vocabulary Score for Boys and Girls, Upper and Lower Socioeconomic Groups, and Total Subsamples by Age from 3 to 5

CA	Boys (N = 30)		Girls (N = 30)		USES (N = 18)		LSES (N = 42)		Total Subsample (N = 60)	
	Mean	SD	Mean	SD	Mean	SD	Mean	SD	Mean	SD
3	60.3	11.5	59.5	10.2	64.1	8.2	58.1	11.4	59.9	10.8
3.5	64.7	9.7	65.4	8.9	67.9	7.7	63.8	9.6	65.1	9.3
4	69.4	10.3	69.1	7.7	72.2	7.8	68.0	9.4	69.3	9.0
4.5	73.8	7.9	74.2	7.7	76.8	5.6	72.7	8.2	74.0	7.8
5	74.5	7.9	77.1	5.9	77.4	6.1	75.1	7.4	75.8	7.0

Table 31. Mean Sound Discrimination Scores A, B, and C with Significance of Differences between Consecutively Tested Age Levels

CA	Score A			Score B			Score C		
	Mean	SD	*t* between Age Levels	Mean	SD	*t* between Age Levels	Mean	SD	*t* between Age Levels
3	50.8	3.9		45.6	5.58		23.8	8.9	
			1.81			1.41			2.88*
3.5	52.1	4.0		47.0	5.06		28.3	8.2	
			1.60			2.66*			3.64*
4	53.3	4.2		49.6	5.64		32.2	9.0	
			.97			1.05			2.94*
4.5	54.0	3.7		50.6	4.78		36.7	7.7	
			2.03**			2.32**			1.91
5	55.2	2.6		52.4	3.65		39.4	7.7	

* Significant at the .01 level.
** Significant at the .05 level.

ments with age are most significant using Score C. The differences do not reach the .01 level of confidence between any ages for Score A, but reach it between 3.5 and 4 years for Score B and between all ages except 4.5 and 5 years for Score C. The differences between these last ages on Scores A and B reach the .05 level, on Score C approach it.

The range in scores obtained with Score C is considerably greater, and the distribution of scores by age tends to be somewhat less skewed than with Scores A or B. The range, medians, means, and degree of skewness obtained for each age level using each of the scoring techniques is presented in Table 32.

With Score A the range of scores for the 3-to-5-year-old sample is 21 points, from 39 to 59. At 5 years of age the range is only 12 points, but at all other ages the range is between 18 and 20 points. The maximum

Table 32. Mean, Median, Range, and Skewness of Sound Discrimination Scores A, B, and C, by Age

Sound Discrimination Score	CA				
	3	3.5	4	4.5	5
Score A					
Mean	50.8	52.1	53.3	54.0	55.2
Median	51.6	53.6	55.0	55.4	55.9
Skewness	−0.61	−1.13	−1.21	−1.13	−0.81
Range	39–58	41–59	42–59	41–59	48–59
Score B					
Mean	45.6	46.9	47.9	50.6	52.4
Median	46.0	47.0	51.5	51.5	53.3
Skewness	−0.22	−0.59	−1.92	−0.56	−0.74
Range	33–57	29–58	30–58	34–58	42–58
Score C					
Mean	23.8	28.3	32.2	36.7	39.4
Median	21.3	28.3	32.5	37.2	41.5
Skewness	0.84	0.00	−0.10	−0.19	−0.82
Range	10–31	9–44	8–55	17–51	15–54

score is obtained by one subject at 3.5, three at 4, three at 4.5, and four at 5 years. Using Score B the range is 30 points. No subject received the maximum score, but one at 3.5, two at 4, one at 4.5, and three at 5 years obtained a score of 58. The range is 17 points at 5 years and from 25 to 30 points at the earlier ages. Using Score C there is a range of 48 points for the total group. The range is 23 points at 3 years, 36 at 3.5, and between 35 and 48 at the three upper age levels. No subject received the maximum score.

That the scores obtained using all three scoring techniques are quite similar in comparing the separate sex groups is evident from Table 33. The boys receive slightly higher scores at 3, the earliest age tested, and the girls receive slightly higher scores at the other ages. The differences between the sexes are not statistically significant with any of the scoring techniques at any age, except that at 5 years using Score A the difference reaches the .05 level.

The higher score is obtained by the USES group at each age tested whether Score A, B, or C is considered (Table 34). The differences are not consistently significantly higher according to any of the scoring methods.

The intercorrelations between the sound discrimination vocabulary score and the sound discrimination Scores A, B, and C are presented in Table 35. They indicate greater similarity between Scores A and B than between either one and Score C. Consistently the correlations

Table 33. Significance of Differences on Sound Discrimination Scores A, B, and C between Boys and Girls by Age

CA	Boys Mean	Boys SD	Girls Mean	Girls SD	t
Score A					
3	51.6	4.2	50.1	3.3	1.54
3.5	51.4	4.3	52.9	3.5	1.48
4	52.4	4.2	54.2	3.9	1.72
4.5	53.4	4.2	54.5	3.0	1.17
5	54.5	3.0	55.9	2.0	2.12**
Score B					
3	46.3	5.5	45.0	5.2	0.94
3.5	45.9	6.0	48.0	4.6	1.52
4	48.3	6.0	50.8	5.5	1.67
4.5	49.9	5.0	51.3	4.3	1.17
5	51.8	3.2	53.0	3.9	1.33
Score C					
3	24.8	9.0	22.7	8.6	0.93
3.5	27.8	8.4	28.7	7.9	0.43
4	32.3	9.7	32.0	8.3	0.13
4.5	36.4	8.1	37.1	7.1	0.34
5	37.8	8.3	41.0	6.8	1.42

** Significant at the .05 level.

Table 34. Significance of Differences on Sound Discrimination Scores A, B, and C between Upper and Lower Socioeconomic Status Groups by Age

CA	USES † Mean	USES † SD	LSES ‡ Mean	LSES ‡ SD	t
Score A					
3	52.4	3.3	50.0	4.5	2.30**
3.5	52.5	4.2	52.0	3.9	0.47
4	54.1	4.1	53.0	4.1	0.98
4.5	55.6	2.7	53.3	3.8	2.66*
5	56.2	2.7	54.7	2.4	1.89
Score B					
3	48.0	5.3	44.6	5.1	2.30**
3.5	47.3	5.6	46.8	5.4	0.32
4	50.7	5.0	49.1	6.2	1.06
4.5	52.3	5.4	49.9	5.4	1.58
5	53.2	6.4	52.0	3.8	0.74
Score C					
3	27.4	7.5	22.2	8.8	2.33**
3.5	30.6	6.2	27.3	8.6	1.67
4	35.3	9.8	30.8	8.6	1.77
4.5	39.9	6.8	35.3	7.9	2.29**
5	42.1	7.1	38.3	7.4	1.88

* Significant at the .01 level.
** Significant at the .05 level.
† N = 18 at each age level.
‡ N = 42 at each age level.

Table 35. Intercorrelations between Sound Discrimination Vocabulary Score and Sound Discrimination Scores A, B, and C; between Score A and Scores B and C; and between Scores B and C, at Each Age Level from 3 to 5

CA	Correlated with Sound Discrimination Score		
	Score A	Score B	Score C
Sound Discrimination Vocabulary Score			
3	.69	.62	.96
3.5	.43	.33	.95
4	.45	.54	.94
4.5	.31	.46	.91
5	.57	.39	.96
Sound Discrimination Score A			
3		.80	.75
3.5		.81	.57
4		.90	.62
4.5		.90	.55
5		.72	.67
Sound Discrimination Score B			
3			.67
3.5			.44
4			.67
4.5			.67
5			.49

Table 36. Mean Sound Discrimination Scores for Boys and Girls, Upper and Lower Socioeconomic Status Groups, and Total Subsamples by Age on Items Where One Test Word Was Not Correctly Identified

CA	Boys (N = 30)		Girls (N = 30)		USES (N = 18)		LSES (N = 42)		Total Subsample (N = 60)	
	Mean	SD	Mean	SD	Mean	SD	Mean	SD	Mean	SD
3	20.9	4.3	20.9	3.8	20.2	3.4	21.2	4.2	20.9	3.8
3.5	19.4	5.7	19.8	4.2	18.2	5.1	20.2	4.6	19.6	4.8
4	16.4	5.1	19.2	5.0	16.1	5.7	18.5	4.8	17.8	5.2
4.5	15.9	5.1	15.4	4.8	14.4	5.5	15.5	4.6	15.2	4.9
5	14.5	4.4	13.7	5.3	12.6	5.3	14.8	5.5	14.1	4.8

between Score C and Score A or B are lower than those between Scores A and B. At the same time the correlation between the sound discrimination vocabulary score and Score C is much higher. Actually they are so highly correlated that at this age level the ability to orally identify the words in the sound discrimination test appears to be a pretty good measure of the ability to discriminate sounds.

Despite the high correlation between the sound discrimination Score

C and the sound discrimination vocabulary score, it cannot be assumed that the child's vocabulary is a good measure of his ability to discriminate sounds. The words in this test have been identified only as being in the child's vocabulary of use. The recognition vocabulary has not been investigated. Whether there is a relationship between the ability to use, produce, and discriminate specific sounds is a problem that needs further investigation. Data gathered in this study can be used to throw some light on this problem.

The subjects accurately indicated the stimulus word in two of three trials in many instances when both words in the test items had not been identified correctly. In Table 36 is given the mean number of correct responses for boys and girls as well as the USES and LSES groups by age when one of the test words was not identified correctly. All words have been presented to each child for identification, and only one word is presented as an aural stimulus. Thus in some instances that one word known is the stimulus word, in others it is not. The stimulus word, even though not used by the subject, may be recognized when presented by the experimenter, since the vocabulary of recognition is larger than the vocabulary of use.

There is a steady decrease in the number of items in which only one word is correctly identified. However, at 3 the mean of these items is just over one third of the total possible score. Even at 5 it is between one fourth and one fifth of the maximum possible score. There are no statistically significant differences between the sexes or the SES groups at any age.

Table 37 presents the mean scores for the sex and SES groups by age on those items in which both of the discrimination words were not identified. The means are decidedly lower than when one word was

Table 37. Mean Sound Discrimination Scores for Boys and Girls, Upper and Lower Socioeconomic Status Groups, and Total Samples by Age on Items Where Both Test Words Were Not Correctly Identified

	Boys (N = 30)		Girls (N = 30)		USES (N = 18)		LSES (N = 42)		Total Subsample (N = 60)	
CA	Mean	SD	Mean	SD	Mean	SD	Mean	SD	Mean	SD
3	5.8	4.0	6.2	3.7	4.6	2.9	6.7	4.0	6.1	3.8
3.5	4.4	2.5	4.3	2.9	3.9	2.4	4.5	3.2	4.3	3.0
4	3.5	3.5	3.0	2.7	2.7	2.4	3.5	3.4	3.2	3.2
4.5	2.5	2.8	2.0	2.5	1.7	1.7	2.5	2.9	2.2	2.8
5	2.1	2.6	1.2	1.4	1.7	1.5	1.6	2.3	1.6	2.1

identified. The mean scores decrease consistently, and quite rapidly, with age. The mean score is about 10 per cent of the possible score at 3 and about 3 per cent at 5.

Discussion. The central problem of the measurement of sound discrimination ability of young preschool children is in finding ways within their level of comprehension to measure the perception of fleeting, intangible sounds. This involves the use of indirect means which may limit or alter the measurement.

In the few studies carried on with young children pictures have been used. This restricts the choice of phonemes to be discriminated, contaminates the measure of the sound discrimination with the child's vocabulary knowledge, and assumes that all test words are equally familiar to him. In the test constructed for the present study, to assure that known words would most likely be included, the test words were taken from the vocabulary items in preschool intelligence tests, from stories for preschool children, and from children's conversations. This excluded the possibility of testing discriminations between sounds such as "v" and "th" which are frequently confused by older children and adults.

The careful selection of words did not result in all words' being known by all children, or even in any one child's knowing all the words pictured. If a word is not known by a child it is, of course, an unsatisfactory instrument for the indirect measurement of sound discrimination. However, the fact that a child does not identify the word pictured need not mean that the word is not known to him. It may not be identified because of the particular picture used to elicit it. It may not be identified because the child does not use it, and yet he might recognize the word if it were said for him. In both the present study and the investigations of Pronovost and his students the recognition of the word, not the use of it, is all that should be required to respond adequately to the task. Yet in the present study the scoring technique that took into account the child's identification by use of the test word as well as the identification of the word uttered as a stimulus seemed to produce the most satisfactory score. Further work needs to be done in this area.

Another problem is inherent in the technique of measurement used. Even though the child identifies both pictured words in a pair, it is probable that they may be unequally familiar to him. Ideally all test words used for discrimination should be equally familiar to the child. This is not accomplished in items such as "ship–chip." There is no way to determine from the techniques used in this study how familiar these words really are to each subject. It is possible that of two known discriminative words, the young child would point to the word more familiar to him. Since the stimulus words were selected randomly, the child may be asked to identify either the more familiar or the less familiar word. Thus, the familiarity of each word plays an undetermined role in the score attained.

The method of presenting the selected pictures to the child must be within his level of comprehension if meaningful results are to be obtained. Judgments of "same" and "different" as used in the Travis-Rasmus test are too difficult for young children. The choice situation must be approached for them in a more concrete manner. Pronovost's students have used the two words making up the discriminative pair as an aural stimulus throughout their investigations. However, in the setup in which the child must identify the stimulus, the revisions have moved toward simplification. In the last revision the child must make a selection from only two sets of paired pictures rather than from four. It is probable that even this technique is too difficult for the young preschool child, although it should be tried.

The present study has used a more simple, but also more indirect method of measurement in an exploratory attempt to measure sound discrimination in the preschool years. The child is presented with pictures of the pair of words and has merely to identify the single word said by the examiner. This technique measures the ability to discriminate between sound pairs only indirectly. It does make possible testing at a lower age level since only one word concept must be dealt with. All the 3-year-old children tested were able to respond to the situation.

Sound Discrimination of Children 6 to 8 Years

The selection of the fifty items used for measuring sound discrimination from 6 to 8 years is described in Chapter II and the test items are presented in Appendix IIB.

Results. That the mean sound discrimination scores continue to increase over this age range is evident from Table 38. The difference between ages 6 and 7 is significant at the .05 level ($t = 2.50$), but that between ages 7 and 8 does not reach this level ($t = 1.69$). The mean scores on the two hundred items from which the fifty items used in this study were selected increased only from 185.4 to 187.3 between the second and the fourth grade, and stayed within one point of the latter score through the sixth grade (49). Since 8-year-olds would be in the second or third grade the lack of significant increments between 7 and 8 years is in agreement with the findings reported for the two-hundred-item test.

Table 38. Mean Sound Discrimination Scores for Boys and Girls, Upper and Lower Socioeconomic Status Groups, and Total Subsamples, by Age from 6 to 8.

CA	Boys (N = 30)		Girls (N = 30)		USES (N = 18)		LSES (N = 42)		Total Subsamples (N = 60)	
	Mean	SD	Mean	SD	Mean	SD	Mean	SD	Mean	SD
6	40.5	8.7	42.9	5.6	43.7	9.0	38.6	10.7	41.7	7.4
7	43.9	6.5	45.4	4.3	47.7	2.3	41.2	11.0	44.7	5.6
8	45.2	3.4	46.9	2.7	47.5	1.4	45.4	3.5	46.1	3.2

The scores of both boys and girls increase steadily with age. Boys consistently receive lower scores than girls. At 6 and 7 years these differences are not statistically significant ($t = 1.27$ and 1.05 respectively), but they reach the .05 level at 8 years ($t = 2.14$). For the entire age range 6 to 8 the mean score of girls is 45.1, SD 4.7, and that of the boys is 43.2, SD 6.9, a difference significant at the .05 level ($t = 2.40$).

At each age level studied the subjects from the USES groups score higher than those from the LSES groups. While the difference between the SES group is not significant at 6 years ($t = 1.89$), it is significant at the .01 level at 7 ($t = 3.68$) and at 8 years ($t = 3.28$). When the subjects from 6 to 8 are combined, the difference is significant at the .01 level ($t = 3.31$). The mean for the USES groups is 46.31, SD 5.76, and that for the LSES groups is 43.22, SD 5.72.

The scores for the 8-year-old boys approximate those of the 7-year-old girls. Here, as in the articulation of speech sounds, the boys are about one year behind the girls at the oldest age included in the study. When the comparison is made between socioeconomic status groups the acceleration of the USES groups is somewhat more than a year.

The distributions of the scores for the groups at all ages are somewhat skewed to the left. On the whole the skewness is slightly greater at the younger ages tested.

Summary

Since different tests were used in the measurement of sound discrimination ability with preschool and with school-age children, the results cannot be considered as if they had been obtained on identical measures although they can be collated.

1. Sound discrimination ability shows a consistent increase with age, but its rate of growth is decelerated at about 4.5 to 5 years of age.

2. No statistically significant difference appears in the sound discrimination ability of boys and girls, at any single age level. During the early

years neither sex consistently receives the higher score, but in later years girls tend to receive higher scores. At the oldest age tested, the mean score of the boy is about equal to that of the girls one year younger.

3. Subjects from the upper socioeconomic status groups receive higher sound discrimination scores than subjects from the lower socioecomonic status groups at each age level, but these differences are not always statistically significant. The higher scores of the upper socioeconomic status groups may be the result of varying ability in sound discrimination, or an indirect reflection of differences in intelligence or in the capacity to deal with abstract concepts of "same" and "different." At the younger ages tested vocabulary knowledge as well is a factor to be considered.

4. In the picture sound discrimination test used with children 3 to 5, three techniques of scoring were tried. There is no real difference among the techniques in comparing sex or socioeconomic status groups. However, the scores obtained by technique C form an essentially normal distribution, do not crowd the ceiling of the test, and show more significant differences between consecutively tested age levels than those obtained using technique A or B. In technique C credit is given for two or more correct responses only if both test words were previously correctly identified.

5. The picture sound discrimination test seems to be a satisfactory preliminary instrument for the measurement of sound discrimination ability in young children. There are several criticisms of the test, however. It is dependent upon the vocabulary of the child and thus may be too highly related to intelligence. It is limited by the words that are likely to appear in the vocabulary of a preschool child, and by the fact that these words must be capable of being pictured. It does not measure sound discrimination ability on all combinations of sound-pairs desired. The testing technique devised by Pronovost and his students should be tried at the lower age levels. The vocabulary load, relation to intelligence, etc., would still be pertinent problems to be met, however. It may be that with the young preschool child a technique using nonsense words may hold more promise.

The chief contribution of the present investigations lies in its exploratory attempt to measure sound discrimination ability at the early preschool ages. In order to attack the problem some arbitrary decisions relating to choice and representation of test words and technique of measurement were made. Many of these may be altered as more evidence is accumulated from further investigation.

V. VERBALIZATIONS

Various aspects of the verbalizations of children can serve as indicators of the level of maturity in language development. The length of the verbalization, the complexity of structure, the grammatical accuracy, and the parts of speech used are considered in the present investigation. Twenty-four thousand remarks, three thousand at each age level, enter into most of the analyses presented in this chapter. The verbalizations of children have been obtained in a controlled child-adult situation described in Chapter II.

Pertinent Studies

Many studies have been made of various aspects of the verbal utterances of young children. Since McCarthy has presented an extensive summary of the literature (28), reference is made only to those studies whose methods and findings are used in direct comparisons.

In her study of language development, McCarthy introduced the technique used in the present study to gather data on a substantial number of young children (27). She obtained 50 verbalizations from 140 subjects between the ages of 18 months and 54 months in a reasonably standardized child-adult situation. Certain toys and books were used to stimulate the verbalization of 20 children within 1.5 months of 18, 24, 30, 36, 42, and 54 months. These 7,000 verbalizations were analyzed according to the length of the responses, the grammatical construction, and the parts of speech used. Davis (5), using a similar technique, included in her sample only children, children with siblings, and twins from 5.5 to 9.5 years of age. The McCarthy technique was modified to include more cowboy, Indian, and other toys or materials aimed at stimulating the speech of boys. Day (10) used essentially the McCarthy technique with twins from 2 to 5. Extensive comparisons are made between these studies and the present investigation since the selection of sample, the procedure of gathering data, and the analyses are very similar.

Williams (54) phonetically transcribed 40 "expression units" of a group of preschool children in play situations. These "expression units" are comparable to the "verbalizations," "utterances," or "sentences" of McCarthy and of Davis. These were verbalizations in which the child had something to express. A unit might be as brief and incomplete as a single word; it might be a grammatically complete and accurate sentence; or it might be several clauses uttered one after another as a loosely integrated sentence. Williams worked out a technique for obtaining a quantitative score of the complexity and grammatical accuracy of the expression. This has been used in the analysis of the data from the present study.

Classification

Dividing utterances. Oral speech differs from written speech in that grammatically incomplete and inaccurate sentences are more frequent. This prohibits the use of the grammatical sentence as a unit for collecting verbal remarks.

The rules as formulated by Davis for the division of comments into "sentences" or "expression units" were followed.

"1. The remark was considered finished if the child came to a complete stop, either letting the voice fall, giving interrogatory or exclamatory inflection, or indicating clearly that he did not intend to complete the sentence.

"2. When one simple sentence was immediately followed by another with no pause for breath, they were considered one sentence if the second statement was clearly subsidiary to the first" (5:44).

In most instances the remarks fell into the first category. The second category is important, however, since young children often express relationships in a series of simple sentences. The real meaning of the child's remarks would be lost unless several verbalizations were considered together as a single expression. These rules agree with Williams' considering a single unit of expression as "several highly connected clauses given together as a more or less integrated unit" (54:10).

Counting words. The central problem in counting the number of words in the verbalization is the functional definition of a word. Opinions differ as to how "word" should be defined. The spoken word of a child or an adult is not necessarily identical with a word in the dictionary. Contractions, elisions, or several dictionary words strung together may function as a single spoken word. To permit comparisons of the results with those of McCarthy, Davis, and Day, the method used by them has been followed in this study with no attempt to justify all the concepts used. The rules followed in counting words are presented in Appendix III A. They were laid down by McCarthy (27:36) and modified by Davis (5:44).

The basic idea underlying the word count is whether or not the child understands the word as a distinct and separate unit. It is assumed that "we are" is meant by the child when "we're" is uttered, so the contraction is counted as two words. On the other hand, the assumption is made that to the child "can't" is a distinct, separate, and independent word rather than a contraction of "can" and "not," so such contractions are counted as one rather than two words. Admittedly, such distinctions are arbitrary. However, there is a substantial advantage in following a classification already set up because then direct comparisons with earlier studies are possible.

Length of Response

Mean number of words. Figure 5 presents the mean leangth of sentence by age as reported by McCarthy, by Davis for her sample of singletons, and as found in the present study. Although in each the mean length of remark increases with age, the verbalizations of children at each age in the current study are longer than those of children in the

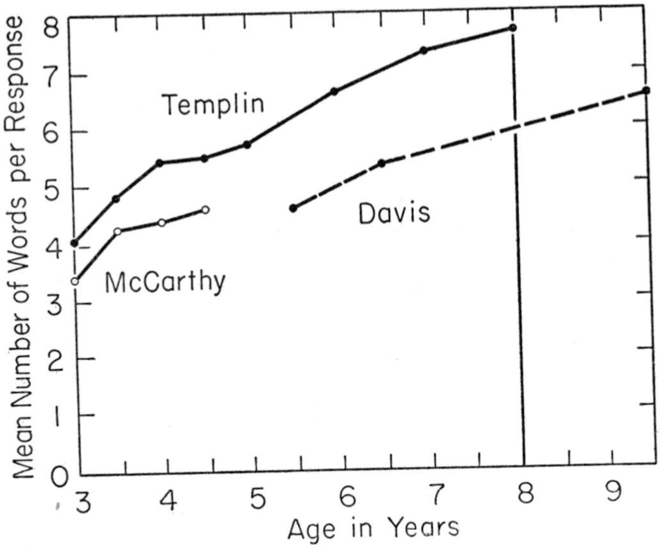

Figure 5. Comparison of Mean Number of Words in 50 Remarks by Age as Reported by McCarthy, Davis, and Templin

studies carried on fifteen or twenty years ago. At the older ages the differences between the results of the studies become even more apparent. While at 3 and 3.5 years the sentences in the present study average about 0.5 of a word longer, at 4 and 4.5 years they are about one word longer. The mean length of utterance at 5.5 years in Davis' study was equal to that of McCarthy's 4.5-year-old sample. In the present study the mean sentence length of the 6-year-olds is approximately equal to that of the 9.5-year-old Davis sample.

These differences are considerable and are statistically significant at the .01 level at all ages except at 3.5 years where the difference reaches the .05 level. At 3, 3.5, 4, and 4.5 years the *t*'s between the mean length of responses in the present study and in the McCarthy study are 3.68, 2.53, 4.76, and 4.21 respectively. The means from the Davis study at 5.5, 6.5, and 9.5 years have been compared with those of the current study at 5, 6, and 8. The *t*'s for each comparison are 5.24, 5.42, and 3.79 respectively.

That longer utterances have been found in the present study is particularly important since the method of obtaining the data so nearly duplicated that of the McCarthy and Davis studies. Factors of sex, intelligence, age, and socioeconomic status are comparable in all three. Since no one person gathered data for a majority of the children in the present study, it is not likely that the obtained difference is merely a reflection of the influence of a particular examiner. This question can, of course, be raised for the McCarthy and Davis studies. It is more likely that the greater amount of linguistic stimulation and the increased permissiveness in child-adult relations in the environment of the present-day child are important factors in determining the results.

In Table 39 the mean number of words used in the 50 utterances for boys and girls separately, for the sexes combined, and for the USES and LSES groups are presented by age. Although the mean length of response increases with age for all groups, in no instance is the difference between consecutive age levels statistically significant.

There is practically no significant difference between the mean length of utterance of boys and girls. At four ages scattered throughout the age range, girls' remarks are slightly longer, at two ages the boys' remarks are longer, and at two ages the length is the same. Only the difference at 5 years reaches statistical significance at the .05 level ($t = 2.08$). McCarthy reported insignificantly longer remarks for the girls in her sample at all ages tested except at 2.5 years. Davis, whose toys were selected to appeal to the boys, found no difference at 5.5 years, but somewhat longer utterances by girls at 6.5 and 9.5 years. In the studies of twins, Day and Davis did not find the mean length of remarks of the girls longer than those of boys.

Girls are frequently reported as uttering longer remarks than boys of the same age, although the differences are usually not statistically significant. McCarthy (28) summarizes fourteen studies of sentence length, including a preliminary report on the relevant part of this study and studies in which no comparisons are made between the sexes. In these she presents sixty-six comparisons between boys and girls at the same ages. Longer sentences were used by girls in forty-eight cases, by boys in fifteen, and by neither sex in three. It should be emphasized, however, that for many of these comparisons the differences are small. As stated, there is no difference in 3 of the 66 comparisons; for the remainder, the difference in mean number of words used per remark is greater than 0.5 words on 20 comparisons, is 0.5 words on 5, 0.4 words on 6, 0.3 words on 8, 0.2 words on 11, and 0.1 words or less on 13 comparisons. Thus in 70 per cent of the comparisions the difference is 0.5 words or less, while in 41 per cent it is only 0.2 words or less.

Table 39 shows that the mean sentence length is greater for the USES groups at every age tested except at 7 years when the length of the response is identical. The difference between the SES groups is significant at the .01 level only at 3.5 and 4.5 years however ($t = 3.28$ and 3.30). McCarthy, Davis, Day, and other investigators have similarly reported that USES groups use slightly longer sentences. Davis found the differences between the social classes consistent, but significant only between twins in these two groups. McCarthy reported significant differences between the USES and LSES groups when subjects 36 and 42 months old were combined and when those 48 and 54 months old were combined. Both McCarthy and Day report the socioeconomic status differences increasing during the preschool years, while Davis reports them decreasing during the school years. These trends for both the preschool and the school years are borne out by the present study.

Five longest remarks. Davis has observed that the mean of the five longest remarks is a good indicator of the development of linguistic skill (6). In Table 40 the mean length of the five longest responses by age is presented for the boys and girls, USES and LSES groups, and the total subsample. The differences in the mean length of these remarks for the subsamples are statistically significant between 3 and 3.5 years, 3.5 and 4 years, and 6 and 7 years ($t = 2.91$, 3.31, and 3.04, respectively). None of the differences between the other consecutive age levels approaches significance. Davis reported the mean of the five longest sentences for her 5.5-year-old sample as 10.3, SD 3.52; that for her 6.5-year-old sample as 12.2, SD 3.36; and that for her 9.5-year-old sample as 15.6, SD 5.48. When these means are compared with the 5-, 6-, and 8-year-old samples in the present study, only the difference at 5 to 5.5 years is significant at the .01 level with a t of 2.94.

The mean lengths of the five longest remarks in the Davis and the

Table 39. Mean Number of Words per Remark of Boys and Girls, Upper and Lower Socioeconomic Status Groups, and Total Subsamples, by Age

CA	Boys (N = 30)		Girls (N = 30)		USES (N = 18)		LSES (N = 42)		Total Subsamples (N = 60)	
	Mean	SD	Mean	SD	Mean	SD	Mean	SD	Mean	SD
3	4.3	1.4	3.9	1.0	4.5	1.4	3.9	1.1	4.1	1.3
3.5	4.5	1.0	4.9	1.0	5.3	1.0	4.4	0.9	4.7	1.0
4	5.2	1.5	5.6	1.3	5.5	0.5	5.4	1.6	5.4	1.5
4.5	5.4	1.6	5.4	0.9	6.1	0.9	5.1	1.4	5.4	1.3
5	5.3	1.4	6.1	1.5	6.1	1.5	5.6	1.5	5.7	1.5
6	6.7	1.4	6.4	1.2	6.9	1.1	6.4	1.4	6.6	1.3
7	7.3	0.8	7.3	1.3	7.3	0.8	7.3	1.1	7.3	1.0
8	7.3	1.4	7.9	1.8	7.7	1.6	7.5	1.6	7.6	1.6

Table 40. Mean Number of Words in Five Longest Remarks of Boys and Girls, Upper and Lower Socioeconomic Status Groups, and Total Subsamples by Age

CA	Boys (N = 30)		Girls (N = 30)		USES (N = 18)		LSES (N = 42)		Total Subsamples (N = 60)	
	Mean	SD	Mean	SD	Mean	SD	Mean	SD	Mean	SD
3	7.95	2.63	7.82	1.83	8.75	2.72	7.52	1.93	7.89	2.27
3.5	8.66	2.08	9.46	3.05	9.99	2.19	8.67	2.00	9.06	2.14
4	10.35	3.05	10.66	3.43	10.64	2.34	10.45	2.89	10.51	2.74
4.5	10.73	3.03	10.78	2.23	11.84	2.26	10.28	2.68	10.76	2.66
5	10.82	2.98	12.63	3.61	12.57	3.73	11.36	3.23	11.73	3.43
6	12.42	2.78	12.11	1.90	13.09	2.23	11.91	2.37	12.27	2.39
7	13.76	1.81	13.37	2.45	13.80	1.71	13.47	2.32	13.57	2.16
8	13.55	2.87	14.75	2.69	14.30	2.70	14.09	2.90	14.15	2.85

Table 41. Median Number of One-Word Remarks of Boys and Girls, Upper and Lower Socioeconomic Status Groups, and Total Subsamples, by Age

CA	Boys (N = 30)		Girls (N = 30)		USES (N = 18)		LSES (N = 42)		Total Subsamples (N = 60)	
	Mdn	Q	Mdn	Q	Mdn	Q	Mdn	Q	Mdn	Q
3	3.5	3.0	5.5	3.9	3.5	2.7	5.7	3.8	4.8	3.3
3.5	3.5	4.3	3.0	2.2	2.0	1.5	5.1	3.5	3.3	2.7
4	3.0	2.5	2.0	3.0	2.3	3.2	2.5	3.1	2.5	2.3
4.5	2.5	1.1	2.5	1.8	2.3	1.1	2.6	1.4	2.5	1.5
5	2.6	1.8	2.0	1.9	2.5	1.8	2.2	1.5	2.4	1.7
6	2.7	0.4	0.8	0.7	1.0	1.0	0.7	0.6	0.7	0.6
7	0.6	0.3	0.6	0.3	0.6	0.4	0.6	0.3	0.6	0.3
8	0.6	0.3	0.6	0.3	0.6	0.4	0.6	0.3	0.6	0.3

present study are less divergent than the mean lengths of all 50 remarks. Davis reports a range of 1 to 56 words among the five longest remarks, and a range in the means of the five longest remarks of 1.4 to 36.4 words. In the present study the five longest remarks of the 5-to-8-year-old subjects range from 3 to 34 words and the range in means of the five longest remarks is from 3.8 to 24.6 words. Thus the increase in the mean length of 50 remarks as found in the present study is not produced by a few children's long remarks, but by generally greater loquacity.

In the present study there are no significant differences in the mean of the five longest remarks uttered by boys and girls with all ages combined. The mean for boys of all ages is 11.03, SD 3.34, and that for girls is 11.45, SD 3.22. There is no consistency in either boys' or girls' using longer remarks: at four age levels the mean for girls is higher, and at the same number the mean for boys is higher. Only at 5 years is a difference statistically significant at the .05 level found ($t = 2.12$, with boys using the longer remarks).

For the entire age range the mean of the five longest remarks of the 144 subjects in the USES sample is 11.87, SD 3.3, and that of the 336 subjects in the LSES sample is 10.97, SD 2.83. This difference is significant at the .01 level of confidence ($t = 2.96$). At seven of the eight single age levels the USES groups have a higher mean length of the five longest remarks. The difference is statistically significant at the .05 level only at 3.5 and 4.5 years ($t = 2.20$ and 2.31 respectively).

One-word remarks. The proportion of one-word remarks uttered may be taken as an indication of language maturity of the subject. The decrease in the median number of such remarks with age for boys and girls, USES and LSES samples, and the total sample is apparent from Table 41. The median rather than the mean is used here because of the variation in the number of subjects not uttering any one-word remarks. At each age tested from 3 to 8 years this number is 6, 14, 22, 13, 16, 38, 49, and 49 out of 60 cases.

There are no significant sex differences in the frequency of use of one-word remarks. At three age levels boys were found to use a lower mean number. For both sexes the decline in the use of such remarks with increasing age is consistent.

Although the mean use of one-word remarks by the LSES groups is greater than that of the USES groups, occasionally the median use by the USES groups is slightly higher. The median differences are greater at those ages when the LSES groups use more such remarks. The mean differences are significantly higher for the USES groups at 3.5 and 5 years ($t = 2.70$ and 2.84 respectively).

Davis reports the mean number of one-word remarks as 10.9, SD 8.85, at 5.5 years; as 9.30, SD 7.04, at 6.5 years; and as 8.34, SD 2.94, at 9.5 years. She does not report medians. In the present study the mean number of one-word remarks is 2.64, SD 2.73, at 5 years; 1.07, SD 2.32, at 6 years; 0.24, SD 0.54, at 7 years; and 0.35, SD 0.89, at 8 years. These means are significantly below those reported by Davis even at the older ages. Since all these one-word remarks enter into the calculation of the mean length of response, they contribute substantially to the differences observed in the mean length of the total remarks as reported in the different studies.

When differences of this magnitude appear in two studies carried on with substantial and comparably selected samples and with quite similar techniques of gathering data, some attempt must be made to explain the divergence in the results. Only two dissimilarities are apparent in the techniques used: some of the toys differed and the number of investigators gathering data varied. However, such dissimilarities should not be sufficient to produce differences of the magnitude observed. The differences are more likely a reflection of the characteristic verbal behavior of children in a child-adult situation at separated periods of time.

Complexity of Verbalizations

Classification of complexity. Both a descriptive and a quantitative method of classifying the complexity of the structure of the remarks was used. To permit comparisons with the McCarthy and Davis investigations, each remark was classified according to its descriptive category. This outline divided all remarks into complete and incomplete sentences. If the sentence was complete, the type of sentence and the type of subordination was further classified; if the sentence was incomplete, the type of incompleteness was classified: e.g., if the subject was omitted it was noted whether the omission was from the main or subordinate clause. The classification outline used by Davis was a modification of that used by McCarthy and is reproduced in Appendix IIIB, page 160.

Williams (54) in his study of interrelations of language skills presented a quantitative classification of the complexity of the sentence. He arbitrarily assigned a score of 0 to unintelligible expressions, 1 to a simple sentence, 2 to a compound sentence, 3 to a complex sentence, and 4 to a compound-complex sentence. In the present study, the classification of utterances according to the McCarthy-Davis outline was used in assigning the weights. A score of 0 was given for all incomplete remarks. These were classified in the McCarthy-Davis outline as incomplete either under IA, functionally complete but structurally incomplete, or as incomplete sentences under II. A score of 1 was given to simple sentences classified IB and IC. A score of 2 was given a simple sentence with two or more phrases or a compound subject or predicate with a phrase classified as IF(1). A score of 3 was given for compound sentences classified as IE. A score of 4 was given for all complex and elaborated compound sentences classified as ID, IF(2), and IF(3).

Some inaccuracies in dealing with incomplete sentences probably were introduced by converting the classification of remarks according to the McCarthy-Davis technique into a Williams weighted score instead of assigning the latter scores directly from the protocols. However, for all other classifications this technique appeared satisfactory and was used because twenty-four thousand remarks had already been classified according to the McCarthy-Davis method.

Quantitative complexity score. Although the quantitative complexity scores as reported in Table 42 increase from 3 to 8 years of age, the increments from age to age are not so stable as they are for most other aspects of language investigated in this study. The girls receive somewhat higher complexity scores at six of the eight age levels considered. Although the difference is statistically significant at 5 years ($t = 2.29$), this is probably related to the fact that boys at 4, 4.5, and 5 did not exhibit the expected increase in complexity of utterance scores.

Unlike most of the other language measures, the complexity score does not consistently differentiate the USES and the LSES groups. The USES groups obtain the higher scores at five of the age levels, however, and the differences when the LSES group receives the higher score are

Table 42. Mean Complexity Score for Remarks of Boys and Girls, Upper and Lower Socioeconomic Status Groups, and Total Subsamples, by Age

	Boys (N = 30)		Girls (N = 30)		USES (N = 18)		LSES (N = 42)		Total Subsamples (N = 60)	
CA	Mean	SD	Mean	SD	Mean	SD	Mean	SD	Mean	SD
3	36.4	19.7	32.2	16.5	40.6	20.4	31.4	16.6	34.3	18.3
3.5	38.1	17.3	43.2	18.2	49.2	19.1	36.9	16.1	40.6	17.9
4	48.0	18.8	54.9	20.7	50.6	14.2	51.8	22.1	51.6	20.1
4.5	50.9	24.0	52.9	16.6	61.8	16.3	47.7	20.9	50.4	24.1
5	50.6	18.8	63.2	23.5	55.6	19.4	57.4	22.3	56.9	21.5
6	71.5	22.1	68.7	17.4	70.5	16.0	69.9	21.4	70.1	22.7
7	69.7	20.0	73.9	16.6	70.0	16.5	72.6	19.2	71.8	18.5
8	74.4	18.7	79.2	28.7	91.0	23.5	71.9	21.3	77.7	33.8

minimal. The differences in favor of the USES groups reach the .01 level of confidence at 4.5 and 8 years ($t = 2.89$ and 2.96 respectively).

The quantitative complexity score is not quite so stable as other language measures used in the study. However, it has the advantage of being a quantitative measure and thus permits some comparisons of grammatical complexity of the obtained remarks with other language skills.

McCarthy-Davis sentence construction categories. In the analysis of the construction of remarks uttered by the children, six major categories were used: (1) functionally complete but structurally incomplete; (2) simple without phrase; (3) simple with phrase; (4) compound and complex; (5) elaborated; (6) incomplete. For each of these categories the percentage of use has been determined and in Tables 43, 44, and 45 comparisons are made with the results of the earlier Davis and McCarthy studies.

The construction analysis of the present study agrees more closely with the findings of McCarthy than with the findings of Davis. There is a tendency particularly at the older ages tested for the more elaborate and mature types of sentence structure to be used somewhat more frequently by the present sample. Davis' results showed considerable divergence from those of McCarthy. Since all results are presented as percentages of the total number of remarks at any given age, the frequency of use of any one category is related to the frequency of use of another. This, of course, means that extreme variation in one category is reflected in all.

Several outstanding differences among the three studies are shown in Table 43. There are many fewer incomplete sentences, particularly at the older age levels, in the present study. The percentage of incomplete sentences was found to decrease with age in the preschool years by both McCarthy and the author. In the present study the percentage levels off at about 6 years. In the Davis study, on the other hand, the number of these responses increases with age. This increase is contrary to expectancy, although incomplete utterances are quite common even in adult speech. In many of the utterances classified as incomplete, words necessary for grammatical accuracy were omitted, e.g., "Saw a train yesterday" instead of "I saw a train yesterday."

In the present study functionally complete but structurally incomplete remarks show a definite and consistent decrease in proportionate use with age. Neither McCarthy nor Davis reports any age trend in the use of this type of remark. In these studies, with the exception of the 3-year-old sample in the McCarthy study, incomplete remarks make up about

Table 43. Mean Percentage of Total Remarks in Each Sentence Construction Category as Found by McCarthy,* Davis,† and Templin

Type of Sentence and Investigator	CA 3	3.5	4	4.5	5	5.5	6	6.5	7	8	9.5
Functionally complete but structurally incomplete											
McCarthy	27.2	30.6	32.0	31.2							
Davis						39.4		32.0			33.6
Templin	28.2	23.8	19.7	19.5	17.2		9.8		9.0	9.4	
Simple without phrase											
McCarthy	45.1	35.3	39.4	36.5							
Davis						29.4		30.8			18.8
Templin	32.0	39.5	37.2	37.6	35.8		38.2		34.1	31.5	
Simple with phrase											
McCarthy	8.7	11.4	10.9	10.4							
Davis						7.8		9.8			11.4
Templin	13.7	16.4	18.5	16.2	16.8		20.7		22.8	21.3	
Compound and complex											
McCarthy	1.5	6.5	6.1	7.0							
Davis						4.6		5.4			6.8
Templin	2.9	3.3	6.9	6.8	8.7		10.8		11.1	15.0	
Elaborated											
McCarthy	1.3	2.3	4.5	5.9							
Davis						3.6		5.6			10.0
Templin	3.1	3.4	6.5	7.5	8.1		11.9		13.4	13.2	
Incomplete											
McCarthy	16.2	13.9	6.8	8.8							
Davis						15.0		16.4			19.4
Templin	16.8	13.1	11.2	12.1	12.6		8.6		10.5	9.5	

* Data based on comprehensible remarks only.
† Data based on analysis of singletons reported.

a third of the remarks at each age. The percentage of functionally complete but structurally incomplete remarks is considerably lower than this in the present study except at the youngest age tested. At 3.5 years slightly less than a fourth of the remarks in the present study are incomplete, and the percentage decreases to between 9 and 10 per cent of the remarks after 6 years.

For simple sentences without phrases, essentially no age relationship is found in the present study. This agrees with the findings of both McCarthy and Davis except at the extremes of the age range tested.

The percentage of simple sentences with phrases in the present study is somewhat higher at the early ages and considerably higher at the later ages tested. An increase from about 14 per cent at 3 to around 21 per cent at 8 years is found. This differs from McCarthy who reported no age trend from to 3 to 4.5, but is in agreement with Davis.

Although compound and complex and elaborated sentences are infrequently used during the preschool period, they are more prevalent in the current study than in the previous ones. Three per cent of the remarks of 3-year-olds are compound and complex and the same percentage elaborated, as compared with slightly less than 1.5 and 1 per cent, respectively, at that age in the McCarthy study. At the older ages tested the increase is particularly apparent. Except for the elaborated sentences at 8 and 9.5 years, the present study finds that the use of these more complicated sentences is at least twice that reported by Davis.

That the percentage of remarks falling into the several constructional categories does not differ substantially between boys and girls is evident from Table 44. This agrees with the findings of Davis and McCarthy. Girls in the present study tend to use slightly more of the advanced types of sentence structure particularly at the older age levels tested.

Table 45 shows that the differences in the percentage of remarks of the USES and LSES groups in each constructional category are not great. Those that do occur tend to be in the expected direction. Youngsters from the USES groups tend to use a greater proportion of the more mature and a smaller proportion of the less mature sentences at any given age. This substantiates the findings of both McCarthy and Davis that "there appears to be a definite trend in the lower group toward more functionally complete remarks and in the upper group toward more complex and elaborated remarks" (5:84).

The use of the various types of sentences throughout the age range studied is shown in Figure 6, where their use by the 8-year-old subsample is taken as a measure of terminal status. There is relatively little change with age in the use of simple sentences without a phrase. The

Table 44. Mean Percentages of Total Remarks in Each Sentence Construction Category for Boys and Girls by Age as Found by McCarthy,* Davis,† and Templin

Type of Sentence and Investigator	CA 3	3.5	4	4.5	5	5.5	6	6.5	7	8	9.5
				Boys							
Functionally complete but structurally incomplete											
McCarthy	31.2	27.2	33.2	31.3							
Davis						36.0		31.8			32.6
Templin	25.4	25.0	22.5	20.8	17.6		10.2		9.2	7.6	
Simple without phrase											
McCarthy	39.9	37.7	36.0	37.9							
Davis						31.8		31.2			19.0
Templin	37.4	39.5	37.5	34.3	37.5		36.8		32.2	33.3	
Simple with phrase											
McCarthy	7.0	10.2	12.3	8.8							
Davis						8.6		9.8			10.2
Templin	14.6	16.3	16.3	15.9	16.2		20.0		23.1	19.5	
Compound and complex											
McCarthy	1.4	7.9	6.5	8.2							
Davis						4.8		5.8			6.2
Templin	2.9	3.1	5.8	6.1	8.0		10.9		10.7	16.0	
Elaborated											
McCarthy	1.7	1.9	5.1	4.4							
Davis						3.2		6.0			10.8
Templin	3.3	2.8	6.2	8.5	6.0		13.0		12.9	11.5	
Incomplete											
McCarthy	19.2	14.9	6.4	9.0							
Davis						15.6		15.4			21.4
Templin	16.3	14.0	10.9	14.0	14.6		8.6		12.5	10.5	

					Girls						
Functionally complete but structurally incomplete											
McCarthy	22.8	35.3	31.0	31.1							
Davis						39.0		27.8			34.2
Templin	30.8	22.5	16.8	18.2	16.8		9.3		8.8	11.2	
Simple without phrase											
McCarthy	50.6	31.8	42.1	34.7							
Davis						29.2		31.2			20.6
Templin	33.2	40.3	36.8	40.7	34.9		39.6		35.8	29.6	
Simple with phrase											
McCarthy	10.6	13.0	9.7	12.2							
Davis						7.8		9.8			12.2
Templin	12.9	16.5	20.0	17.2	17.2		20.9		22.5	19.5	
Compound and complex											
McCarthy	1.4	4.5	5.8	5.6							
Davis						4.6		8.0			6.0
Templin	2.9	4.3	7.9	7.1	10.1		10.6		11.3	16.0	
Elaborated											
McCarthy	0.9	2.8	4.0	7.8							
Davis						4.2		6.4			11.8
Templin	2.8	4.0	6.8	6.5	10.2		10.8		13.8	15.1	
Incomplete											
McCarthy	13.0	12.5	7.1	8.6							
Davis						15.2		16.8			15.2
Templin	17.2	12.1	11.4	10.1	10.5		8.5		7.3	8.5	

* Data based on comprehensible remarks only.
† Data based on analysis of singletons reported.

Table 45. Mean Percentage of Total Remarks in Each Sentence Construction Category for Upper and Lower Socioeconomic Status Groups by Age as Found by McCarthy,* Davis,† and Templin

Type of Sentence and Investigator	CA 3	3.5	4	4.5	5	5.5	6	6.5	7	8	9.5
Upper Socioeconomic Status Groups (USES)											
Functionally complete but structurally incomplete											
McCarthy		20.4‡		20.5§							
Davis						34.2		28.4			32.0
Templin	26.0	20.2	18.4	11.6	16.1		12.0		9.1	7.0	
Simple without phrase											
McCarthy		44.5‡		41.7§							
Davis						31.4		31.4			20.0
Templin	36.4	39.2	38.6	40.2	32.2		36.0		29.5		30.4
Simple with phrase											
McCarthy		13.2‡		12.3§							
Davis						8.4		9.0			12.2
Templin	15.3	21.5	19.3	18.3	17.6		17.4		22.2	18.0	
Compound and complex											
McCarthy		6.3‡		12.3§							
Davis						5.2		8.2			6.8
Templin	4.2	5.3	6.0	8.0	8.8		10.4		12.7	19.0	
Elaborated											
McCarthy		2.9‡		6.3§							
Davis						4.2		6.6			13.6
Templin	4.7	4.9	6.0	9.0	8.4		13.1		14.0	16.0	
Incomplete											
McCarthy		12.4‡		6.7§							
Davis						16.6		16.4			15.4
Templin	13.3	8.6	11.4	12.0	15.8		9.9		12.3	8.8	

Lower Socioeconomic Status Groups (LSES)

Functionally complete but structurally incomplete											
McCarthy		34.7‡		37.4§							
Davis						40.4		31.2			35.2
Templin	27.7	24.1	20.9	21.8	16.5		8.5		8.6	10.0	
Simple without phrase											
McCarthy		32.4‡		34.5§							
Davis						29.6		31.0			19.6
Templin	33.2	37.7	35.9	34.7	52.1		37.4		34.4	30.6	
Simple with phrase											
McCarthy		6.3‡		9.1§							
Davis						8.0		10.8			10.2
Templin	12.5	13.5	17.3	15.1	15.7		21.9		23.2	22.8	
Compound and complex											
McCarthy		1.6‡		5.6§							
Davis						4.4		5.6			5.6
Templin	2.2	2.9	6.7	5.3	8.6		9.9		9.9	12.6	
Elaborated											
McCarthy		0.6‡		4.2§							
Davis						3.4		5.6			9.2
Templin	2.3	2.1	6.8	6.6	7.6		10.9		12.5	11.2	
Incomplete											
McCarthy		16.0‡		8.8§							
Davis						14.2		15.8			20.2
Templin	17.1	15.1	10.6	12.0	10.6		7.6		7.7	9.8	

* Data based on comprehensible remarks only.
† Data based on analysis of singletons reported.
‡ Includes subjects 30 and 36 months old.
§ Includes subjects 48 and 54 months old.

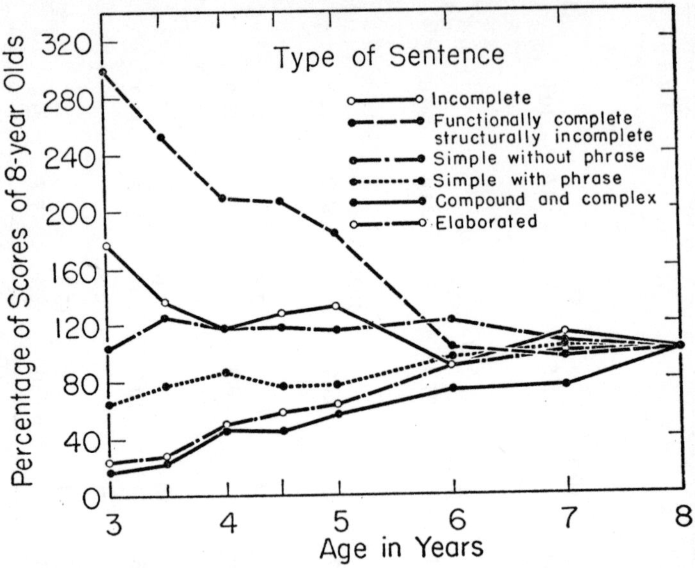

FIGURE 6. PERCENTAGE OF USE BY AGE OF VARIOUS STRUCTURAL CATEGORIES IN 50 REMARKS WITH THE USE BY THE 8-YEAR-OLD SUBSAMPLE TAKEN AS A MEASURE OF TERMINAL STATUS

use of incomplete sentences, whether or not they are functionally complete, decreases considerably over this age range. The decrease is greatest for the sentences that are structurally incomplete but functionally complete. Use of all the sentences involving subordination and coordination, i.e., simple sentences with a phrase, compound, complex, and elaborated sentences, increases with age.

Classification of complete sentences. The complete sentences used at 3, 4.5, 6, and 8 years were classified as declarative, interrogative, imperative, and exclamatory. It was possible to classify 9,644 complete sentences at these ages. The number and percentage of each of these used by boys and girls, USES and LSES groups, and the total subsample at each age are presented in Table 46.

For the entire age sample the declarative sentence is by far the most common, interrogative next, imperative after that, and exclamatory least common. The proportionate use of these sentence types by age groups varies: the use of the declarative sentence increases from 3 to 8 years; the use of the imperative sentence decreases; the use of the interrogative sentence is relatively constant from 3 to 6 years but falls sharply by 8 years; the use of the exclamatory sentence is infrequent at all ages and

Table 46. Number and Percentage of Classified Types of Sentences Used by Boys and Girls, Upper and Lower Socioeconomic Status Groups, and Total Subsamples, by Age

CA	Boys (N = 30)		Girls (N = 30)		USES (N = 18)		LSES (N = 42)		Total Subsamples	
	N	%	N	%	N	%	N	%	N	%
Declarative Sentences										
3	710	68.3	597	68.5	370	66.7	937	69.2	1,307	68.4
4.5	871	74.1	983	80.9	620	71.3	1,234	81.1	1,854	77.5
6	1,070	80.3	1,014	75.7	644	79.0	1,440	77.5	2,084	78.0
8	1,158	86.6	1,220	91.5	731	91.2	1,647	88.1	2,378	89.0
Total	3,809	78.0	3,814	80.2	2,365	77.8	5,258	79.7	7,623	79.0
Interrogative Sentences										
3	193	18.6	154	17.7	115	20.8	232	17.1	347	18.2
4.5	217	18.5	164	13.5	184	21.1	197	13.0	381	15.9
6	220	16.5	260	19.4	126	15.4	354	19.1	480	18.0
8	130	9.7	75	5.6	56	7.0	149	8.0	205	7.7
Total	760	15.5	653	13.7	481	15.8	932	14.1	1,413	14.7
Imperative Sentences										
3	117	11.3	102	11.7	57	10.3	162	11.9	219	11.5
4.5	67	5.7	57	4.6	49	5.6	75	4.9	124	5.2
6	33	2.5	61	4.6	37	4.5	57	3.1	94	3.5
8	25	1.9	23	1.7	10	1.2	38	2.0	48	1.8
Total	242	5.0	243	5.1	153	5.0	332	5.0	485	5.0
Exclamatory Sentences										
3	19	1.8	18	2.1	12	2.2	25	1.8	37	1.9
4.5	20	1.7	12	1.0	17	2.0	15	1.0	32	1.3
6	10	0.7	4	0.3	9	1.1	5	0.3	14	0.5
8	24	1.8	16	1.2	5	0.6	35	1.9	40	1.5
Total	73	1.5	50	1.0	43	1.4	80	1.2	123	1.3

bears little relation to the age group tested. The shift in the use of the interrogative sentence may be a function of the difference in the child-adult relations at the preschool and school ages. Age trends for the separate sex and SES groups are similar to those for the total subsample.

The use by the 8-year-old subsample of each classified type of sentence is taken as a measure of terminal status. Table 47 shows that the 3-year-olds use about half as many declarative sentences and over four times as many interrogative sentences as the 8-year-olds. It should be noted that exclamatory sentences represent such a small proportion of total remarks that the observed fluctuations may be accounted for merely by chance.

Subordinate clauses. There were 1,473 subordinate clauses, classified as noun, adjective, or adverb clauses, used by the 3-, 4.5-, 6-, and 8-year-old subjects. The number of subordinate clauses used increases substantially with age. Only 111 such clauses are used by the 3-year-olds and 293 by the 4.5-year-old subjects. This number increases to 489 subordinate clauses at 6 years and to 580 at 8 years. Thus of all the subordinate clauses, 7.5 per cent are used by 3-year-olds, 20.0 by the 4.5-year-olds, 33.1 per cent by the 6-year-olds, and 39.4 by the 8-year-olds.

For the age range studied, 13.8 per cent of the subordinate clauses are adjectival, 35.0 per cent are nominal, and 51.2 per cent are adverbial. Very few (1.7 per cent) adjective clauses are used by 3-year-olds. Because of the infrequent appearance of subordination at 3 years, a substantially larger sample of children's speech is needed to obtain a stable picture of the characteristic use of subordination at this age. Nevertheless, the present findings at the preschool level are presented because of the paucity of published information on this age.

The great increase in the frequency of use of all types of subordination with age is seen in Table 48. The 8-year-olds use five times as much subordination as the 3-year-old subjects: the use of adjective clauses increases nearly twelve times; noun clauses seven times; and adverbial clauses four times. This, however, is not an accurate picture of subordination since over 50 per cent of the subordinate clauses used are adverbial, about a third are nominal and 15 per cent are adjectival. A comparison of the percentage of noun, adjective, and adverb clauses used at 3, 4.5, 6, and 8 years indicates that the proportion of adverb clauses decreases, while, in general, the proportion of the others increases with age.

Despite the differences in the frequency in use of these subordinate clauses there is great similarity in the curves of development when their

Table 47. Percentages of Use by 8-Year-Old Subsample of Declarative, Interrogative, Imperative, and Exclamatory Sentences Attained by Total Subsamples, by Age

CA	Declarative	Interrogative	Imperative	Exclamatory
3	55.0%	169.0%	456.0%	92.5%
4.5	78.1	185.9	258.3	80.0
6	87.7	234.1	195.8	35.0
8	100.0	100.0	100.0	100.0

Table 48. Number and Percentage of Various Types of Subordinate Clauses Used by Boys and Girls, Upper and Lower Socioeconomic Status Groups, and Total Subsamples, by Age

	Boys (N = 30)		Girls (N = 30)		USES (N = 18)		LSES (N = 42)		Total Subsamples	
CA	N	%	N	%	N	%	N	%	N	%
					Noun Clauses					
3	20	36.4	13	23.2	16	37.2	17	25.0	33	29.7
4.5	38	25.2	46	32.4	36	26.1	48	31.0	84	28.7
6	96	36.8	93	40.8	67	41.6	122	37.2	189	38.7
8	121	41.6	98	33.9	72	34.6	147	39.5	219	37.8
Total ..	275	36.3	250	35.0	191	34.7	334	36.2	525	35.6
					Adjective Clauses					
3	5	9.1	1	1.7	4	9.3	2	2.9	6	5.4
4.5	24	15.9	16	11.3	24	17.4	16	10.3	40	13.7
6	32	12.2	35	15.4	12	7.5	55	16.8	67	13.7
8	35	12.0	47	16.3	25	12.0	57	15.3	82	14.1
Total ..	96	12.7	99	13.8	65	11.8	130	14.1	195	13.2
					Adverbial Clauses					
3	30	54.5	42	75.1	23	53.5	49	72.1	72	64.9
4.5	89	58.9	80	56.3	78	56.5	91	58.7	169	57.6
6	133	51.0	100	43.8	82	50.9	151	46.0	233	47.6
8	135	46.4	144	49.8	111	53.4	168	45.2	279	48.1
Total ..	387	51.0	366	51.2	294	53.5	459	45.2	753	51.2

use by the 8-year-old subsample is taken as a measure of terminal status. This is evident in the graphic comparison in Figure 7.

For the several ages combined, there is no difference in the amount of subordination used by boys or girls. In the 50 remarks, boys over the entire age range used a mean number of 6.3 subordinate clauses and girls used 6.0. The lack of significant difference between the sexes extends to each type of subordinate clause: the mean number of noun clauses is 2.3 for the boys and 2.1 for the girls; the mean number of

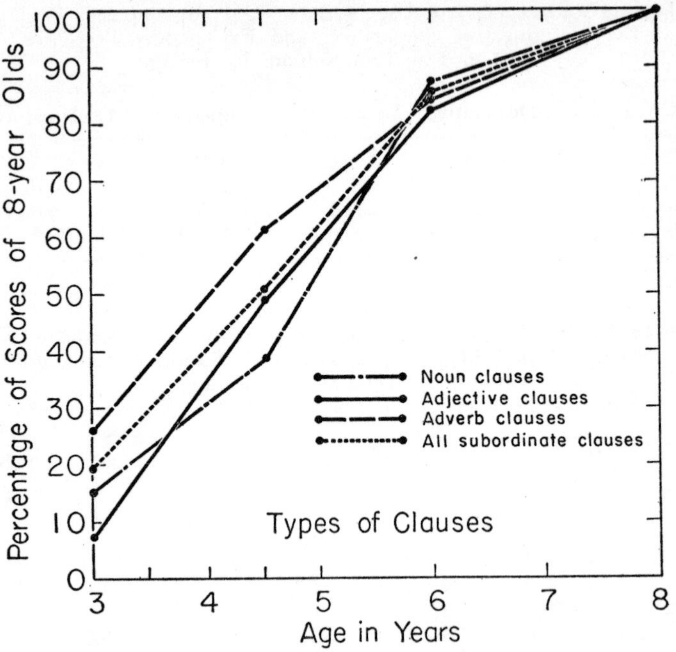

FIGURE 7. PERCENTAGE OF USE OF NOUN, ADJECTIVE, ADVERB, AND ALL SUBORDINATE CLAUSES BY AGE COMPARED WITH THE USE BY THE 8-YEAR-OLD SUBSAMPLE TAKEN AS A MEASURE OF TERMINAL STATUS

adjective clauses is .8 for both sexes; the mean number of adverbial clauses is 3.2 for the boys and 3.1 for the girls. The fact that neither sex consistently uses more subordination is also reported by Davis. In general, although somewhat less stable, the trend in the use of the various types of subordinate clauses with age is similar for both sexes and for the total subsample.

For the sample as a whole, however, the USES subjects use more subordination than the LSES: a mean of 7.64 subordinate clauses in the 50 remarks as contrasted with 5.49. The difference in the use of the adjective and noun clauses is not great: the means are .9 and .8 for adjective clauses; 2.7 and 2.0 for noun clauses. The SES groups differ most in their use of adverbial clauses. Nevertheless, the difference between a mean of 4.1 and 2.7 clauses is not statistically significant.

The frequency of use of the several types of subordination by the USES and LSES groups does not differ consistently either in the present study or in that reported by Davis. Comparisons between the percent-

Table 49. Percentages of Various Types of Subordinate Clauses Used at Different Age Levels as Found by Davis and by Templin

CA	Investigator	Noun Clauses	Adjective Clauses	Adverbial Clauses
3	Templin	29.7%	5.4%	64.9%
4.5	Templin	28.7	13.6	57.7
5.5	Davis	48.3	23.3	28.3
6	Templin	38.8	13.7	47.5
6.5	Davis	48.2	20.1	31.2
8	Templin	39.5	14.1	46.4
9.5	Davis	31.5	16.5	52.0

Table 50. Number and Percentage of Types of Adverbial Clauses Used by Subsamples

CA	Type of Adverbial Clause					
	Time	Condition	Causal	Result	Misc.*	Total
			Number			
3	17	19	19	4	13	72
4.5	64	45	30	9	21	169
6	58	81	38	29	27	233
8	90	79	57	15	38	279
Total	229	224	144	57	99	753
			Percentage			
3	23.6%	26.4%	26.4%	5.6%	18.0%	100.0%
4.5	37.9	26.6	17.8	5.3	12.4	100.0
6	24.9	34.8	16.3	12.4	11.6	100.0
8	32.3	28.3	20.4	5.4	13.6	100.0
Total	30.5	29.7	19.1	7.6	13.1	100.0

* Clauses of place, manner, comparison, concession, and purpose.

ages of noun, adjective, and adverb clauses found in the present study and in Davis' study are made in Table 49. Since the reported percentages in the literature vary not only with age, but with the type of material analyzed, comparisons with other investigators are less valid than those with Davis. In both studies, the adjective clauses are consistently the least frequently used. In the present study adverb clauses are most frequently used throughout the age range studied. This does not agree with the findings of Davis, except at the 9.5-year level. In the earlier school years Davis finds noun clauses more frequent. In the present study, however, there is no shift in the proportions of noun, adjective, and adverb clauses during the early school years. In addition, the proportionate use of the several subordinate clauses found is in substantial agreement with that reported by Davis for her 9.5-year-old sample.

For the entire age range, 30.5 per cent of the 753 adverbial clauses were clauses of time, 29.7 per cent clauses of condition, 19.1 per cent causal, 7.6 per cent result, and 13.1 per cent clauses of place, manner, comparison, concession, and purpose combined. Table 50 shows that no age trends are observable for the separate types of adverbial clauses. The data have not been analyzed by sex and SES levels since the sample of clauses is not adequate when the sample is thus subdivided.

Grammatical Inaccuracies in Sentence Structure

Inaccuracies in grammatical construction are common among young children. These are not directly comparable to the grammatical errors of the older child, adolescent, or adult. As correct grammatical usage is being built up, these inaccuracies may be indications of growth toward more mature forms of expression. The grammatical errors of the adult, on the other hand, are inaccuracies which occur after knowledge and experience of correct usage should have been established.

Despite some grammatical inaccuracies, most of the remarks of children are grammatically correct. The percentage of remarks that have no grammatical errors increases from 48.0 per cent at 3 years to 57.9 per cent at 4.5 years to 73.7 per cent at 6 years to 76.1 per cent at 8 years. The percentages of correct remarks are very similar for boys and girls at 6 and 8 years. At the earlier ages tested, while the difference is somewhat greater, neither sex consistently uses more grammatically correct remarks.

The errors have been classified, both according to those that have resulted in incomplete sentences and according to specific grammatical errors.

Errors resulting in incomplete sentences. As previously noted, with increasing age fewer remarks are incomplete. At 3 years of age 16.8 per cent and at 8 years of age 9.5 per cent of the utterances were incomplete. Of all remarks collected over the eight age levels 2,812 were incomplete utterances.

Table 51 shows that the number of errors resulting in incomplete sentences is about cut in half, from 504 at 3 to 259 at 6 years of age, and is quite consistent from 6 to 8 years. For the group as a whole, the most frequent error was the omission of the subject in either the main or a subordinate clause. Examples of such remarks are "Put on my tennis shoes just before you come," or "Yes, works on the railroad."

The distribution of errors at each age level varies considerably. One

Table 51. Number and Percentage of Each Incomplete Sentence Category, by Age *

Category	CA 3	3.5	4	4.5	5	6	7	8	Total
			Number						
Subject omitted	145	122	104	105	93	85	126	85	865
Verb omitted	101	95	85	98	80	30	21	33	543
Subject and verb omitted	41	22	31	53	70	68	33	42	360
Fragmentary or incomprehensible	119	43	37	13	12	9	9	27	269
Article omitted	31	36	33	28	39	9	17	8	201
Loosely strung together	8	15	15	13	12	14	46	46	169
Main clause incomplete	15	12	28	26	33	25	16	5	160
Preposition missing	22	13	8	7	11	2	3	4	70
Miscellaneous †	22	21	18	19	30	17	13	35	175
Total	504	379	359	362	380	259	284	285	2,812
			Percentage						
Subject omitted	28.7	32.1	29.0	29.0	24.4	32.7	44.3	29.7	30.6
Verb omitted	20.0	25.1	23.7	27.1	21.0	11.6	7.4	11.6	19.2
Subject and verb omitted	8.2	5.8	8.6	14.7	18.4	26.2	11.6	14.7	12.7
Fragmentary or incomprehensible	23.5	11.3	10.3	3.6	3.2	3.5	3.2	9.5	9.5
Article omitted	6.2	9.5	9.2	7.6	10.3	3.5	6.0	2.8	7.2
Loosely strung together	1.6	4.0	4.2	3.6	3.2	5.4	16.2	16.2	6.0
Main clause incomplete	3.0	3.2	7.8	7.2	8.7	9.7	5.6	1.8	5.7
Preposition missing	4.4	3.4	2.2	1.9	2.9	.8	1.1	1.4	2.9
Miscellaneous †	4.4	5.6	5.0	5.3	7.9	6.6	4.6	12.3	6.2
Total	100.0	100.0	100.0	100.0	100.0	100.0	100.0	100.0	100.0

* N = 60 in each age group.

† Items D, E, I, J, M, and N under "Incomplete sentences" in Appendix III, B are included.

of the chief differences is the result of the decline in the proportion of fragmentary or incomprehensible utterances. At 8 years the percentage of fragmentary or incomprehensible utterances increases. Whether this is a real shift, a function of the particular sample used in this study, or a function of the percentage technique, is difficult to know. There were 119 such errors at the 3-year level, only 9 at 6 and 7 years, and 27 at 8. This absolute increase could be accounted for by a very few 8-year-old children's using a substantial number of fragmentary responses.

Sentences that are loosely strung together account for 1.6 per cent of the errors at 3 years and increase to 16.2 per cent at 7 and 8 years. There is a substantial decrease in the proportion of errors that are due to missing prepositions, particularly the preposition introducing the infinitive. Although these errors are never common, they are much more frequent at the early ages when such language constructions are beginning to be used. Although the shift is not so obvious, there is a tendency for proportionately fewer articles to be omitted by older children whose sentence structure is more complex. Sentences in which both subjects and verbs are omitted increase proportionately with age, since there is little change with age of such errors.

Grammatical errors. Specific grammatical errors have been tabulated in the remarks of the 3-, 4.5-, 6-, and 8-year-olds. In Table 52 the frequency of occurence of grammatical errors by age, and the frequency of the error per one thousand words used is reported. The most frequent error at all age levels is the use of "got" for "have." Disagreement between verb and subject ranks second. The occurrence of all errors decreases from 3 to 8 years of age – with the exception of the use of colloquialisms and slang, which increases. Only slightly fewer errors than those reported by Davis are recorded in the present study. The error classifications used in the two studies are not identical, so it is not possible in all instances to make direct comparison. However, a rank-order correlation of frequency of occurrence of nine identical error classifications is .68. The number of errors rather than the frequency per one thousand words was used to determine the rank so that fewer equal ranks resulted. Since the difference in the total frequency of error in the two studies is not great, comparisons can be made between the specific classifications of errors they have in common. Disagreement between verb and subject occurred approximately four times in every thousand words used in the current study, and seven times in every thousand words in the Davis study. The word "got" for "have" or "have got" was used about eight times in a thousand words in this study as compared with three times reported by Davis. The present study finds that the use

Table 52. Summary of Grammatical Deviations by Age *

Type of Deviation	Number of Deviations in Protocols					Frequency per 1,000 Words				
	3	4.5	6	8	3–8	3	4.5	6	8	3–8
"Got" for "have"	119	150	164	136	569	10.0	9.2	8.3	6.0	8.0
Verb not in agreement with subject	67	89	54	45	255	5.4	5.5	2.7	2.0	3.6
Auxiliary omitted	54	94	39	19	206	4.5	5.8	2.0	0.8	2.9
Colloquialisms and slang	24	56	46	78	204	2.0	3.4	2.3	3.4	2.9
Beginning sentence with "and"	38	69	27	45	179	3.4	5.5	1.4	2.0	2.5
Errors in conjugation	42	46	24	18	130	3.5	2.8	1.2	0.8	1.8
Errors in word order	24	25	12	22	83	2.0	1.5	0.6	1.0	1.2
Noun and pronoun: case	12	33	8	9	62	1.0	2.0	0.4	0.2	0.9
"Ain't"	8	19	25	9	61	0.7	1.2	1.3	0.4	0.9
Redundancy	12	9	11	26	58	1.0	0.6	0.6	1.1	0.8
Double negative	6	17	9	11	43	0.5	1.0	0.5	0.5	0.6
Errors in use of preposition	20	9	4	9	42	1.6	0.6	0.2	0.2	0.6
Noun and pronoun: gender and number	18	17	3	2	40	1.5	1.0	0.2	0.0	0.6
"Can" for "may"	7	7	5	2	21	0.6	0.5	0.3	0.0	0.3
Comparison of adjectives or adverbs	1	1	3	2	7	0.0	0.0	0.2	0.0	0.1

* N = 60 in each age group.

of colloquialisms and slang has increased about five times in every thousand words as compared with the Davis study. These appeared about three times in every thousand words as compared to 0.06 times earlier.

Errors in usage indicate that certain grammatical constructions are beginning to appear. For the entire age range errors in the use of the auxiliary verb occurred 2.9 times per thousand words, but such errors were about a fifth as frequent per thousand words at 8 as at 3 years. Nevertheless the auxiliary verb was used from 3 years of age on. At 3 years it was used correctly 50 times and omitted 54. At 4.5 it was used correctly 104 times and omitted 94 times. This type of verbal construction is used incorrectly about as frequently as it is used correctly in the early years of its use. At 6 years, however, it was used correctly 145 times and omitted 39, and at 8 years it was used 129 and omitted only 19.

The future tense is used by these subjects. In 301 instances it was used correctly. About one sixth of the correct usage occurred at 3 and 4.5 years and about one third at 6 and 8 years. There are only 57 instances in which an error in the use of the future tense occurs. Thus, only about one sixth as many errors as correct usages of the future tense were found. Of these errors about half were made at the 3-year level, and only seven such errors in tense were made at the 6- and 8-year levels combined.

Parts of Speech

Each word in the remarks of all the subjects was classified as a noun, verb, or other part of speech. A "miscellaneous" category was included for unintelligible words, proper names, "ain't," etc. Following the McCarthy classification, this permits direct comparison with her results. The mean percentages of parts of speech used in 50 remarks by subjects 3 through 8 years of age based on the total number of words are presented in Table 53. The percentages based on the number of different words used in these remarks are presented in Table 54.

The total number of words upon which these percentages of parts of speech are based at the single age levels varies from approximately 12,000 at 3 years through approximately 22,000 at 8 years, and includes a total of over 125,000 words for the entire age range. By the time a child begins to use sentences, the formal structure of the sentence imposes restrictions which partially determine the relative proportions of use of the various parts of speech. Before the child uses sentences, the classification of words into parts of speech is not justifiable. Soon after the child begins to use sentences, considerable stability in the proportion of the various parts of speech has been reported by various investigators, par-

Table 53. Mean Percentages of Various Parts of Speech Used by Subjects 3 to 8 Based on Total Number of Words Uttered

CA *	Noun	Verb	Adjective	Adverb	Pronoun	Conjunction	Preposition	Article	Interjection	Miscellaneous
3	17.7	22.6	6.3	10.0	19.4	1.5	6.5	6.8	2.1	7.1
3.5	17.1	23.0	6.9	9.9	19.2	2.3	6.9	6.5	1.8	6.5
4	16.3	23.1	6.7	10.1	20.3	2.8	6.9	6.8	1.3	5.7
4.5	16.5	23.6	7.7	10.0	18.9	2.5	6.8	7.3	1.2	5.6
5	16.1	23.5	7.5	10.6	20.0	2.6	6.7	6.7	0.8	5.4
6	17.1	25.0	7.6	10.0	19.3	2.6	7.6	7.0	1.0	3.1
7	17.0	24.0	7.3	10.4	18.0	3.3	8.0	7.9	1.4	2.8
8	17.0	24.3	7.4	9.1	17.8	3.7	7.9	8.1	1.2	2.9

* N = 60 in each age group.

Table 54. Mean Percentages of Various Parts of Speech Used by Subjects 3 to 8 Based on the Number of Different Words Uttered

CA *	Noun	Verb	Adjective	Adverb	Pronoun	Conjunction	Preposition	Article	Interjection	Miscellaneous
3	25.5	23.4	8.8	11.5	12.1	1.1	5.8	2.2	2.0	7.6
3.5	23.8	24.1	9.8	11.6	11.4	1.6	6.6	2.0	2.0	7.2
4	24.2	24.0	10.3	12.2	10.4	1.6	6.0	1.7	1.6	8.0
4.5	25.0	23.3	10.9	12.4	10.5	1.4	5.5	1.7	1.4	7.9
5	23.7	23.9	11.0	13.4	10.4	1.6	5.7	1.7	0.9	7.7
6	25.9	24.4	12.1	12.8	9.2	2.2	5.9	1.6	1.3	4.8
7	26.0	24.1	11.9	12.9	9.2	2.2	6.1	1.5	1.7	4.2
8	27.4	24.2	11.9	12.4	8.7	2.5	5.6	1.5	1.3	4.5

* N = 60 in each age group.

ticularly when all words used are considered. The youngest subjects in the present study are already beyond the age when extensive change in proportion of various parts of speech is observed.

When the percentages are calculated on total number of words used, little change in the percentage of use of the various parts of speech is found. Part of the differences that are found can be accounted for by the much smaller proportion of words classified in the miscellaneous category after 5 years of age. This stability in the distribution in parts of speech of all words uttered after 3 years agrees with the results of the McCarthy study on preschool children. In the current study the percentage of each of the different parts of speech is in close agreement with that reported by McCarthy. After three years the percentage of nouns used by her sample was stabilized near 20 per cent, verbs around 25 per cent, adjectives around 15 per cent, adverbs around 7 per cent, pronouns around 20 per cent, conjunctions around 4 per cent, prepositions around 7 per cent, interjections around 1 per cent, and miscellaneous less than 1 per cent.

When the percentages are based upon the number of different words used, although similarity throughout the age range is most characteristic, some slight shifts with age do appear. This, too, agrees with the McCarthy findings. The percentage of use of pronouns decreases about one third between 3 and 8 years of age. This results from normal vocabulary growth in which nouns, verbs, adjectives, and adverbs can continue to increase in relation to total vocabulary, whereas pronouns, prepositions, articles, and interjections must decrease since by comparison relatively few are in the language. The percentages are roughly comparable with those reported by McCarthy, which are nouns 38 per cent, verbs 26 per cent, adjectives 12 per cent, adverbs 7 per cent, pronouns 6 per cent, conjunctions 1.5 per cent, prepositions 3 per cent, interjections 2 per cent, and miscellaneous 2 per cent.

The differences in the characteristic proportions of the various parts of speech when calculated on the total number of words and the number of different words used are the result of the restrictions imposed by formal language structure.

Summary

Twenty-four thousand utterances of children from 3 to 8 years have been analyzed according to length, grammatical complexity, grammatical accuracy, and the parts of speech used.

1. The following statements can be made concerning the length of the verbalization. (a) Responses are significantly longer in the present study

than in the earlier studies of Davis and McCarthy. This difference becomes greater when the older subjects are compared. (b) Few significant differences in the length of the responses of boys and girls are found. The upper socioeconomic status groups use longer responses at practically every age level tested, and in some instances the differences are statistically significant. (c) The mean length of the five longest remarks in the present study is not substantially different from that reported by Davis, although the range is somewhat less than that reported by Davis. While essentially no differences were found in the mean length of the five longest remarks used by boys and girls, the upper socioeconomic status groups consistently use longer remarks than the lower socioeconomic status groups. (d) In the present study many fewer one-word remarks are found than in the earlier Davis study. No consistent sex or socioeconomic status trends are found.

2. Concerning the complexity of the sentence, the following can be said. (a) A modification of the Williams technique of quantifying the complexity of the sentence was partially satisfactory. With this scoring status groups consistently use longer remarks than the lower socioeco-economic status differences appear. (b) In comparing the structural analysis of the present study with those of Davis and McCarthy, proportionately fewer incomplete sentences have been found at practically all age levels. There is a consistent decrease in the proportionate use of structurally incomplete but functionally complete remarks with age; more simple sentences with phrases are used by the children in the present study; and there is a steady increase with age in the use of the more complex and elaborated forms of the sentence. In agreement with the findings of Davis and McCarthy no age relationship was found in the use of the simple sentence without phrases. (c) There is no essential difference in the use of the various types of sentences by boys and girls. This agrees with the studies of Davis and McCarthy. (d) Differences in the use of the several types of sentences are not great for the different socioeconomic status groups. The differences which do occur, however, are in the direction of the more advanced type of sentence structure being used more frequently by the upper socioeconomic status group. (e) When the sentence usage of the 8-year-old sample is taken as a measure of terminal status over the five-year span studied, there is a decrease in the use of incomplete sentences, little change in the use of simple sentences without a phrase, and an increase in all in the use of all types of sentences that involve increasing complexity of sentence structure such as coordination or subordination. (f) For both sexes and both socioeconomic status groups the declarative sentence is the most com-

mon, interrogative next, and the other types are infrequently used. (g) The use of subordination greatly increases over the five-year span studied. At all ages, and for both sexes and both socioeconomic status groups, however, the adverbial clauses are most frequent, the nominal next, and the adjectival clauses least frequent. (h) Considerable variation is found in the use of the various types of adverbial clauses.

3. About half of the remarks of 3-year-old children are grammatically correct. Errors resulting in incomplete sentences decrease with age. The specific grammatical errors made are similar to those reported by Davis. All errors except those associated with the use of slang and colloquialisms decrease over the age range studied. This may reflect the more liberal attitude toward such usage at the present time.

4. After the age of 3 the parts of speech used in both the total number of words and the different words uttered show little change. This is in agreement with other studies and is an indication that the language of children is functioning similarly to the language of adults. At this age the structure of adult grammar has already imposed the pattern of word selection upon the children.

VI. VOCABULARY

Vocabulary and its interrelations have long been a topic of interest. This chapter presents some of the problems associated with its measurement, the results of the investigation of the vocabularies of recognition and use, and their relationship to intelligence in children from 3 to 8 years.

Measurement of Vocabulary

Great discrepancies in the estimated size of children's vocabularies appear in the literature. These differences can be traced to such factors as the kind of vocabulary measured, the operational definition of "word" adopted, the criteria accepted for knowledge of a word, and the type of vocabulary test used.

The estimated size of vocabulary varies depending upon whether the vocabulary of use or the vocabulary of understanding is sampled. The vocabulary of use is made up of those words that are actually produced or used in oral and written speech. The vocabulary of understanding consists of those words that are recognized or understood when heard or read. Although there is substantial overlap in the words in the two vocabularies, they are not identical. The vocabulary of understanding is the larger from infancy on. Just as the infant responds to words before he uses them, so the child and the adult respond to many words they never use. Thus, estimates of the size of the vocabulary of understanding are always larger than those of the vocabulary of use.

The operating definition of a word which an experimenter accepts influences the estimate of vocabulary size. Such definitions vary greatly. Seashore in his work has defined a word as a "dictionary item." By this definition any bold-faced entry in the dictionary is counted as a word. Although neither additional meanings nor variant spellings are counted as separate words, compound words in bold-faced type are so counted. This technique of counting results in more words than Thorndike's method, which classifies such variants of a word as plurals, adverbs, comparatives and superlatives, verb forms and past participles as single words rather than as separate ones (51).

Words can be understood or known in differing degrees of completeness. The criteria which are frequently used to denote "knowledge of a word" include the recognition of the commonest meaning of a word in the identification of a picture, an object, or a synonym; a definition or explanation of the word; and the use of the word in a sentence (40). These are the criteria used in the present study. It should be noted that this study, like most investigations of children's vocabularies, is not concerned with the completeness with which the meaning or meanings of a word are understood. Many words have multiple meanings. The question of whether a word with several meanings is really "known" when only one or two meanings are understood is not faced. Although such investigation has been done at the adult level (34), there is need for similar work with children.

On the whole, the estimated size of vocabulary varies directly with the size of the sample of words from which the vocabulary test words are drawn (33, 41, 43). Thus a vocabulary test made up of a sample of words from the Thorndike *Junior Dictionary* results in a smaller estimated vocabulary than one based on a sample of words from an unabridged dictionary. This is partly a function of the selection of words to be included in the smaller dictionaries and partly the result of a wider representation of information more likely to be sampled by words drawn from the larger ones. The question of how small a sample of words can be used to predict knowledge of the total word sample is at present being investigated by the author.

While both published tests used in the current study measure the vocabulary of recognition, only the English Recognition Vocabulary Test of Seashore and Eckerson provides for an estimate of vocabulary size. These estimates are large since the test words are drawn from the Funk and Wagnall unabridged dictionary and since Seashore's definition of a word as a "dictionary item" is used.

The vocabulary of use is not sampled by any published or standardized test. Rather, measures are obtained secondarily in the verbalizations of the children and in connection with the measurement of sound discrimination ability during the preschool years. Thus the vocabulary of use is determined in two specific situations, but the total vocabulary of use is not ascertained.

Vocabulary of Recognition

The vocabulary of recognition is measured by the Ammons Full-Range Picture Vocabulary Test administered to the subjects 5 years of age and younger, and the Seashore-Eckerson English Recognition Vocabulary Test administered to the 6-to-8-year-old subjects. In the former the children identify in pictures the words uttered by the examiner. The latter is a multiple-choice test.

Table 55. Mean Scores on Ammons Vocabulary Test for Boys and Girls, Upper and Lower Socioeconomic Status Groups, and Total Subsamples, by Age

	Boys (N = 30)		Girls (N = 30)		USES (N = 18)		LSES (N = 42)		Total Subsample (N = 60)	
CA	Mean	SD	Mean	SD	Mean	SD	Mean	SD	Mean	SD
3	13.4	3.4	12.3	2.9	13.4	3.5	12.6	3.1	12.8	3.2
3.5	15.5	2.8	14.6	2.7	16.1	2.6	14.6	2.7	15.1	2.8
4	16.8	3.0	17.0	3.0	17.7	3.4	16.6	2.8	16.9	3.0
4.5	18.4	3.6	18.6	2.8	19.9	2.8	17.9	3.2	18.5	3.2
5	19.4	3.3	21.5	3.2	20.7	3.1	20.3	3.6	20.4	3.4

Ammons Full-Range Picture Vocabulary Test. Table 55 shows a steady increase with age in mean scores on the Ammons vocabulary test for boys and girls, USES and LSES groups, and subsamples over the preschool years tested. The differences between the scores of consecutive age subsamples are all significant at the .01 level (t values range from 2.81 to 4.18). For girls differences significant at the .01 level (t values above 3.19) are found between all ages except 4 and 4.5 where $t = 2.13$. For the boys, however, the differences in scores are not significant at the .05 level between any of the consecutive age levels tested. For the USES groups, only between the two youngest ages is the difference significant at the .05 level ($t = 2.62$). For the LSES groups the difference reaches the .01 level between all consecutively tested ages (t values all above 3.15) except between 4 and 4.5 years ($t = 2.00$).

When all preschool subsamples, that is, the 3-to-5-year subsamples, are combined, the difference between the mean score for boys, 16.7, SD 3.88, and girls, 16.8, SD 4.33, is not statistically significant. At each age level except at 5 years the difference between the mean scores obtained by boys and girls is not significant (t at 5 years = 2.52). Neither sex consistently receives the higher score.

The difference between the mean score of 17.6, SD 4.1, for all 3-to-5-year-old USES subjects and that of 16.4, SD 4.1, for all LSES subjects is significant at the .05 level ($t = 2.18$). The USES group receives the higher score at each age level. The differences are statistically insignificant at 3, 4, and 5 years, but reach the .05 level at 3.5 and 4.5 years ($t = 2.04$ and 2.45 respectively).

In the sample upon which Ammons and Holmes established their norms, thirty subjects covered each entire year span of 2, 3, 4, and 5 years (1). The mean chronological age for the respective age groups was 30.0, 41.5, 53.2, and 64.9 months. The same number of boys and girls was tested at each age. Over the entire age range the children were selected proportionate to the 1940 census distribution for each occupational group of fathers with children under 5 years of age. The mean vocabulary scores by age are reported as 11.8, SD 3.6, at 3 years; 16.6, SD 3.9, at 4 years; and 21.0, SD 4.4, at 5 years. These means are somewhat higher than those reported in the present study at 3 and 4 years and somewhat lower than reported at 5 years.

To compare more adequately the mean vocabulary scores obtained in the two studies, the 3- and 3.5-year-olds in the present one were combined into a new 3-year-old group containing 120 subjects, and the 4- and 4.5-year-olds were similarly combined into a new 4-year-old group. There was no comparable 5.5-year-old group to combine with the 5-year-old group of 60 subjects. The mean age of these new 3- and 4-year-old groups is about equal to that of comparable groups in the Ammons and Holmes sample; the 5-year-old sample is several months younger. The mean scores on the Ammons test for these groups are 13.9, SD 3.2, at 3 years, 17.7, SD 3.2, at 4 years, and 20.4, SD 3.4, at 5 years. The difference between these scores and those reported for comparable ages by Ammons and Holmes is significant at 3 years at the .05 level ($t = 2.5$) but is not significant at 4 or 5 years ($t = 1.3$ and 0.7 respectively). For the 3- and 4-year-old groups, when the mean ages are approximately equal, the higher score is obtained by the subjects in the current study; for the 5-year-old groups the higher score is attained by the older Ammons subjects.

When the data from the present study are combined into whole-year intervals, the scores tend to be quite similar to those reported by Ammons and Holmes. However, because of the rapid increment in vocabulary test scores over this preschool age range, norms of performance at half-year intervals are more useful since they are more sensitive to such growth.

The Seashore-Eckerson English Recognition Vocabulary Test. An estimation of the number of words in both basic and total vocabulary is made from performance on the Seashore-Eckerson test. The total vocabulary includes all basic words plus derived and compound words. In estimating vocabulary, each basic word and each compound word represents 505 words in the Funk and Wagnall unabridged dictionary, and each derived word represents 4,450 words. These values were determined by the method used in selecting the test words.

The Seashore-Eckerson test was devised as a group test, and, as such, is of particular use with older children. From the most extensive study of vocabulary of primary-grade children using this test, M. K. Smith has determined the test words to be used with these younger school-age children (47). She measured the vocabulary of 867 subjects from first grade through high school. The test was administered individually and orally to 44 children in first grade, 40 in second grade, and 59 in third grade.

In the administration of the test to these primary-grade children, each child was first asked to define a word; then, if he was unable to do this, he was given four possible meanings of the word from which to choose the correct one. In preliminary work it was determined that the results were not satisfactory if four synonyms were presented in series. For this reason, M. K. Smith recast the synonym choices into short questions, each repeating the test word. In scoring the test, she credited any correct meaning of the word which the child could give even though the definition offered was not included in the alternate choices, "for example, the child might not know 'poker' as a game, but know it as a fire-tool" (47:325).

The manual prepared by M. K. Smith was followed in the present study, although there was one possible difference in the technique of administration in the use of leading questions. M. K. Smith reports that "When all other questions failed, leading questions were asked and only half-credit was given for correct replies to such questions" (47:325). It is a nice problem to know how far an examiner can go in the use of leading questions without actually teaching the child. The examiners in the present investigation were trained to ask the child to define or describe a test word, to tell about it, or to use it in a sentence, but to avoid the use of leading questions. It is probable that this difference in administration would have a minimal effect on the results of the study since such extensive probing to determine whether or not the child knew any one accepted meaning of a test word was necessary in very few instances.

In scoring the Seashore-Eckerson test at the upper elementary and secondary grade levels, a correction for guessing is made. The number of basic test words known is determined by multiplying all incorrect items by 1.33 and then subtracting this product from the total number of items attempted. In the current study, the use of the correction factor in scoring has been questioned because of the individual administration of the test and the use of the shorter test devised for primary-grade children. Since all the tests were administered individually, greater control of guessing was obtained than in group administration. Also in the use of the selected primary test words, all words are presented to the child until he no longer identifies several words correctly. This probably means that the child gets some items wrong which he might not have attempted had he had free choice. Since the number of items attempted figures in the scoring, this is important. These same factors, of course, were present in the testing of primary grade children in M. K. Smith's study. However, her method of scoring at the primary-grade level is not described completely enough so that one can be assured whether or not the present study follows it precisely.

To meet the uncertainty about scoring, the responses used to estimate the size of basic and total vocabulary were scored by two methods in the present study: (1) an "uncorrected score" was obtained in which the total number of items correct was taken without the application of the correction factor for guessing; and (2) a "corrected score" was obtained in which the correction factor was applied.

Although the 99 words selected by Smith for use with primary-grade children appeared difficult when inspected by the author, they were satisfactory when used with the children. Many words were defined spontaneously. Over 60 per cent of a sample of 40 subjects drawn at each age level defined 20 or more words spontaneously. More than 85 per cent of the 6-year-olds spontaneously defined 10 or more words. Such definitions were not so prevalent among the 7- and 8-year-olds, probably because these older children were able to handle the multiple-choice items more readily. For the 6-year-old group, the proportion of incorrect choices was not equally distributed among the four choice positions. Words in the final position were chosen incorrectly in nearly two fifths and those in the initial position in about one fourth of the possible instances.

Basic vocabulary. Table 56 presents the number of words in the estimated basic vocabulary from 6 to 8 years as based on Smith's study and upon the medians of the corrected and uncorrected scores in the present study. The M. K. Smith estimations have been read from a graph presenting medians, Q's, and ranges for the single age levels since the exact figures were not reported.

The use of corrected or uncorrected scores makes a substantial difference in the number of words estimated in the basic vocabulary. In the current study, the basic vocabulary as estimated on the basis of the medians of the uncorrected scores is 1.4 to 1.8 times as large as those estimated for the same ages on the basis of the medians of the corrected scores.

If the estimation of basic vocabulary in the current study is based on the uncorrected scores, the agreement with Smith is greater. Such comparisons indicate that the median scores upon which the estimations

Table 56. Comparison of Median Number of Words (in thousands) in Estimated Basic Vocabulary According to Age as Reported by Templin and M. K. Smith Using the Seashore-Eckerson English Recognition Vocabulary Test

	Templin					
	Estimation Based on Corrected Score		Estimation Based on Uncorrected Score		Smith	
CA	Mdn	Q	Mdn	Q	Mdn	Q
6	7.8	2.5	14.4	2.6	16.1	4.6
7	12.4	3.8	19.2	4.0	18.5	4.4
8	17.6	4.4	25.1	3.8	23.0	4.4

Table 57. Mean Number of Words (in thousands) in Estimated Basic Vocabulary of Boys and Girls, Upper and Lower Socioeconomic Status Groups, and Subsamples by Age Based on Corrected and Uncorrected Seashore-Eckerson English Recognition Vocabulary Test Scores

	Boys (N = 30)		Girls (N = 30)		USES (N = 18)		LSES (N = 42)		Total Subsample (N = 60)	
CA	Mean	SD	Mean	SD	Mean	SD	Mean	SD	Mean	SD
	Estimation Based on Corrected Scores									
6	8.9	3.9	8.1	4.2	11.4	4.1	6.8	3.7	8.5	4.1
7	13.5	7.3	12.9	5.4	15.0	6.1	11.5	6.6	13.2	6.5
8	18.3	6.9	18.0	6.2	21.9	6.0	16.6	6.1	18.2	6.6
	Estimation Based on Uncorrected Scores									
6	14.8	4.1	13.9	4.2	16.9	4.6	12.7	5.6	14.4	4.2
7	19.6	6.5	18.7	5.7	21.5	5.1	17.1	7.0	19.2	6.2
8	25.1	5.8	24.5	5.6	28.3	4.9	23.4	5.3	24.8	5.7

are based differ by knowledge of only a few words in the vocabulary test. The greatest discrepancy between these estimations, 2,119 words at 8 years, is a difference of about 4 test words between the medians of the raw scores. When the uncorrected score is used, the higher estimations appear in the Smith study at 6 and 7 years and in the present one at 8 years. The Smith estimations are consistently higher than those in the present study based on the corrected scores. Nevertheless, it must be recognized that these lower estimations are still considerably above reports using other tests and measures (43).

The estimations of size of basic vocabulary based on both corrected and uncorrected mean scores are presented in Table 57 for boys and girls, USES and LSES groups, and for subsamples by age. The estimations based on the corrected mean scores are lower in all instances than comparable ones based on the uncorrected mean scores.

Since the distributions of estimations for subsamples are only slightly skewed, medians for the separate sex and SES groups are not presented in the Appendix. When the estimations are based on the corrected means and medians, the measures of skewness are .16, .13, and .09 at 6, 7, and 8 years respectively. When they are based on the uncorrected mean and median scores, they are identical or very similar, and the measures of skewness range between .00 and .06.

The increase in size of estimated basic vocabulary is significant at the .01 level between consecutively tested age subsamples. For the uncorrected scores the t is 4.97 between 6 and 7 years and 5.21 between 7 and 8 years. For the uncorrected scores the t values are 4.74 and 4.19 between the same ages.

The range in estimated basic vocabulary size is substantial at each age: based on the corrected scores, the ranges at 6, 7, and 8 years are 13, 30, and 23 thousand words; based on the uncorrected scores they are 13, 20, and 26 thousand words at the same ages. With the exception of the range as estimated by the corrected scores at 7 years, each of these is smaller than the 20,000-, 23,000-, and 33,000-word ranges reported by Smith at these ages.

The estimated basic vocabulary of boys, based on either the corrected or uncorrected means, is consistently higher than that of girls at the same ages. However, the difference between the sexes in the size of estimated basic vocabulary is not statistically significant at any age level. Since M. K. Smith has not reported an analysis by sex, no comparison with her data is possible.

The estimated basic vocabulary of the USES groups is larger than that of the LSES groups at each age regardless of whether the estimation is based on the corrected or the uncorrected means. Using either the corrected or the uncorrected scores in estimating, the differences are significant at the .01 level at 6 years ($t = 4.12$ and 3.29) and at 8 years ($t = 3.11$ and 3.49). This level of confidence is not reached at 7 years, although the .05 level is approached for the corrected and is passed for the uncorrected scores ($t = 1.98$ and 2.72). This substantial difference in the estimated basic vocabulary of USES and LSES groups is probably related, at least in part, to the difference in intelligence between the groups.

Total vocabulary. In the estimation of size of total vocabulary the number of words represented by those compound and derived words correctly defined is added to the number of words in the estimated basic vocabulary. Since estimations based on corrected and uncorrected scores have been made for basic vocabulary, similar estimations are made for total vocabulary. In Table 58 estimations based on medians in the present study and those read from a graph published by Smith for the same age levels are presented. As with the basic vocabulary, the estimations for total vocabulary based on the uncorrected score are consistently larger. In addition, at all three age levels, the Smith estimations are higher than those in the present study. However, the estimations based on the corrected and uncorrected median scores are substantial. Those based on the uncorrected scores are more similar to those of Smith than to those based on the medians of the corrected scores in this study.

From Table 59 it is evident that the estimated total vocabulary of

Table 58. Comparison of Median Number of Words (in thousands) in Estimated Total Vocabulary According to Age as Reported by Templin and M. K. Smith Using the Seashore-Eckerson English Recognition Vocabulary Test

	Templin					
	Estimation Based on Corrected Scores		Estimation Based on Uncorrected Scores		Smith	
CA	Mdn	Q	Mdn	Q	Mdn	Q
6	13.0	6.0	18.8	5.3	21.0	7.0
7	21.6	7.6	24.4	7.0	26.5	9.0
8	28.3	7.2	35.0	8.1	38.0	8.5

Table 59. Mean Number of Words (in thousands) in Estimated Total Vocabulary of Boys and Girls, Upper and Lower Socioeconomic Status Groups, and Subsamples by Age Based on Corrected and Uncorrected Seashore-Eckerson Recognition Vocabulary Scores

	Boys (N = 30)		Girls (N = 30)		USES (N = 18)		LSES (N = 42)		Total Subsample (N = 60)	
CA	Mean	SD	Mean	SD	Mean	SD	Mean	SD	Mean	SD
					Estimation Based on Corrected Scores					
6	15.1	7.5	13.9	7.4	19.2	8.2	12.5	6.0	14.5	7.6
7	20.9	12.1	19.3	8.3	24.0	10.9	18.7	10.1	20.1	10.6
8	28.7	12.4	28.9	11.1	34.4	11.8	25.0	10.7	28.8	11.9
					Estimation Based on Uncorrected Scores					
6	21.2	8.2	20.0	7.5	25.0	9.1	18.7	6.3	20.6	7.8
7	26.7	11.0	25.0	8.4	29.6	9.6	24.2	9.5	25.8	9.9
8	35.3	11.6	34.6	10.2	39.4	10.6	32.8	10.4	34.9	11.0

boys and girls, USES and LSES groups, and total subsamples based on uncorrected mean scores is consistently larger than that based upon the means of corrected scores.

The distributions of the estimations of the total vocabulary of the subsamples are only slightly skewed at 6 years (measure of skewness is .59 for the corrected and .69 for the uncorrected scores) and they are less skewed at the other ages (range .02 to .42). The medians for the various subgroups have not been presented in the Appendix.

The increase in estimated size of total vocabulary between subsamples at consecutively tested age levels is statistically significant between consecutively tested age levels for both estimations. Using the estimations based on the corrected mean score the t is 3.31 between 6 and 7 years and 4.22 between 7 and 8 years. Using the estimations based upon the means of the uncorrected scores, the t is 3.17 and 4.76 for the same comparisons.

The differences between the estimated vocabularies of boys and girls are small and not statistically significant at any age level. For the estimations based on the means of the corrected scores the highest t is 0.63; for those based on the uncorrected means it is 0.67. Boys have the larger estimated total vocabulary based upon the uncorrected scores at three ages, and at two ages when the estimate is based upon the means of the corrected scores.

Using either the means of the corrected or uncorrected scores for estimation of total vocabulary, the estimated size of vocabulary of the LSES groups at each age level is smaller than that of the USES groups. These differences for the corrected mean score estimations are significant at the .01 level at 6 and 8 years ($t = 3.11$ and 2.91 respectively) but that at 7 years is insignificant ($t = 1.77$). The differences between the two socioeconomic status groups when the estimations are based on the uncorrected scores do not reach the higher level of confidence at any age, but the t values of 2.68 at 6 years, 2.00 at 7 years, and 2.22 at 8 years of age are just significant at the .05 level.

Vocabulary of Use

Although no attempt has been made to determine the total vocabulary of use, the number of different words used in the 50 utterances obtained for the study of grammatical construction and the number of sound discrimination test words correctly identified provide a measure of vocabulary of use in two specific situations.

Number of different words used in 50 verbalizations. Since 50 remarks were available from all subjects, the number of different words appearing is taken as a measure of the vocabulary of use in a sample of oral speech obtained under specific conditions. The mean number of different words used by boys and girls, USES and LSES groups, and subsamples is presented in Table 60. For the subsamples at each age level the distribution of the number of different words used is quite normal. At 8 years the measure of skewness is .51 and at other ages it ranges from .06 to .38.

The increase in the number of different words used from one test age to another is steady. The differences are significant at the .01 levels between the three earliest ages and at the age when most children are introduced to school for the first time. The t between 3 and 3.5 is 2.87, between 3.5 and 4 years it is 3.52, between 5 and 6 years it is 2.92. Between 6 and 7 years it is 2.14 and between the other consecutive ages it ranges from 1.15 to 1.70. These increments with age in the number of different words used could reflect the size of the total vocabulary of use. On the other hand, in a measure such as this they could be associated with the increased loquacity of older children.

The mean number of different words used by girls from 3 to 8 years combined is 132.0, SD 33.8; that used by boys is 129.5, SD 37.1. This difference is not statistically significant since t is .07. For the separate age levels the differences between the sexes are not statistically significant at any age except at 6 years where the difference reaches the .05 level (t values range from .12 to 2.40). Neither sex consistently uses more different words: boys use more different words at three of the age levels tested and girls at five of them.

The USES group composed of all ages combined used more different words than the LSES group, a difference significant at the .01 level ($t = 3.43$). The mean number of words used by the USES groups is 138.9, SD 33.0; that by the LSES group is 127.3, SD 35.9. At each age level the USES subjects use more different words, but only at 3.5 years does the difference reach the .01 level of confidence ($t = 2.80$) and at 4.5 and 7 years the .05 level ($t = 2.33$ and 2.16). The differences at all other age levels are not statistically significant (t ranges from 1.24 to 1.91).

Table 61 presents the total number of words used by the boys and girls, USES and LSES groups, and subsamples by age. By comparing Tables 60 and 61, the proportion of different words used to all words uttered in 50 remarks is apparent. This ratio is approximately one different word for slightly over every two words uttered. The ratio shows little variation over the age range tested and among subsamples, sex, and SES groups.

Table 60. Mean Number of Different Words Used in 50 Remarks by Boys and Girls, Upper and Lower Socioeconomic Status Groups, and Subsamples by Age

	Boys (N = 30)		Girls (N = 30)		USES (N = 18)		LSES (N = 42)		Total Subsamples (N = 60)	
CA	Mean	SD	Mean	SD	Mean	SD	Mean	SD	Mean	SD
3	94.3	29.9	90.7	21.4	102.4	26.7	88.3	24.6	92.5	26.1
3.5 ...	100.6	20.5	109.0	19.4	115.0	17.9	100.4	19.8	104.8	20.4
4	115.7	28.9	125.2	25.3	127.8	27.1	117.3	27.2	120.4	27.6
4.5 ...	128.6	28.3	125.4	16.5	136.2	17.4	123.0	28.1	127.0	23.9
5	125.8	26.5	139.1	26.1	141.3	25.6	128.6	26.9	132.4	27.2
6	155.2	25.8	138.8	27.0	151.0	23.9	138.6	42.2	147.0	27.6
7	156.0	29.1	159.4	24.9	164.1	22.6	145.8	42.3	157.7	27.2
8	164.7	28.1	168.4	30.6	173.8	30.1	163.4	28.4	166.5	29.5

Table 61. Mean Total Number of Words Used by Boys and Girls, Upper and Lower Socioeconomic Status Groups, and Total Subsamples in 50 Consecutive Remarks

	Boys (N = 30)		Girls (N = 30)		USES (N = 18)		LSES (N = 42)		Total Subsamples (N = 60)	
CA	Mean	SD	Mean	SD	Mean	SD	Mean	SD	Mean	SD
3	213.3	70.9	196.5	48.1	209.9	20.8	202.8	58.8	204.9	61.3
3.5	223.0	47.6	242.7	51.7	263.7	47.0	219.6	46.3	232.9	50.8
4	258.5	76.4	279.1	67.0	277.4	61.7	265.1	76.6	268.8	72.6
4.5	269.9	80.0	271.5	45.8	302.3	44.8	257.1	67.9	270.7	65.3
5	266.7	70.2	305.7	75.1	302.6	75.6	279.2	74.1	286.2	75.5
6	335.4	71.0	320.5	59.0	343.4	53.2	305.0	95.7	328.0	65.9
7	366.8	41.8	359.3	58.7	363.7	40.2	342.6	93.3	363.1	51.3
8	364.0	69.4	393.6	88.0	386.8	80.0	375.4	80.8	378.8	80.9

Sound discrimination vocabulary. For the subjects 5 years of age and under scores on the vocabulary used in the preschool sound discrimination test were presented by age in Table 30. Steady increases in the scores occur between consecutively tested age levels, but these differences are not statistically significant.

The mean of 68.5 for all the boys over the age range tested is not significantly different from that of 69.1 for the girls. At three age levels the girls receive higher scores, but at no age level are the differences between the sexes significantly different at the .05 level or higher.

For the entire USES group the mean score is 71.7, SD 7.16, and that of the entire LSES group is 67.5, SD 9.31. This difference does not reach the .05 level of confidence ($t = 1.88$). At each age level the USES subjects receive the higher scores. Only at 3 and 4.5 years does the difference reach the .05 level ($t = 2.31$ and 2.25). The t values at the other ages range between 1.28 and 1.79.

Specific words. The 480 subjects used 6,144 different words in the 50 remarks of all subjects compared with 2,033 different words used by Davis' subjects (5:109). Since in the present study over half of the subjects are in the preschool age range, the discrepancy in the number of different words is even greater than a simple word count would indicate.

Despite this difference there is great similarity in the words used most frequently. Davis reports 175 words used 100 or more times; there are 178 words used this frequently in the present study. The ten most frequently used words in the present study include the first seven words and the ninth, thirteenth, and sixteenth most frequently used in the Davis study.

In both studies 25 words were used 900 or more times. Twenty of these words are identical in both studies. These are is, the, a, this, I, and, to, here, he, they, go, one, that, there, it, of, in, up, got, and have. The other 5 words used at least 900 times in the present study are on, you, we, my, and she. The same words in the Davis study were used between 234 and 897 times. The 5 words used as often as 900 times in the Davis study but not in the present one are "Indian," "these," "are," "horse," and "them." Unlike any other of the most frequently used words, "Indian" and "horse," are related to the materials used in the testing situation by Davis.

Relation of Intelligence to Vocabulary Measures

A substantial relationship between intelligence and vocabulary has long been recognized. For the separate age levels in the current study, the r's (correlations) between the IQ or IQ-equivalent and scores on the measures of vocabulary of recognition and of use are presented in Table 62. No correlations between intelligence and recognition vocabulary could be calculated for the preschool subjects since the IQ-equivalent which is used as a measure of intelligence at this age is based upon the score obtained on the Ammons Full-Range Picture Vocabulary Test. No other preschool recognition vocabulary test was given.

On the whole, the correlations presented are substantial, although somewhat lower than frequently reported. The magnitude of the correlations is similar between the Stanford-Binet IQ and either the basic or total recognition vocabulary as estimated by the uncorrected scores on the Seashore-Eckerson test. Although only the r's with the vocabulary estimations based on the uncorrected scores are presented, they agree

Table 62. Product-Moment Correlations between IQ or IQ-equivalent and Several Vocabulary Measures

Vocabulary Measure	Correlated with IQ or IQ-equivalent *							
	Age 3*	Age 3.5*	Age 4*	Age 4.5*	Age 5	Age 6	Age 7	Age 8
Corrected Seashore-Eckerson basic vocabulary..						.50	.55	.56
Corrected Seashore-Eckerson total vocabulary...						.54	.65	.54
Uncorrected Seashore-Eckerson basic vocabulary..						.50	.55	.64
Uncorrected Seashore-Eckerson total vocabulary...						.52	.65	.53
Number of different words in 50 remarks.......	.57	.40	.56	.57	.27	.26	.28	.20
Sound discrimination vocabulary...	.51	.66	.42	.46	.36			

* IQ-equivalent based on Ammons Full-Range Picture Vocabulary Test score.

quite closely with those between intelligence and the corrected vocabulary scores. The r's between IQ and the basic vocabulary estimated from the corrected scores are .50 at 6, .57 at 7, and .56 at 8. Only at the highest age is any considerable difference in magnitude of correlation noted.

The correlations between intelligence and the two measures of vocabulary of use show somewhat similar and yet distinctive trends with age. The correlations with sound discrimination vocabulary, after the earliest age tested, seem to show some decrease with age. The correlations with the number of different words in 50 remarks, on the other hand, are similar at the first four age levels and then drop sharply at 5, and continue at the lower magnitude. This break occurs at the age most children enter school and not at the age at which the measure of intelligence was shifted.

The magnitude of the correlations between intelligence and the number of different words used in 50 remarks from 3 to 4.5 years agrees reasonably with those at the older ages tested between intelligence and the vocabulary of recognition. Even at these younger ages the correlations are much smaller than the .83 to .85 reported by Ammons and Holmes between their vocabulary test and that of the Stanford-Binet, Form L.

The substantial decrease in the relationship between the number of different words used in 50 remarks and intellectual ability after 5 years of age may indicate that this is not a satisfactory measure of vocabulary of use throughout the age range tested. The number of words in the total vocabulary of use increases with age during the developmental period. Thus, if a sufficiently large sample of speech were obtained, the number of different words used would reflect the total vocabulary of use. It is probable that 50 remarks provide a sample large enough to reflect the number of words the young child actually uses, but it is likely that a larger sample of speech is necessary to be sensitive to the total number of words used by older children. That the sample of speech is too small is a more likely explanation than that the relationship between the number of different words used and intelligence decreases during the early developmental period.

The correlations between intelligence and sound discrimination vocabulary tend to decrease with age, but a sharp break in the magnitude of the correlations is not apparent. The decrease here may again be a function of the measure of vocabulary used. Although at 5 years there is still considerable ceiling to the test, the variability of the groups has decreased considerably. Correlations calculated between the two measures of vocabulary of use in specific situations do not show a decrease with age nor a break at 5 years. The correlations between the sound discrimination vocabulary and the number of different words used in 50 remarks is .45 at 3 years, .37 at 3.5 years, .39 at 4 years, .57 at 4.5 years, and .49 at 5 years.

Summary

1. The increase in the vocabulary of recognition is substantial from age to age and is continuing with no apparent deceleration at the oldest ages tested. This holds for the Ammons Full-Range Picture Vocabulary Test at 5 years and for both the basic and total vocabulary estimations on the Seashore-Eckerson English Recognition Vocabulary at 8 years.

2. No significant differences in the recognition vocabulary scores of boys and girls at separate ages nor for the entire preschool age range appear on the Ammons test. On the Seashore-Eckerson test boys from 6 to 8 consistently attained higher scores which were not statistically significant.

3. On the Ammons test during the preschool years and the Seashore-Eckerson during the primary grades, the upper socioeconomic status groups consistently attain higher scores than the lower socioeconomic status groups, and the differences tend toward statistical significance.

4. Although there is considerable agreement between mean scores of the 3-to-5-year-old subjects and those for comparable age groups reported by Ammons and Holmes, because of the half-year age intervals during a period of rapid vocabulary growth the current study presents more sensitive norms.

5. The Seashore-Eckerson English Recognition Vocabulary Test was scored both using and omitting the correction factor. The estimations based on the corrected scores were lower than those based on the uncorrected, but nevertheless, large. The estimations based on the uncorrected scores were, in most instances, lower than those made by M. K. Smith, but they tended to agree more with the Smith estimations than with those based on the corrected scores.

6. The vocabulary of use as measured by the sound discrimination vocabulary and the number of different words used in 50 remarks continued to show an increase throughout the age ranges tested. For both measures no sex differences were found, but the upper socioeconomic status groups knew more words than the lower socioeconomic status groups.

7. Although many more different words were used in the children's 50 remarks than were reported by Davis, there is high agreement in the specific words used most frequently.

8. Correlations between intelligence and the vocabulary measures were somewhat lower than reported by other investigators. In the correlations of intelligence with the number of different words used in 50 remarks a sharp break in the magnitude of the correlations occurs at 5 years.

VII. INTERRELATIONSHIPS AMONG SEVERAL LANGUAGE SKILLS

Since measures of different language skills were obtained for the same children, the interrelationships among them have been explored at several age levels over a five-year span.

PERTINENT STUDIES

Only a few studies of the interrelationships among language skills have been reported in the literature. Of these, several are concerned with the relationships that exist in the language of children with speech or reading disorders. To the author's knowledge only two published studies make any extensive investigation of the interrelationships among these skills in children who are not speech defectives. Of these, the most extensive is the study by Williams and his associates published in 1937 (54). This study has been referred to previously in the discussion of articulation and sentence structure. The major contribution for purposes of the present investigation is in the analysis of the interrelationships among several language abilities.

In the Williams study two vocabulary measures, a measure of speech sound articulation, and several measures of oral expression based on 40 verbal utterances of the subjects, were included. Vocabulary was tested by the Van Alstyne Picture Vocabulary Test and by the Smith-Williams Vocabulary Test. Articulation was measured using a modification of the technique developed by Wellman *et al.* The verbal utterances were obtained in free play situations.

Williams reports two analyses of the data. One, using a varying number of tests on 70 to 130 children ranging in age from 2.5 to 6.5 years, provides little basis for satisfactory comparisons. The second, however, furnishes the best comparative data available. This analysis is made on 38 children between 3 and 4 years who were tested on all the language measures. Specific comparisons between this analysis and the present study are reported in this chapter.

A study recently reported by Schneiderman investigated some interrelationships of intelligence, speech, and language among 70 first-grade children ranging in age from 6 years to 7 years and 1 month (39). The intelligence of each child was measured on the Chicago Non-Verbal Examination. A combined language score was derived from the scores on three languages measures, weighted so that each would make an equal contribution. The language skills measured included spoken vocabulary, the mean length of spontaneous utterance, and a teacher rating of each child's ability to express himself. The spoken vocabulary was measured using the Van Alstyne Picture Vocabulary Test. Spontaneous utterances were obtained as definitions of 15 words taken from among the first 500 words on the Gates Reading Vocabulary List for Children. The teacher rating took account of the amount of language, the accuracy of word usage, and general facility in use of words for expressing needs and ideas. Articulation ability was measured in the children's spontaneous responses to the Test Cards accompanying the Speech Improvement Cards developed by Bryngelson and Glaspey.

Since Schneiderman's study is one of the few in which the analysis of the interrelationships of several language variables was possible in the same children, it is unfortunate that no correlations between articulation and the several language scores are reported either in the published article or in the unpublished thesis. However, whenever possible, comparisons with the present study are made.

Analysis of the Data

To study the interrelationships of the various language skills, correlation, terminal status, and the significance of the differences between consecutively tested age levels are used. Product-moment correlations between the several variables have been determined for the total subsamples at each age level. The N used in computing all correlations presented in this chapter is 60. No correlations are reported for the separate sex or SES groups. With an N of 60 an r above .30 is significant at the .01 level, and an r of .21 satisfies the .05 level of confidence.

Terminal status measures are presented for each major language area tested. Consistent with the earlier chapters, the terminal status scores are presented for boys and girls, USES and LSES groups, and for total subsamples. The terminal status score, like any percentage, depends for stability upon the size of the sample and the magnitude of the raw scores being considered. In this study, the N at each age level varies from 18 for the USES groups to 30 for the boys and girls to 42 for the LSES groups to 60 for the total subsample. The range of raw scores varies considerably, but for these major measures is always substantial.

For each major language measure, the mean score of the subjects at the oldest age tested is taken as a measure of terminal status and the percentage of this score attained by each younger age group is calculated. With the scores of the 8-year-old subjects taken as a measure of terminal status, comparisons are made of the development of articulation, sentence structure, sound discrimination as measured in paired nonsense syllables, and vocabulary as measured by the Seashore-Eckerson English Recognition Vocabulary Test. The scores of the 5-year-old subjects were taken as a measure of terminal status when a different test of any language area was used with the preschool and the school-age subjects. These include sound discrimination and vocabulary. Although different tests were used to measure articulation at the preschool and the school ages, terminal status scores were not taken at both 5 and 8 years since the same sounds were measured throughout the age range.

Throughout this monograph reference has been made to the significance of the differences between consecutively tested age subsamples. These are brought together for the major measures in this chapter.

Correlation Analysis

In Table 63 the intercorrelations among the various language skills are presented separately for each age subsample. In interpreting them it must be remembered that different measures of intelligence, sound discrimination, and vocabulary are used at the preschool and at the school ages. At 6, 7, and 8 years of age the IQ is based most frequently on the Stanford-Binet which was administered by kindergarten teachers. The IQ-equivalent is the only measured approximation of intelligence at the preschool level. The correlations with IQ-equivalent are presented in Table 63 under the heading "Ammons Vocabulary" since the scores are based upon that test.

Of the 189 correlations presented, 76 per cent are significant at the .01 level and only 12 per cent do not reach the .05 level of confidence. The magnitude of the intercorrelations varies with the language areas tested, the particular test used, and the age of the subsample being considered. The highest correlations are found between sound discrimination and sound discrimination vocabulary. At each of the preschool ages tested (sound discrimination vocabulary scores are available only on preschool children) the r's are about .90. The intercorrelations among the measures related to sentence structure are only slightly lower. Of the 24 correlations reported among the length of remark, the complexity of remark, and the number of different words used, only 6 fall between .5 and .7, while 18 are above .75. This is not unexpected since these three sentence variables would seem necessarily to be intimately dependent upon one another. Although there is considerable variability in the magnitude of the correlations between the several vocabulary measures and other language variables, they are generally in a lower range. Of the 70 correlations among these variables, only one reaches .6. The mean correlation reported for the Ammons vocabulary test and both the Seashore-Eckerson scores is somewhere between .3 and .4.

Although no marked age trends are evident, some differences are apparent in the magnitude of the correlations at different ages. For those language areas in which the same test was used over the age span covered in this study, essentially no age trends are found in the intercorrelations among length of response, complexity of response, and number of different words used. The size of the correlations among these sentence variables is substantial throughout the age range. The correlations between these measures and total articulation score tend to decrease slightly with age. This decrease in the relationship of sentence

Table 63. Product-Moment Correlations among Major Measures by Age

Measure	CA 3	3.5	4	4.5	5	6	7	8
Total articulation versus:								
Sound discrimination	.59	.42	.58	.41	.44	.67	.69	.47
Length of remark	.62	.47	.27	.26	.52	.45	.23	.18
Complexity of remark	.66	.57	.30	.49	.35	.46	.08	.15
Number of different words	.65	.53	.41	.34	.62	.34	.24	.19
Ammons vocabulary	.47	.48	.24	.41	.27			
Sound discrimination vocabulary	.54	.42	.52	.42	.42			
Corrected basic vocabulary						.34	.45	.40
Uncorrected basic vocabulary						.39	.46	.38
Intelligence quotient						.37	.39	.29
Sound discrimination versus:								
Length of remark	.45	.23	.32	.40	.69	.40	.36	−.01
Complexity of remark	.49	.25	.40	.37	.50	.41	.25	.05
Number of different words	.49	.44	.45	.49	.54	.26	.37	.02
Ammons vocabulary	.37	.63	.48	.05	.12			
Sound discrimination vocabulary	.93	.95	.94	.91	.96			
Corrected basic vocabulary						.44	.46	.58
Uncorrected basic vocabulary						.51	.49	.52
Intelligence quotient						.54	.47	.45
Length of remark versus:								
Complexity of remark	.89	.81	.88	.90	.59	.91	.68	.77
Number of different words	.91	.85	.93	.89	.91	.84	.68	.80
Ammons vocabulary	.55	.26	.24	.52	.26			
Sound discrimination vocabulary	.42	.21	.27	.54	.61			
Corrected basic vocabulary						.32	.16	.06
Uncorrected basic vocabulary						.39	.19	.03
Intelligence quotient						.39	.08	.15

Table 63 *continued*

Measure	CA 3	3.5	4	4.5	5	6	7	8
Complexity of remark versus:								
Number of different words...	.87	.77	.69	.76	.80	.82	.52	.68
Ammons vocabulary	.54	.29	.30	.46	.31			
Sound discrimination vocabulary	.45	.28	.31	.33	.43			
Corrected basic vocabulary..						.29	−.18	.12
Uncorrected basic vocabulary						.36	−.03	.13
Intelligence quotient						.26	.00	.30
Number of different words versus:								
Ammons vocabulary	.57	.40	.56	.57	.49			
Sound discrimination vocabulary	.45	.37	.39	.47	.27			
Corrected basic vocabulary..						.22	.31	.17
Uncorrected basic vocabulary						.28	.31	.19
Intelligence quotient						.26	.28	.22
Ammons vocabulary versus:								
Sound discrimination vocabulary	.51	.66	.42	.46	.36			
Corrected basic vocabulary versus:								
Uncorrected basic vocabulary						.91	.94	.91
Intelligence quotient						.50	.57	.56
Uncorrected basic vocabulary versus:								
Intelligence quotient						.50	.55	.64

variables with articulation may be spurious, resulting from the large number of maximum scores attained at the older ages. However, it may be a true reflection of language growth in the earlier years. At this time when the variation in articulatory skill among children of the same age is greater, articulation may actually be more closely related to talkativeness, size of vocabulary, and the use of complex grammatical expressions.

Schneiderman does not report correlations between articulation and her combined language score. However, when her subjects were divided into upper, middle, and lower groups on the basis of the magnitude of this score, the differences in the mean articulation scores obtained by the three groups were statistically significant ($F = 4.3$). When the subjects in these groups were matched on MA and CA, the differences among their articulation scores were no longer differentiated significantly as the F was reduced to 2.0. In both analyses the trend in the articulation scores was the same: the group receiving the highest combined language score made the fewest articulation errors, the middle group made slightly more such errors, and the lowest group made the most articulation errors.

Since different tests were used to measure sound discrimination and vocabulary at the preschool and the school ages, terminal status measures for these language skills are taken at both 5 and 8 years. For sound discrimination the trends in the size of the correlations differ for the two. From 3 to 5 there is essentially no trend in the size of the correlations between sound discrimination and the length of response, the complexity of response, the number of different words used, and the total articulation score. From 6 to 8 years, however, there is a tendency for all the correlations between sound discrimination and these language variables to decrease with age. Although this decrease is somewhat irregular, it is still apparent at the oldest ages tested. This may be in part a function of the reduction in SD as the ceiling of the sound discrimination test is approached. Because of this it would have been of value to extend these measures to older age levels.

For the subsamples from 3 to 5 years, the correlations of both sound discrimination score and sound discrimination vocabulary with the various language variables are quite similar. Over the entire age range the correlations between total articulation and sound discrimination scores decrease slightly. Correlations between the various language variables and sound discrimination vocabulary at the preschool age also decrease slightly as age is increased. At the younger ages a difference is found in the magnitude of the correlations between the Ammons vocabulary score and both sound discrimination score and sound discrimination vocabulary. From 3 to 5 years the correlations between the Ammons vocabulary scores and sound discrimination decrease, while those with sound discrimination vocabulary do not vary with age. From 6 to 8 years the correlations between sound discrimination and the Seashore-Eckerson vocabulary scores do not vary regularly with age, while those between sound discrimination and IQ decrease slightly, although they are not markedly related to age. The correlations with the Ammons scores and the other language variables at the preschool ages resemble trends found at the older ages in correlations with IQ more than those found with other vocabulary measures.

Vocabulary is another of the language areas in which different tests are used in measurement. During the preschool years the correlations between Ammons vocabulary and sound discrimination scores decrease with age. At this period all other correlations with either the Ammons vocabulary scores or the sound discrimination vocabulary show no real age trends. From 6 to 8 years the correlations between the corrected and uncorrected Seashore-Eckerson basic vocabulary scores also bear little relation to age. During the early school years there is a tendency for the magnitude of the correlations between vocabulary and length and complexity of response to decrease some with age. The number of different words used in the responses may be looked upon as a measure of vocabulary of use. With this vocabulary measure a decrease in correlations is noted with articulation and sound discrimination, but there is little relation to age with both length and complexity of remark.

The decrease in the magnitude of these correlations at the older ages may indicate that at these ages the samples of language obtained in spontaneous utterances in a child-adult setting are not long enough for the complexities of sentence structure and the larger vocabulary of use to become apparent. Schneiderman has reported a correlation of .17 between sentence length and vocabulary with 6-to-7-year-old children. This is considerably lower than the .32 and .39 found with the Seashore-Eckerson test at 6 years in the present study, but it is in close agreement with the correlations of .16 and .19 reported at 7 years.

There is no consistent trend in the relationships between the measures of intelligence and the various language variables over the age range studied. For the 6-to-8-year-old subjects only the correlations of IQ with sound discrimination and the two Seashore-Eckerson basic vocabulary scores reach any substantial magnitude. No comparisons can be made with a similar vocabulary measure at the preschool ages. The relation between IQ and sound discrimination increases slightly, which contrasts with the relation found during the preschool years. The correlations between IQ and articulation are substantial, dropping only at the highest CA tested.

During the school years there is a tendency for the relationships of the three measures of sentence development with IQ-equivalent to decrease. During the preschool years the size of the correlations tends to be unstable, particularly in the early years. This may reflect the inadequacy of the intellectual measure or the inadequacy of the sample of speech obtained in the utterances of the youngsters. It is probably the latter. Reasonably it is expected that intelligence is related to the length and complexity of sentence and to the number of different words a child uses. To determine the really meaningful relations which probably obtain among these variables, longer samples of speech are needed at the older ages included in this study.

Agreement with the findings of Schneiderman is close on two of the three possible comparisons of correlations between language variables and intelligence which can be made. She reports an r of —.35 between articulation score and MA for 6-to-7-year-olds. The IQ obtained on a restricted age of two months in the present study may be considered an intellectual unit comparable to the MA over a wider age range. In the present study the r between IQ and articulation score for 6-year-olds is .37 and for 7-year-olds it is .39. Since the articulation score used by Schneiderman is an error score and that used in the present study is a measure of correct articulation, these three correlations are nearly identical. This close agreement exists in spite of the fact that a verbal test was used in the present study to measure intelligence while Schneiderman used a nonverbal test.

The correlation of .48 reported by Schneiderman between vocabulary and MA is essentially equal to the .50 found at 6 years with both the corrected and uncorrected basic Seashore-Eckerson vocabulary scores and with the .55 and .57 found at 7 years in the present study. Schneiderman reports a correlation of —.003 between MA and sentence length whereas the comparable correlations in the present study are .39 and .08 at 6 and 7 years respectively. This difference could be accounted for partially by the use of verbal and nonverbal intelligence tests. It is more likely, however, that the relative adequacy of the samples of verbalizations is the more important factor. In the present study the relationship between sentence length and IQ-equivalent is considerably higher at the preschool ages. This may indicate that the size of the sample of verbalization at these ages is sufficiently large to include more adequately the range of variations in the complexity of sentence structure which is likely to occur.

The intercorrelations among the language variables are presented in Table 64 with intelligence partialled out. For the subsamples from 3 to 5 the Ammons scores are partialled out; for the subsamples from 6 to 8 the Stanford-Binet IQ's are partialled out. The magnitude of all of these correlations is substantial. Essentially the same intercorrelations are highest, middle, or lowest as found for the zero-order correlations. The correlations between sound discrimination and sound discrimination vocabulary are still highest and range in the .90's. Those among the length of response, the complexity of response, and the number of different words are next high.

The trends with age in the magnitude of the correlations are essentially similar to those evident in Table 63. The correlations of sound discrimination with length of response, complexity of response, and number of different words vary irregularly. This is more evident at the older ages than at the younger ages, and particularly in correlations with articulation and sound discrimination.

In Table 65 the zero- and first-order intercorrelations reported by Williams on 3-to-4-year-old children are compared with the comparable correlations on 3.5-year-old subjects in the present study. The particular

Table 64. Product-Moment Correlations among Major Measures by Age with Intelligence Partialled Out

Measure	CA 3*	3.5*	4*	4.5*	5*	6	7	8
Total articulation versus:								
Sound discrimination	.53	.42	.34	.14	.58	.27	.15	.14
Length of remark	.44	.41	.35	.06	.48	.36	.22	.14
Complexity of remark	.55	.51	.25	.37	.30	.40	.09	.07
Number of different words	.53	.42	.34	.14	.58	.27	.15	.14
Sound discrimination vocabulary	.45	.18	.48	.44	.41			
Corrected basic vocabulary						.19	.30	.30
Uncorrected basic vocabulary						.26	.32	.26
Sound discrimination versus:								
Length of remark	.32	.09	.24	.45	.69	.24	.37	−.06
Complexity of remark	.37	.09	.31	.39	.50	.33	.28	−.10
Number of different words	.37	.26	.25	.57	.57	.15	.28	−.09
Sound discrimination vocabulary	.93	.92	.93	.99	.99			
Corrected basic vocabulary						.23	.27	.44
Uncorrected basic vocabulary						.33	.31	.34
Length of remark versus:								
Complexity of remark	.84	.79	.87	.84	.56	.91	.68	.71
Number of different words	.87	.84	.99	.85	.93	.83	.99	.81
Sound discrimination vocabulary	.38	.12	.16	.37	.18			
Corrected basic vocabulary						.16	.14	−.03
Uncorrected basic vocabulary						.24	.18	−.09
Complexity of remark versus:								
Number of different words	.82	.75	.66	.68	.78	.81	.52	.66
Sound discrimination vocabulary	.24	.12	.21	.15	.37			
Corrected basic vocabulary						.19	−.22	−.07
Uncorrected basic vocabulary						.27	.03	.09
Number of different words versus:								
Sound discrimination vocabulary	.22	.15	.21	.28	.12			
Corrected basic vocabulary						.11	.18	.06
Uncorrected basic vocabulary						.18	.19	.06
Corrected basic vocabulary versus:								
Uncorrected basic vocabulary						.89	.91	.87

* IQ-equivalents based on Ammons Full-Range Picture Vocabulary Test scores.

intelligence test upon which Williams obtained the MA used in his computations is not reported. Although several comparable language areas are measured by Williams and by the author, only in the classification of the complexity of the verbal expressions of the children was the technique used in the two studies identical. If the number of different

Table 65. Comparison of the Correlations of Several Language Skills with Intelligence and the Intercorrelations among the Language Skills as Reported by Williams * on 3-to-4-Year-Old Children and by Templin † on 3.5-Year-Old Children

Measure	Correlation				
	Reported by Williams (N = 38) ‡				
	Articulation	Length of Response	Complexity of Response	Van Alstyne Vocabulary	Smith-Williams Vocabulary
Intelligence	.12	.78	.59	.52	.47
Articulation		.60	.62	.16	.01
Length of response	.69		.80	.56	.37
Complexity of response	.60	.67		.56	.41
Van Alstyne vocabulary	.57	.28	.36		.59
Smith-Williams vocabulary	.08	.04	.22	.76	
	Reported by Templin (N = 60) §				
	Articulation	Length of response	Complexity of Response	Sound Discrimination Vocabulary	Number of Different Words
Intelligence	.48	.26	.29	.66	.40
Articulation		.47	.57	.42	.53
Length of response	.41		.81	.21	.85
Complexity of response	.51	.79		.28	.77
Sound discrimination vocabulary	.18	.12	.12		.40
Number of different words	.42	.84	.75	.15	

* Williams used the MA.

† Templin used the IQ-equivalent based on the Ammons Full-Range Picture Vocabulary Test.

‡ Zero-order correlations are above and to the right of the diagonal. Partial correlations holding CA and MA constant are below and to the left.

§ Zero-order correlations are above and to the right of the diagonal. Partial correlations holding IQ-equivalents constant are below and to the left.

words used in the verbal expressions is taken as a rough measure of vocabulary of use, there is little agreement in the correlations between the several measures of vocabulary and the other measures either within or between the Templin and Williams studies. The agreement in the correlations between IQ and IQ-equivalent are somewhat closer. The problem of the real relation of these variables to intelligence is not adequately faced at the 3-to-4-year levels since comparable measures are not available. The divergence in the results also emphasizes the fact that vocabulary is not a unit characteristic; there are different vocabularies which need to be studied and identified.

The agreement of the intercorrelations among articulation, length of response, and complexity of response as reported by the author and by Williams is high when the zero-order correlations are considered, but lower when intelligence is partialled out. The agreement among these correlations may be much closer than is apparent in this comparison. The differences in the magnitude of correlations with the various vocabulary measures are related to the basic question of adequate vocabulary measurement. This is an area which needs further investigation. The differences in the relationship with intelligence are probably tied up with the measure of intelligence used. The IQ-equivalent used in this study behaves somewhat more like a measure of vocabulary than intelligence. Some of the observed differences in the two studies are probably merely a reflection of the variation in size of samples.

Terminal Status Analysis

Figures 8 and 9 present graphically the percentage of terminal status scores attained at each age on the major language measures. In Table 66 the exact percentages are shown.

The Ammons Full-Range Picture Vocabulary Test and the sound discrimination vocabulary test were given only to preschool children. Different sound discrimination measures were given to the preschool and the school-age children. On these three measures the achievement of the 5-year-old subsamples is taken as a measure of terminal status. Direct comparisons cannot be made with those measures in which the scores attained by 8-year-old subjects were taken as a measure of terminal status.

Of the three measures in which the scores of the 5-year-old subsamples were taken as a measure of terminal status, the sound discrimination vocabulary shows the least growth over the two-year span. There is an increment of only about 20 per cent. For both the Ammons vocabulary test and the sound discrimination test the increment over this same period is approximately 40 per cent. The 3-year-olds have achieved about 60 per cent of the attainment of the 5-year-olds in these language areas. This is within the range of percentages obtained on the other major language measures when the scores of the 5-year-olds were taken as a terminal status measure. In total articulation and complexity of response, for example, the 3-year-old subsample attains about 60 per cent of the score of the 5-year-olds. The mean number of different words used in the responses, the total number of words used, and the mean

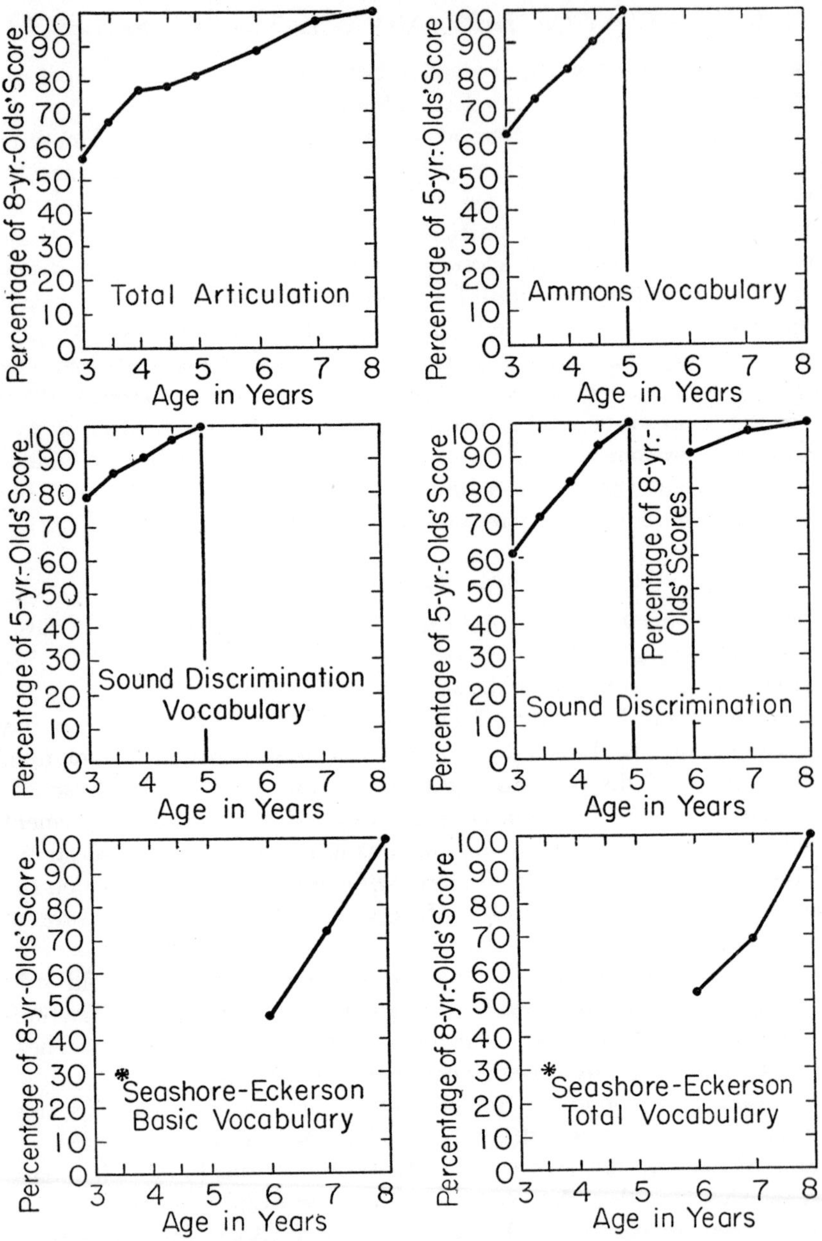

FIGURE 8. PERCENTAGE BY AGE OF THE USE OF THE 8-YEAR-OLD SUBSAMPLE TAKEN AS A MEASURE OF TERMINAL STATUS ON ARTICULATION, SOUND DISCRIMINATION, AND VOCABULARY MEASURES

* The corrected vocabulary scores have been used in the calculations.

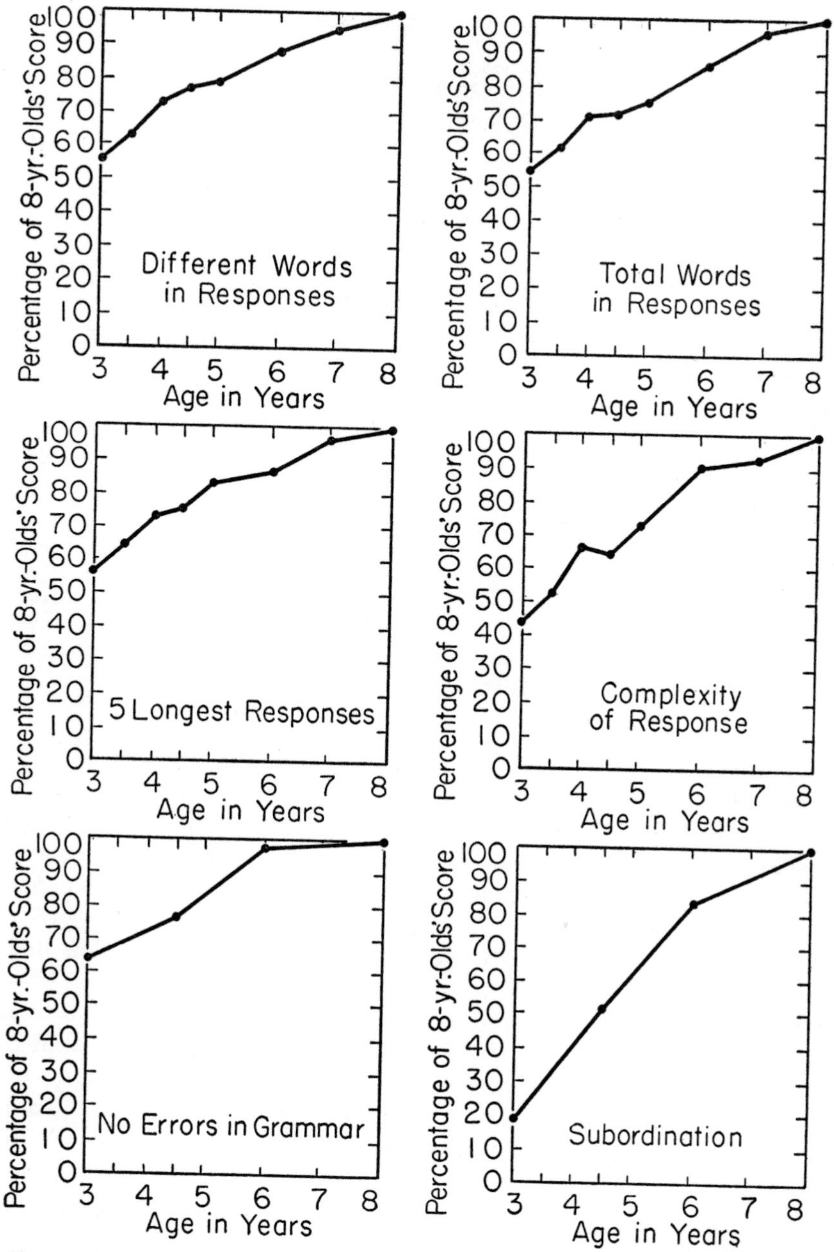

FIGURE 9. PERCENTAGE BY AGE OF THE USE OF THE 8-YEAR-OLD SUBSAMPLE TAKEN AS A MEASURE OF TERMINAL STATUS ON VERBALIZATION MEASURES

Table 66. Percentage of Scores of 8-Year-Old Subsample on the Major Language Measures Attained by Total Subsamples by Age

Measure	CA 3	3.5	4	4.5	5	6	7	8
Total articulation.....	55.8	67.0	76.2	77.3	81.0	89.9	96.9	100.0
Ammons vocabulary...	62.4	73.7	82.4	90.2	100.0			
Sound discrimination vocabulary	79.0	85.9	91.4	97.6	100.0			
Seashore-Eckerson basic vocabulary *....						46.8	72.7	100.0
Seashore-Eckerson total vocabulary *.....						52.0	69.8	100.0
Number of different words	55.5	62.9	72.3	76.3	79.5	88.3	94.7	100.0
Sound discrimination..						90.5	97.0	100.0
Sound discrimination Score C.............	60.4	71.8	81.7	93.1	100.0			
Total words in response	54.1	61.5	71.0	71.5	75.5	86.6	95.9	100.0
5 longest responses....	55.7	64.0	73.6	75.3	82.9	86.7	95.9	100.0
Complexity of response	44.1	52.3	66.4	64.9	73.2	90.2	92.4	100.0
No grammatical errors	63.0			76.0		96.8		100.0
Use of subordination..	19.1			50.5		84.3		100.0

* The corrected vocabulary scores have been used.

length of the five longest responses of the 3-year-olds are about at 70 per cent of the attainment of the 5-year-olds. This increment of about 30 per cent over these two years indicates that skill in these language variables is increasing more rapidly than in sound discrimination vocabulary but less rapidly than in total articulation, complexity of utterance, and Ammons vocabulary score.

Comparisons made at the 3-year level show that at this age less than 50 per cent of the achievement of the 8-year-olds has been attained in articulation, length of responses, and the number of different words; about 40 per cent of the degree of complexity of sentences; and about 20 per cent of the use of subordination.

While the Seashore-Eckerson tests were given only to 6-, 7-, and 8-year-olds the comparisons at these ages can be made with any measure taken as a measure of terminal status. At least 85 per cent of the achievement of the 8-year-old subsamples is attained by 6-year-olds on all language measures except the two basic scores on the Seashore-Eckerson vocabulary test. For these, approximately 50 per cent of the growth achieved by 8 years occurs between 6 and 8. Other investigators have reported substantial maturity in language in the early school years, but continued growth in vocabulary until well into adulthood. Since deceleration in growth usually occurs as maximum performance is being reached, the finding of proportionately more vocabulary increment in the early school years is in keeping with the findings of other investigators.

On these same language measures the scores of 8-year-old girls are taken as terminal status measures and the percentages of such terminal status achieved by both boys and girls is presented in Table 67. The scores of the 8-year-old boys are not taken as measures of terminal status since the scores of the two sexes are not sufficiently different to justify such separate consideration. On all variables except subordination and sound discrimination the 3-year-old boys achieve from 1.0 to 11.2 per cent more of the scores of the 8-year-old girls than do 3-year-old girls. At this age the mean achievement of the boys is 4 percentage points higher than that of the girls. However, this acceleration for the boys does not hold throughout the age range studied. On the whole, 8-year-old boys attain slightly higher scores than girls on only three of the measures: Seashore-Eckerson vocabulary scores, use of subordination, and total articulation. On the latter the boys at 7 years about equal the attainment of the 6-year-old girls. In the other two areas, the boys are somewhat superior to the girls throughout the age range. On all the other language variables reported in Table 67 the achievement of boys and girls is about equal at 8 years of age. For several preceding test intervals, boys tend to receive scores about equal to those of girls one test interval younger.

In Table 68 the terminal status scores of the USES and the LSES groups are presented with the scores of the 8-year-old USES sample taken as a measure of terminal status. The achievement of the 3-year-old LSES group on all measures reported here is lower than that for the USES group at this same age. The differences between the 3-year-old USES and LSES groups range from 1.9 to 12.4 percentage points with a mean difference of 7.1 points. When the lowest age at which any test was used is considered in the comparison, the maximum range of differences is extended to 21.1 points with a mean of 8.7.

The greatest retardation of the LSES group is on the vocabulary scores. At 6 years the LSES group has reached about one third to two fifths of the scores of the 8-year-old USES group, while at 6 years the USES group has achieved somewhat over half the scores of the 8-year-old USES group. At this age only one score, "No grammatical errors," reaches 90 per cent of the terminal status measures. The others are all below 85 per cent of the attainment of the USES 8-year-olds. This is in

Table 67. Percentage of Scores of 8-Year-Old Girls Attained by Boys and Girls from 3 to 8 Years on Major Language Measures

Measure	CA 3	3.5	4	4.5	5	6	7	8
				Girls (N = 30)				
Total articulation.....	52.9	70.9	75.2	78.8	85.1	94.2	99.9	100.0
Ammons vocabulary...	57.2	67.9	79.1	86.5	100.0			
Sound discrimination vocabulary	77.2	84.8	89.6	96.2	100.0			
Seashore-Eckerson basic vocabulary *						44.8	71.4	100.0
Seashore-Eckerson total vocabulary *						48.1	66.8	100.0
Number of different words	53.9	64.7	74.3	74.5	82.6	82.4	94.7	100.0
Sound discrimination..						91.5	96.8	100.0
Sound discrimination Score C............	55.4	70.0	78.0	90.5	100.0			
Total words in responses	49.9	61.7	70.9	69.0	77.7	81.4	91.3	100.0
5 longest responses....	53.0	64.1	72.3	73.1	85.0	82.1	90.6	100.0
Complexity of response	40.7	54.5	69.3	66.8	79.8	86.7	93.3	100.0
No grammatical error..	57.2			82.3		97.4		100.0
Use of subordination..	19.4			49.1		78.9		100.0
				Boys (N = 30)				
Total articulation.....	59.0	63.3	76.4	76.4	77.3	86.3	94.4	100.6
Ammons vocabulary...	62.3	72.1	78.1	85.6	90.2			
Sound discrimination vocabulary	78.2	83.9	90.0	95.7	96.6			
Seashore-Eckerson basic vocabulary *						49.3	74.8	101.4
Seashore-Eckerson total vocabulary *						52.2	72.3	99.4
Number of different words	56.0	59.7	68.7	76.4	74.7	92.2	92.6	97.8
Sound discrimination..						86.4	93.6	96.4
Sound discrimination Score C............	60.5	67.8	78.8	88.8	92.2			
Total words in responses	54.2	56.7	65.7	68.6	67.8	85.2	93.2	92.5
5 longest responses...	53.9	58.7	70.2	72.7	73.4	84.2	93.3	91.9
Complexity of response	46.0	48.1	60.6	64.3	63.9	90.3	88.0	93.9
No grammatical error..	68.4			69.2		95.5		99.3
Use of subordination..	19.3			52.3		90.3		100.7

* The corrected vocabulary scores have been used.

Table 68. Percentage of Scores of 8-Year-Old Upper Socioeconomic Status Group Attained by Upper and Lower Socioeconomic Status Groups from 3 to 8 Years on Major Language Measures

Measure	CA 3	3.5	4	4.5	5	6	7	8
Upper Socioeconomic Status Groups (USES)								
Total articulation	57.5	68.3	80.2	83.5	86.6	91.0	98.9	100.0
Ammons vocabulary	64.7	77.8	85.5	96.1	100.0			
Sound discrimination vocabulary	82.8	87.7	93.3	99.2	100.0			
Seashore-Eckerson basic vocabulary *						52.2	68.6	100.0
Seashore-Eckerson total vocabulary *						55.6	69.8	100.0
Number of different words	58.9	66.2	73.5	78.4	81.3	86.9	94.4	100.0
Sound discrimination						92.0	100.4	100.0
Sound discrimination Score C	65.1	72.7	83.8	94.8	100.0			
Total words in responses	54.3	68.2	71.7	78.2	78.2	88.8	94.0	100.0
5 longest responses	61.2	69.9	74.4	82.8	87.9	91.5	96.5	100.0
Complexity of response	44.6	54.1	55.6	67.9	61.1	77.5	76.9	100.0
No grammatical error	67.7			89.9		95.0		100.0
Use of subordination	20.7			66.3		77.5		100.0
Lower Socioeconomic Status Groups (LSES)								
Total articulation	53.9	64.9	72.0	73.0	76.8	82.7	89.2	97.8
Ammons vocabulary	60.9	70.5	80.2	86.5	98.1			
Sound discrimination vocabulary	76.9	84.5	89.3	95.9	97.0	81.3	86.7	95.6
Seashore-Eckerson basic vocabulary *						31.1	52.8	75.7
Seashore-Eckerson total vocabulary *						43.5	54.3	72.6
Number of different words	50.8	57.8	67.5	70.8	74.0	79.8	84.0	94.0
Sound discrimination						81.3	86.7	95.6
Sound discrimination Score C	52.7	64.8	73.2	83.8	91.0			
Total words in responses	52.4	56.8	68.5	66.5	72.2	78.9	88.6	97.1
5 longest responses	52.6	60.6	73.1	71.9	79.4	83.3	94.2	91.5
Complexity of response	34.5	43.8	56.9	52.4	63.1	76.8	79.8	79.0
No grammatical error	57.9			66.3		92.8		95.1
Use of subordination	14.4			32.0		67.8		76.9

* The corrected vocabulary scores have been used in the calculations.

sharp contrast to the picture presented by the two sexes where the scores of the boys on all the measures were at least 84 per cent of those of the 8-year-old girls. At 8 years of age the LSES group has achieved about three fourths that of the 8-year-old USES group. The LSES group does not reach the achievement of the 8-year-old USES group on any of the language variables.

Increments between Consecutively Tested Age Levels

In Table 69 the *t* values of the differences between the achievement of the subsamples at consecutively tested age levels are summarized for the major language measures. It should be pointed out that only the differences between consecutively tested ages are considered. If such an increment is statistically significant, it is important. However, the lack of significance is not equally important when the development of youngsters is considered. Although increments between consecutively tested age levels are not statistically significant, the increments between more widely spaced age intervals may be. The trend of change is of psychological significance, and must be recognized.

Of the 197 comparisons presented, in only 4 is there a reversal so that the younger age group receives the better score. For the one-word remarks the better score is the lower score, but for all other measures presented the better score is the higher one. Of course it is expected that over the age range studied, children will increase in the language abilities measured with an increase in age. However, the few small reversals which occurred indicate that the tests used and the sample selected were reasonably satisfactory.

One of the most interesting findings concerning these age trends is the substantial number of significant increments in all areas tested. Nearly half of all comparisons made reach at least the .05 level of confidence. In the language score between 3 and 3.5 years, the earliest ages tested, 19 of the 28 increments are significant at the .05 or .01 levels. Of those that are not statistically significant, three of the articulation measures — vowels, diphthongs, and nasals — have attained a high level of accuracy at 3 years of age and show no significant increments throughout the age range tested. Among the others, the four articulation scores (on plosives, semivowels, final consonants, and initial double-consonant blends) show a significant increment between 3.5 and 4 years, the next older consecutively tested ages. The differences in the number of one-word remarks used at the several ages become significant only at the school ages.

A difference is apparent in the patterns of increment among the

Table 69. *t* Values Showing Significance of Difference between Consecutively Tested Age Levels on Major Language Measures †

Measure	CA						
	3–3.5	3.5–4	4–4.5	4.5–5	5–6	6–7	7–8
Articulation							
Total articulation	2.96*	2.46**	0.51	0.98	2.48**	2.63*	1.93
Consonant elements	2.43**	2.84*	0.98	0.47	2.72*	2.52**	1.85
Double-consonant blends	2.91*	2.25**	0.32	1.15	2.27**	2.42**	2.00**
Triple-consonant blends	3.56*	2.22**	0.20	1.18	2.09**	2.44**	1.50
Vowels	0.17	0.08	0.00	0.09	0.33	0.17	0.00
Diphthongs	0.19	0.07	0.07	0.18	0.10	0.00	0.00
Nasals	1.55	1.57	0.38	*0.81*	1.67	1.88	1.00
Plosives	1.88	2.68*	*0.63*	0.62	4.11*	0.82	0.20
Fricatives	2.54**	2.18**	1.60	0.42	2.45**	2.75*	2.04**
Combinations	1.96	3.15*	0.93	0.31	1.24	0.13	0.17
Semivowels	1.63	2.59*	0.07	0.68	2.11**	1.72	0.11
Initial consonants	2.43**	2.50**	0.60	0.33	2.00**	2.23**	2.00**
Medial consonants	2.50**	2.14**	0.83	0.43	3.17*	1.75	1.67
Final consonants	1.63	3.00*	1.50	0.57	2.75*	2.50**	2.00**
Initial double blends	1.45	2.61*	0.09	0.69	1.03	3.05*	1.34
Final double blends	2.60*	4.28	0.44	1.55	2.75*	2.15**	1.83
Final reversed double blends	2.41**	1.73	0.79	1.05	2.34**	2.28**	2.12**
Initial triple blends	3.13*	1.77	*0.48*	1.15	0.93	1.84	1.67
Final triple blends	2.73*	0.52	*0.52*	1.58	0.46	1.77	0.87
Final reversed triple blends	3.45*	2.43**	0.94	0.94	3.02*	3.11*	1.27
Sound discrimination							
Sound discrimination score						2.50**	1.69
Sound discrimina- Score C	2.88*	3.64*	2.94*	1.91			
Vocabulary							
Number of different words	2.87*	3.52*	1.40	1.15	2.92*	2.14**	1.70
Sound discrimination vocabulary	2.83*	2.52**	3.07*	1.33			
Ammons vocabulary	4.18*	3.40*	2.81*	3.33*			
Seashore-Eckerson basic (uncorrected)						4.97*	5.21*
Seashore-Eckerson basic (corrected)						4.74*	4.19*
Seashore-Eckerson total (uncorrected)						3.17*	4.76*
Seashore-Eckerson total (corrected)						3.31*	4.22*
Verbalization							
Length of remark	2.72*	3.14*	0.15	1.20	3.23*	3.26*	1.27
5 longest remarks	2.91*	3.31*	0.51	1.76	1.00	3.04*	1.26
One-word remarks	1.87	0.04	0.49	1.38	3.83*	2.73*	2.69*
Complexity score	1.98**	3.16*	0.30	1.56	3.28*	0.45	1.19

† Italicized figures indicate better score attained by younger subsample.
* Significant at the .01 level.
** Significant at the .05 level.

several language measures tested. The development of correct articulation, on the whole, shows most significant increments between consecutively tested age levels from 3 to 4 years and again from 5 to 7 years. No significant differences are found between 4 and 5 years. This could be a function of the particular sample tested, but this is a questionable explanation, since increments which are statistically significant do appear for the other language measures between these age levels. It is reasonable to find that accuracy in articulation increases substantially during the early preschool years when child language first begins to function as adult language, and again when children begin to attend school.

Sound discrimination shows significant increments throughout most of the preschool years and again between the youngest ages after school entry, despite different tests being used at the two ages. However, somewhat different patterns obtain for the preschool children when the picture sound discrimination test is scored using different scoring techniques. Using Score A, only the increment between 4.5 and 5 years reaches the .05 level ($t = 2.03$). Using Score B the increment between 3.5 and 4 years reaches the .01 level ($t = 2.66$) and that between 4.5 and 5 years reaches the .05 level ($t = 2.32$). Table 69 shows that three of the four increments obtained using Score C are significant at the .01 level and the fourth approaches the .05 level. Scoring techniques A, B, and C are described in Chapter IV.

Throughout the age range the measures of vocabulary of recognition show increments consistently significant at the .01 level. The measures of vocabulary of use are less consistent, but seven out of the eleven increments are significant at the .05 level or higher.

Among the verbalizations, the length and complexity of remarks show the greatest significant increments in the earliest years tested and in the early school years. The actual mean and median number of one-word remarks decreases substantially during the early preschool years. In the early school years, however, when the range of such performance becomes restricted, the decrements become statistically significant.

Summary

1. There is substantial interrelationship among the language skills measured, but the magnitude of the relationship varies with the skill measured.

2. The highest correlations are found between sound discrimination score and sound discrimination vocabulary. Intercorrelations among measures related to sentence structure are only slightly lower. On the

whole, the correlations between vocabulary and the other language skills are of lower magnitude.

3. There are no marked age trends in the correlational pattern. However, there is a tendency for the intercorrelations among the verbalization measures and articulation to decrease with age. This is also true for sound discrimination and articulation over the entire age range; for sound discrimination and Ammons vocabulary scores from 3 to 5, and for either sound discrimination score and the verbalization scores from between 6 to 8. No consistent age trends occur either among the verbalization intercorrelations or between any of the language variables and intelligence.

5. With intelligence partialled out, the magnitude of the intercorrelations is somewhat reduced, although their rank order and the pattern of relation to age remains essentially the same, as was found for the zero order correlations.

6. With the achievement of the 8-year-old subsample taken as a measure of terminal status for those skills measured over the entire age range, the 3-year-olds have achieved about 50 per cent of the scores of the 8-year-olds in articulation, length of remark, and number of different words used; about 40 per cent in the complexity of verbalization; and about 20 per cent in the use of subordination.

7. When the achievement of the 8-year-old girls is taken as a measure, the growth patterns of boys and girls are similar and neither sex exhibits any consistent retardation.

8. When the achievement of the 8-year-old upper socioeconomic status group is taken as a measure of terminal status, the growth patterns of the upper socioeconomic status and the lower socioeconomic status groups are similar, and the lower socioeconomic status group is slightly retarded.

9. Nearly half of the increments in language scores obtained by consecutively tested age groups are statistically significant.

10. The several language skills measured show different patterns of increments. In articulation substantial growth occurs in the earliest years measured except in a few types of sounds in which a high level of accuracy of articulation has already been achieved by 3 years. With the exception of these, the articulation subscores show the most significant increments between 3 and 4 years and between 5 and 7 years. Sound discrimination scores and the length and complexity of verbalizations follow a similar pattern. Vocabulary shows significant increments throughout the age range tested. In the use of one-word remarks a significant decrement occurs during the school years.

VIII. SUMMARY AND CONCLUSIONS

This study was conducted to secure normative data on several language skills and to study the interrelationships among them. The sample included 480 children, 240 boys and 240 girls between the ages of 3 and 8, divided into eight subsamples by age. Because of the more rapid growth in language at the earlier ages, the subsamples were selected at half-year intervals between 3 and 5 years and at year intervals between 5 and 8 years. Each subsample, composed of 30 boys and 30 girls, was a discrete age group with the actual age range only one month older or younger than the designated age. Each subsample was selected to form a representative sample according to father's occupation as classified on the Minnesota Occupational Scale.

Measures of four language skills were obtained for each child: articulation of speech sounds, sound discrimination, vocabulary, and verbalizations. The measures of articulation and sound discrimination were devised by the author; the measures of vocabulary and verbalizations were ones previously used by other investigators.

The articulation of 176 speech sound elements was tested in words either spontaneously uttered or repeated after the examiner. These test sounds included 69 consonant elements, 71 double-consonant blends, 19 triple-consonant blends, 12 vowels, and 5 diphthongs. Although the same sounds were measured throughout the age range tested, they were sometimes measured in different words for children under 5 and over 6 years.

Different measures of sound discrimination were used at the preschool and school ages. For testing the preschool children, a picture sound discrimination test was devised. In this test the child, in response to a stimulus word uttered by the examiner, chose between two pictures of objects whose names were acoustically similar except for one sound. There were 59 paired items in the test. The sound discrimination ability of school-age children was assessed by a test made of the 50 most discriminating items from 200 previously devised. In this test the child identified a pair of nonsense syllables spoken by the examiner as either the "same" or "different."

Several measures of both vocabulary of recognition and vocabulary of use were used in the study. The vocabulary of recognition was measured at the preschool level by the Ammons Full-Range Picture

Vocabulary Test and at the school age by the Seashore-Eckerson English Recognition Vocabulary Test. The latter was used to estimate the number of words in the children's basic and total vocabulary. Two measures of the vocabulary of use were obtained on the preschool children and one on the school-age children. The number of different words used in 50 verbalizations provided a measure for all subjects and the identification of words used in the sound discrimination test, referred to as the sound discrimination vocabulary, provided a second measure on the preschool children.

Using the technique developed by McCarthy, 50 utterances were obtained from all the subjects in a child-adult situation in which toys and books were used. Most of the verbalizations were consecutive remarks and all included in the study were complete utterances of the children.

Each child included in the sample was individually tested on the four language skills. The author assessed the speech sound articulation of all subjects and administered the sound discrimination test to all school-age children. The measures in the other language skills were obtained by the author, several graduate assistants in the University of Minnesota Institute of Child Welfare, and one undergraduate major in the Nursery School–Kindergarten-Primary teacher training program.

Children 5 years of age and younger were tested in their homes, in nursery schools in Minneapolis and St. Paul, and in kindergartens in the Minneapolis public schools. All older children were tested during school hours in rooms provided in the Minneapolis public schools. With few exceptions the battery of measurements was administered in two sessions with each child.

Age Trends

Two methods were used to determine the age trends evident in the several language skills measured in the present study: the use of the terminal status concept and the significance of differences between consecutively tested age levels.

At 3 years of age, the youngest age tested, substantial growth has already occurred in the language areas tested. The over-all accuracy of articulation of speech sounds by the 3-year-olds is approximately 50 per cent that of the 8-year-olds. Taking the achievement of the oldest subsample tested as a terminal status measure, proportionate attainment at the younger ages varies for the type of speech sound, type of consonant sound, and the position of the consonants. At 3 years the accuracy of articulation of vowels and diphthongs has reached about 90 per cent of the attainment of the 8-year-olds; that of the consonant elements about 60 per cent; that of the double-consonant blends about 40 per cent; and that of the triple-consonant blends about 30 per cent of the 8-year-old subsample.

By 8 years essentially mature articulation of speech sounds has been attained. At this age about 95 per cent correct articulation, as measured on the 176-item test, has been reached. Only 14 sound elements are not articulated correctly by 90 per cent of the children, and, with the exception of the "hw," most of these sound elements approach this level of accuracy. The achievement of mature articulation at this age agrees with studies on less representative samples.

Terminal status scores in sound discrimination are taken at both 5 and 8 years, since two different tests are used to measure this ability. The increment in scores between 3 and 5 is about 40 per cent. Between 5 and 8 years, however, only a 10 per cent increment occurs. Since there is only a slight increment in score between the last two age levels tested, it would seem that by 8 years of age the ceiling in sound discrimination ability, as measured on the test used in this study, is being pushed.

Different growth patterns are seen for the various aspects of verbalizations studied. The mean length of remark of the 3-year-old subsample is about 55 per cent as long as that of the 8-year-olds. At the oldest ages studied, the length of verbalizations is still increasing. No real change with age is apparent for the parts of speech used in the verbalizations. The use of various parts of speech is in large measure determined by the grammatical structure of a language. By 3 years of age, children's speech already is conforming to these demands. This is emphasized by the fact that the speech of 3-year-olds is about two thirds as grammatically accurate as that of the 8-year-olds. Complexity of grammatical construction increases with age, and is continuing to increase at the oldest age tested. This is seen in the increase in both the use of subordination, and in the Williams complexity score. Over the 5-year age range studied the increase in this latter score is about 60 per cent of the achievement of the oldest subsample tested.

The measures of the vocabulary of recognition available on the subjects in the present study are more satisfactory than the measures of the vocabulary of use.

The vocabulary of recognition for both the preschool and the school years shows continued substantial increment even when the oldest ages tested are reached. This is in keeping with studies reporting increase in vocabulary size into adulthood. The vocabulary of use shows a similar but less definite trend.

Sex Differences

The more precocious language development of girls is frequently referred to in the literature of child development. The present study has not entirely substantiated this, especially at the separate age levels. When the performance of boys and girls is compared over the entire age range, girls tend to receive higher scores more frequently than the boys, but the differences are not consistent and are only infrequently statistically significant.

In Table 70 the *t* values for the comparisons of the scores of boys and girls on 33 of the major language measures are presented for the age subsamples. In the 230 comparisons made, the girls received the better score 133 times, the boys 84 times, and no differences occurred 13 times. For the number of one-word remarks the smaller number is the better

Table 70. *t* Values Showing Significance of Differences between the Sexes on Major Language Measures †

Measure	CA 3	3.5	4	4.5	5	6	7	8
Articulation								
Total articulation	*1.17*	1.43	*0.23*	0.51	1.40	1.67	2.07**	*0.34*
Consonant elements	*0.74*	1.52	0.43	1.10	1.61	1.94	1.67	0.67
Double-consonant blends	*1.36*	1.32	*0.24*	0.31	1.16	1.70	2.03**	*0.65*
Triple-consonant blends	*1.33*	1.08	*0.71*	0.28	1.55	1.72	2.23**	*0.13*
Vowels	0.97	1.28	*0.54*	*1.41*	0.00	0.00	1.82	0.00
Diphthongs	0.00	0.22	1.36	1.25	0.00	0.00	0.00	0.00
Nasals	0.00	1.56	1.79	0.37	*0.68*	1.41	*0.90*	*0.97*
Plosives	*0.19*	1.38	*0.15*	0.85	1.03	1.52	*0.17*	1.87
Fricatives	*0.78*	1.12	*0.28*	0.81	*0.72*	1.59	2.14**	0.21
Combinations	*0.55*	0.00	0.07	1.15	1.12	1.33	1.26	0.70
Semivowels	*1.18*	1.33	0.59	1.20	0.90	1.36	2.22**	*1.32*
Initial consonants	*0.48*	0.14	0.26	0.82	1.38	1.93	2.50**	0.00
Medial consonants	*1.63*	1.00	0.25	0.66	1.27	1.46	1.44	1.23
Final consonants	*1.73*	1.44	0.26	*0.45*	1.26	1.44	1.90	0.59
Initial double blends	*0.48*	0.14	*0.06*	0.82	1.38	*1.93*	*2.50***	0.00
Final double blends	*1.63*	0.99	*0.25*	0.66	1.27	*1.46*	*1.44*	1.23
Final-reversed double blends	*1.73*	1.44	*0.06*	*0.45*	1.26	*1.44*	*1.90*	0.59
Initial triple blends	*1.22*	0.99	*1.29*	0.39	1.22	*1.44*	*2.51***	0.37
Final triple blends	*0.91*	0.48	*0.46*	0.00	0.91	*0.97*	*1.83*	1.37
Final-reversed triple blends	*1.31*	1.19	*0.14*	0.24	1.82	*1.56*	*1.80*	0.22

† Italicized figures indicate better score obtained by boys.
** Significant at the .05 level.

Table 70 *continued*

Measure	CA 3	3.5	4	4.5	5	6	7	8
Sound discrimination								
Sound discrimination score						1.27	1.05	2.14**
Sound discrimination Score C.	*0.93*	0.43	0.13	0.34	1.42			
Vocabulary								
Number of different words.	*0.54*	1.81	1.09	*0.52*	1.81	*2.40* **	0.50	0.46
Sound discrimination vocabulary	*1.46*	0.33	*1.11*	0.10	1.11			
Ammons vocabulary. .	*1.36*	*1.27*	0.25	0.24	2.52**			
Seashore-Eckerson basic (uncorrected). . .						*0.85*	*0.54*	*0.45*
Seashore-Eckerson basic (corrected).						*0.77*	*0.36*	*0.15*
Seashore-Eckerson total (uncorrected). . .						*0.59*	*0.67*	0.02
Seashore-Eckerson total (corrected).						*0.63*	*0.60*	*0.07*
Verbalization								
Length of remark. . . .	*1.08*	1.54	1.11	0.12	2.08**	*0.88*	*0.57*	1.45
5 longest remarks. . . .	*0.22*	1.19	0.37	0.07	*2.12* **	*0.50*	*0.70*	1.67
One-word remarks. . .	*1.11*	1.12	1.32	0.99	0.94	*0.53*	*0.49*	0.16
Complexity score. . . .	*0.90*	1.07	1.35	0.38	2.29**	*0.52*	0.89	0.77

score; for all other measures the better score is the higher score. On the whole, the statistically significant differences are found between the two sexes only sporadically. None of the differences reaches the .01 level of confidence and 15 reach the .05 level. In 4 of the latter cases the boys' score is better.

The boys tend to receive language scores which are higher, though not at a statistically significant level, at 3 years of age and to a lesser degree at 4, 6, 7, and 8 years. This may be related to the particular sample measured. Higher scores of the 3-year-old boys appear in all the language skills measured. The scores of the 4-year-old boys exceed those of the girls in a substantial number of the articulation measures, although not in the other language skills. The higher scores of the boys in the 6-to-8-year-old range is particularly apparent in the vocabulary of recognition. At these ages it is the boys who occasionally receive higher scores on verbalizations and on the more difficult articulation measures. Nevertheless, with the exception of the recognition vocabulary scores, girls obtain the greater proportion of higher scores in each area.

It may be that the test used to measure recognition vocabulary at the older ages, because of the method used in its construction, is comparable to a range of information test.

Using the terminal status scores, it is interesting to note that in the articulation of the consonant sounds particularly, the boys took about one test interval longer than the girls to reach a comparably mature level of articulation. Even though the actual differences are not great, eight of them reached the .05 level of confidence at the older ages tested.

In general, the results reflect the findings of earlier studies showing that girls tend to exceed in articulation of sounds at the older ages and boys in word knowledge. Yet the differences between the sexes are somewhat less pronounced than is frequently stated. It may be that the differences which have appeared in the literature have been overemphasized in the past. It may also be that over the years differences in language ability of the two sexes have actually become less pronounced in keeping with the shift toward a single standard in child care and training in the last few decades.

Socioeconomic Status Differences

Consistent differences in the performance of the USES and the LSES groups have been found throughout the study. When the SES samples over the entire age range are combined, the performance of the USES group is consistently higher than that of the LSES group, and for nearly all measures these differences are statistically significant. Since the level of intellectual ability of these two SES groups is significantly different, it may be that some of these results reflect this factor. It should be recognized, however, that the linguistic environment provided by USES and LSES homes is likely to vary and that the correlation between intelligence and the several language skills is not consistent.

The USES group receives higher scores quite regularly at each level and for all language measures than the LSES group at the same age. In Table 71, out of a possible 230 comparisons, the LSES group receives the higher score in only 13 instances. Although the USES group usually attains a higher level of performance, the differences are significant at the .01 level in only 30 of the comparisons, and at the .05 level in 38. Thus in about 28 per cent of the comparisons the scores of the USES group are significantly higher. This, however, is a considerably greater difference than that found between the scores of boys and girls.

The significant differences are scattered over the entire age range, with a slightly greater concentration of significant differences appearing only at 4.5 years. The greatest number of significant differences seem to be concentrated in the articulation of vowels, medial and final consonants, in the grammatical complexity of the verbalizations, and in the vocabulary of recognition at the older ages. When the same measure was used throughout the age range, differences significant at the .05 level or higher were found for at least four age levels. For the Seashore-Eckerson measure of recognition vocabulary, the differences were significant below the .05 level in only two instances, and at the .01 level

Table 71. *t* Values Showing Significance of Differences between Upper and Lower Socioeconomic Status Groups on Major Language Measures †

Measure	CA 3	3.5	4	4.5	5	6	7	8
Articulation								
Total articulation	0.65	0.63	2.09**	2.13**	1.89	1.50	2.50**	1.46
Consonant elements	0.78	0.98	2.69*	1.98	1.47	0.21	2.67*	2.45**
Double-consonant blends	0.93	0.39	1.69	1.99	2.05**	1.41	2.47	1.14
Triple-consonant blends	0.64	0.52	1.64	2.36**	1.96	0.42	1.49	0.91
Vowels	3.00*	2.00**	2.98*	2.98*	2.98*	0.00	1.43	2.13**
Diphthongs	1.00	0.00	0.21	0.00	0.00	0.00	0.00	0.00
Nasals	*0.32*	0.02	0.86	1.48	0.63	0.01	*0.01*	*0.01*
Plosives	1.55	1.68	4.10*	2.66*	3.31*	1.41	*1.15*	1.47
Fricatives	*0.71*	0.98	1.00	1.33	1.06	1.07	2.27**	2.69**
Combinations	0.15	0.49	1.46	1.17	0.53	*0.25*	2.32**	1.61
Semivowels	*0.05*	0.35	1.03	1.50	2.17**	0.64	2.84*	0.00
Initial consonants	0.61	0.46	1.58	0.99	1.48	0.69	1.30	1.05
Medial consonants	*0.35*	1.14	2.91*	2.18**	1.21	0.39	2.09**	2.31**
Final consonants	1.21	1.20	2.35**	2.53**	1.88	2.04**	3.26*	1.69
Initial double blends	1.08	0.91	1.11	1.24	2.30**	0.05	1.82	1.59
Final double blends	0.80	0.94	1.21	2.29**	2.48**	0.98	1.47	2.67*
Final-reversed double blends	1.29	0.68	0.47	2.33**	1.44	1.47	2.17**	1.01
Initial triple blends	1.25	0.20	0.84	1.95	2.13**	0.21	1.11	1.39
Final triple blends	0.00	0.42	0.74	2.00**	1.41	1.68	0.61	0.67
Final-reversed triple blends	0.39	0.88	3.10*	2.74*	1.81	0.34	2.17**	0.57
Sound discrimination								
Sound discrimination score						1.89	3.68*	3.28*
Sound discrimination Score C	2.33**	1.67	1.77	2.29**	1.88			

† Italicized figures indicate better scores attained by LSES group.
* Significant at the .01 level.
** Significant at the .05 level.

Table 71 *continued*

Measure	CA 3	3.5	4	4.5	5	6	7	8
Vocabulary								
Number of different words...	1.91	2.80*	1.37	2.33**	1.73	1.44	2.16**	1.24
Sound discrimination vocabulary...	2.31**	1.75	1.79	2.25**	1.28			
Ammons vocabulary	0.85	2.04**	1.20	2.45**	0.34			
Seashore-Eckerson basic (uncorrected)						3.29*	2.72*	3.49*
Seashore-Eckerson basic (corrected)..						4.12*	1.98	3.11*
Seashore-Eckerson total (uncorrected)						2.68*	2.00**	2.22**
Seashore-Eckerson total (corrected)..						3.11*	1.77	2.91*
Verbalization								
Length of remark	1.66	3.28*	0.36	3.30*	1.21	1.49	0.00	0.45
5 longest remarks	1.74	2.20**	0.27	2.31**	*1.20*	1.84	0.61	0.27
One-word remarks	0.30	2.70*	0.03	2.84*	0.34	0.11	−0.15	1.45
Complexity score.	1.69	2.44**	*1.20*	2.89*	*1.80*	0.60	*2.60***	2.96*

in eight. Except in the articulation of diphthongs, nasals, and initial consonants, some of the differences between the two SES groups were significant in all language skills measured.

Evaluation of Techniques of Measurement

In future studies of language skills, the modification or refinement of the techniques of measurement is probably the most important consideration. The techniques used in measurement are basic in determining the type and accuracy of the results obtained. The techniques used in this investigation have, on the whole, followed the conventional and traditional methods used previously. Only in the measurement of sound discrimination in preschool children was a new and somewhat imaginative procedure tried. Traditional methods are useful since they permit comparisons with other studies. However, in order to increase understanding of the development and the interrelationships of language skills, exploration and experimentation with new techniques is needed.

Comparison with Earlier Studies

Since language production is an aspect of behavior that may be expected to vary considerably with the linguistic environment, it is interesting to compare the results of this study with those of earlier studies. No comparisons over any substantial period of time are possible for sound discrimination. In the areas of articulation and vocabulary one is impressed with the stability of results over a period of time among studies using comparable methods, but carried on with different samples and by different investigators. The order of development of correct production of specific speech sounds reported in studies over a twenty-year period is remarkably similar. This similarity appears also in the substantial agreement in the age at which accuracy of articulation was achieved. This is true despite the representative character of the present sample and the more selective character of those of the Poole and Wellman *et al.* studies. Sex differences found in the present study are on the whole similar to those reported by Poole, although they differ somewhat from those reported by Wellman *et al.*

In the area of vocabulary, the measures of recognition vocabulary show substantial agreement with the earlier studies. Agreement at the preschool ages is close between the published data of Ammons and Holmes and the present study using the Ammons Full-Range Picture Vocabulary Test. In agreement with the earlier publications, the estimations of basic and total vocabulary based on the Seashore-Eckerson English Recognition Vocabulary Test between 6 and 8 years are large. Depending upon the technique used in scoring the Seashore-Eckerson test the extent of the agreement with the published results of M. K. Smith varies.

The most commonly used words in comparable child-adult situations separated by a twenty-year period are similar. The specific words most frequently used are articles, pronouns, and verbs, in agreement with other studies.

When this study is compared with the earlier studies of verbalizations, both similarities and differences become apparent. Essentially, the patterns of growth in sentence length and complexity, and in the use of various parts of speech reported earlier are substantiated. Differences occur, however, in the increased loquacity of children in child-adult situations and in a tendency for children of the same age to use more mature language than they did twenty-five years ago. That is, children talk more; and their language is somewhat more mature than that reported by Davis and McCarthy, in that at any age fewer one-word remarks and simple and incomplete sentences are uttered and more complex sentences and adverb clauses are used. These are means, however, and the upper limit of sentence length is no greater, but actually somewhat smaller than reported by Davis.

Perhaps the increase in mean length of response accounts for some of the increase in the complexity of grammatical construction. It is surely difficult to increase the length of a remark substantially without a corresponding increase in the complexity of that remark, but this is probably not the complete explanation of increased complexity. Even if it were, however, the greater loquacity of present-day children is in itself an important finding.

There has been much popular discussion in recent years about the increased activity of children. This has been observed in a variety of their behaviors. Among the language skills measured, verbalizations are the most likely to reflect the linguistic environment. Years ago McCarthy showed the importance of this in her findings. It has been emphasized and refined in studies of only children, children with siblings, twins, children in institutions, etc. The increased talkativeness found in the present study would seem to reflect an increased amount of adult language in the child's environment whether as a result of increased viewing of TV, more inclusion in family activities, general permissiveness toward the child's behavior, or other factors.

Suggestions for Future Research

Having completed this normative study, my suggestions for further research deal with the problems of language study in general and of the study of specific language skills.

1. Of primary importance in future study is the development and exploration of techniques used in the study of language. This means not only the use of electronic devices and various acoustic techniques, but a refinement and shift in the procedure used to study articulation, vocabulary, and the sentence. The question can be raised whether sounds in words should be considered at all in the study of articulation of speech sounds. It may be that the study of sounds in syllables or in phrases may provide a more acceptable unit of measurement. In the measurement of vocabulary many problems and questions are apparent. One example is the need to determine when a word is really "known." This is a basic question which demands techniques of study different from those currently used with children to explore possible answers. In the study of verbalizations questions concerning the size of sample and the conditions under which the verbalizations are obtained need to be studied. For all techniques the reliability of the measurement needs to be explored.

2. Language behavior of children should be described in greater detail and from different points of view. The mean, median, and range of performance is not adequate. There are many basic problems which

need to be investigated in relation to this more refined description. In articulation, one such problem is the development of a criterion to determine how accurate the production of a sound should be before it can be considered as "learned." Furthermore, the shift of this criterion for acceptable production of a sound or phoneme with the increasing age of a child demands study. It may be that an acceptable production of an "s" sound for a 3-year-old would not be similarly classified if an 8-year-old produced it. In the area of vocabulary there is need to determine children's vocabularies of use. No adequate records of sizable samples of speech of a substantial number of young children in a variety of situations are available. Similarly, the grammatical structure used in child-adult and peer group situations should be compared and explored.

3. In order to learn more about the actual development and interrelationships of language skills, longitudinal studies must be done. It is through these that the interrelations of language as it is developed will be better understood.

4. There is need to study in greater detail the impact of the environment upon the language development of children. This should include attention to the broad cultural environment so that changes over time can be investigated. The environment also includes the factors in the USES and LSES groups which are important in bringing about differences in language production such as were found in the present study. The effect of more mature adult language has frequently been alluded to. The effect of varying peer group pressures also needs investigation.

5. In this investigation a beginning to the study of the interrelation of language skills was made. This needs to be continued with more refined and precise techniques.

6. The relation to the language development of children and their social acceptability, their perception, and cognition needs further investigation.

7. In 1937 Williams purposed his investigation as a preliminary study essential to the construction of a scale of language development in children. This is a worthwhile goal which, as yet, has not been reached. The present study should provide materials useful for the construction of such a scale.

APPENDIXES, BIBLIOGRAPHY, AND INDEX

APPENDIX I. LIST OF SCHOOLS FROM WHICH SUBJECTS WERE SELECTED

Elementary Schools in Minneapolis

Adams	Hawthorne	Pratt
Blaine	Holmes	Seward
Calhoun	Lafayette	Washington
Clay	Madison	Webster
Clinton	Monroe	

Nursery Schools in Minneapolis

Beth El	Mrs. Solie's
Buckingham	Parkway
Corcoran	Phyllis Wheatley
Elliott Park	Pillsbury Neighborhood House
Emanuel Cohen	Pillsbury Annex
Margaret Barry Kindergarten	Rosemary
Margaret Barry Nursery	Southeast
Northeast Neigborhood House	Unity
Oak Park	University of Minnesota

Nursery Schools in St. Paul

Wilder, Edgerton Avenue   Wilder, Leech Street   Wilder, Marshall Avenue

APPENDIX II. PREVIOUSLY UNPUBLISHED TESTS USED IN STUDY

A. ARTICULATION TEST WORDS USED WITH 3-TO-5-YEAR AND 6-TO-8-YEAR SUBSAMPLES IN THE MEASUREMENT OF SPEECH SOUNDS

Sound	Test Word for 3–5-Year Subsamples	Test Word for 6–8-Year Subsamples
	Consonant Sounds	
Nasals		
m–	*m*outh*	*m*yself
–m–	ma*m*a	a*m*ount
–m	gu*m**	dru*m*
n–	*n*ail*	*n*umber
–n–	o*n*ion	ba*n*ana
–n	sto*n*e*	spoo*n*
–ng–	swi*ng*ing	swi*ng*ing
–ng	swi*ng*	agi*ng*
Plosives		
p–	*p*ie*	*p*ipe
–p–	o*p*en	u*p*on
–p	soa*p**	pi*p*e
t–	*t*oes*	*t*able
–t–	ska*t*ing	ou*t*ing
–t	ba*t**	ska*t*e
k–	*c*ards*	*c*onduct
–k–	va*c*uum cleaner	a*c*orn
–k	ra*k*e*	tru*ck*
b–	*b*eans*	*b*uckle
–b–	rhu*b*arb	rhu*b*arb
–b	tu*b*	tu*b*e
d–	*d*ish*	*d*angle
–d–	wa*d*ing	ra*d*io
–d	brea*d**	sle*d*
g–	*g*oat*	*g*ift
–g–	bi*gg*est	bi*gg*est
–g	pi*g**	do*g*
Fricatives		
f–	*f*eet*	*f*orth
–f–	ele*ph*ant	ele*ph*ant
–f	kni*f*e	mu*ff*
th–	*th*inner	*th*umb
–th–	play*th*ing	any*th*ing
Fricatives *continued*		
–th	ba*th**	clo*th*
s–	*s*eat*	*s*ilk
–s–	my*s*elf	gla*ss*es
–s	mou*s*e*	gra*ss*
sh–	*sh*ip*	*sh*oes
–sh–	spla*sh*ing	spla*sh*ing
–sh	fi*sh**	fre*sh*
v–	*v*acuum cleaner	*v*alentine
–v–	dri*v*ing	dri*v*ing
–v	sto*v*e*	sto*v*e
t͟h–	*th*ose	*th*ere
–t͟h–	ba*th*ing	ba*th*ing
–t͟h	smoo*th*	smoo*th*
z–	*z*ipper	*z*ipper
–z–	fro*z*en	pre*s*ent
–z	pea*s**	shoe*s*
–zh–	plea*s*ure	plea*s*ure
–zh	gara*g*e †	gara*g*e †
Combinations		
hw–	*wh*istle	*wh*istle
–hw–	black and *wh*ite	black and *wh*ite
ch–	*ch*ip*	*ch*erry
–ch–	rea*ch*ing	rea*ch*ing
–ch	pea*ch**	scra*tch*
j–	*j*umped	*j*ump
–j–	a*g*ing	a*g*ing
–j	pa*g*e	ca*g*e
Semivowels		
r–	*r*ing*	*r*eaching
–r–	che*rr*y	che*rr*y
–r	ca*r**	the*r*e
l–	*l*amb*	*l*arge

*Words common to articulation and sound discrimination measures.

† "Rouge" was presented as a second stimulus word if "garage" was pronounced "guroj."

Sound	Test Word for 3–5-Year Subsamples	Test Word for 6–8-Year Subsamples
Semivowels *continued*		
–l–	yellow	valentine
–l	bell*	wheel
h–	house*	help
–h–	ship ahoy	ship ahoy
w–	wading	work
–w–	flowing	flowing
y–	yellow	yellow
–y–	onion	onion
Double Consonant Blends		
Initial		
pl–	pleasure	pleasure
pr–	prompt	present
tr–	train*	truck
tw–	twinkle	twine
kl–	clown*	cloth
kr–	cracker	cracker
kw–	quilt	quilt
bl–	blocks*	blotter
br–	bread*	brother
dr–	drum*	drum
gl–	glass*	glasses
gr–	grass*	grass
fl–	flowing	flowing
fr–	frozen	fresh
thr–	three*	throw
shr–	shrink	shrink
sk–	skating	skate
sl–	sleep*	sled
sm–	smooth	smooth
sn–	snow	snow
sp–	spoon	spoon
st–	stairs*	stove
sw–	sweep*	swinging
Final		
–pl	apple	apple
–pr	zipper	zipper
–tr	blotter	blotter
–kl	buckle	buckle
–kr	cracker	cracker
–bl	bubble	table
–br	rubber	rubber
–dr	odor	odor
–gl	giggle	giggle
–gr	bigger	bigger
–fl	ruffle	ruffle
–fr	offer	offer
–shr	masher	masher
–sk	ask	ask
Final *continued*		
–sl	whistle	whistle
–sm	o'possum	o'possum
–sp	grasp	grasp
–st	biggest	biggest
Final-reversed		
–lp	help	help
–rp	sharp	sharp
–rt	squirt	squirt
–lk	milk	silk
–rk	work	work
–lb	bulb	bulb
–rb	rhubarb	rhubarb
–rd	card*	word
–rg	iceberg	iceberg
–lf	myself	myself
–rf	wharf	wharf
–rth	earth	forth
–ks	books	talks
–lz	boils	boils
–zm	chasm	chasm
–ngk	shrink	shrink
–mp	lamp*	jump
–nt	elephant	elephant
–nd	sand*	bend
–kt	conduct	conduct
–pt	jumped	tripped
–ft	gift	gift
–lth	health	health
–tl	bottle	bottle
–lt	quilt	quilt
–rm	arm	arm
–rn	horn*	acorn
–mr	hammer	hammer
–nr	thinner	runner
–thr	mother	brother
Triple Consonant Blends		
Initial		
skr–	scratch	scratch
str–	string*	straw
skw–	squirt	squirt
spl–	splashing	splashing
spr–	spread*	sprinkle
Final		
–skr	whisker	whisker
–str	aster	aster
Final-reversed		
–rst	burst	burst

APPENDIX IIA *continued*

Sound	Test Word for 3–5-Year Subsamples	Test Word for 6–8-Year Subsamples	Sound	Test Word for 3–5-Year Subsamples	Test Word for 6–8-Year Subsamples
Final-reversed *continued*			Vowels *continued*		
–ngkl	twin*kle*	sprin*kle*	ă	b*a*ck*	*a*ster
–nggl	da*ngle*	da*ngle*	ŏ	cl*o*cks*	bl*o*tter
–kst	ne*xt*	ne*xt*	ŭ	g*u*n*	th*u*mb
–mpt	pro*mpt*	pro*mpt*	o͝o	b*oo*ks	h*oo*d
–mbr	nu*mber*	nu*mber*	o͞o	*soup**	t*u*be
–mps	gli*mpse*	gli*mpse*	ō	c*o*ne*	thr*ow*
–rch	chu*rch*	chu*rch*	ô	b*a*ll*	str*aw*
–rj	la*rge*	la*rge*	ȧ	*u*pon	*a*mount
–jd	ca*ged*	ca*ged*	ûr	h*or*se*	b*ir*d
–ntth	mo*nth*	mo*nth*	Diphthongs		
–lfth	twe*lfth*	twe*lfth*	ū	m*u*sic	m*u*sic
Vowels			ā	s*ai*l*	r*a*dio
ē	b*ee*ts*	wh*ee*l	ī	t*ie**	tw*i*ne
ĭ	p*i*n*	mus*i*c	ou	cl*ou*d *	*ou*ting
ĕ	r*e*d*	*a*nything	oi	b*oi*ls	b*oi*ls

B. SOUND DISCRIMINATION TEST USED WITH 6-TO-8-YEAR-OLD SUBJECTS

1. āzh–āzh
2. ōsh–ōsh
3. ēth–ēzh
4. ēv–ēzh
5. thā–tā
6. hwē–wē
7. pā–bā
8. zā–zā
9. āwā–ālā
10. ēj–ēzh
11. āf–āp
12. ōs–ōth
13. ālā–ālā
14. āth–āt
15. sā–zā
16. fē–vē
17. rī–wī
18. sā–shā
19. fā–sā
20. ās–āf
21. ēs–ēch
22. āhwā–āhwā
23. āwā–āvā
24. sā–thā
25. ēk–ēt
26. ārā–āvā
27. shā–chā
28. rō–yō
29. āj–āch
30. zhā–jā
31. āyā–ālā
32. thā–jā
33. thā–shā
34. shā–zhā
35. āz–āz
36. ōv–ōz
37. hwō–rō
38. thā–zā
39. ēmē–ēngē
40. āsh–āzh
41. tā–dā
42. vē–hwē
43. dā–gā
44. rā–rā
45. āsh–āch
46. ēf–ēv
47. sā–sā
48. hā–gā
49. ēth–ēch
50. jē–chē

C. SOUND DISCRIMINATION TEST USED WITH 3-TO-5-YEAR-OLD SUBJECTS*

1. *keys* — peas
2. *chairs* — stairs
3. mouse — *mouth*
4. *dish* — fish
5. bell — *ball*
6. pin — *pig*
7. clocks — *blocks*
8. bat — *bath*
9. *sail* — pail
10. *card* — car
11. bread — *red*
12. *peach* — peas
13. *seat* — feet
14. bag — *back*
15. horn — *corn*
16. *stone* — stove
17. gun — *drum*
18. *nail* — mail
19. *box* — blocks
20. *coat* — goat
21. star — *car*
22. *bread* — bed
23. pen — *pin*
24. back — *bat*
25. *grass* — glass
26. *clown* — cloud
27. pail — *nail*
28. *cap* — cup
29. *rake* — lake
30. *blocks* — socks
31. thread — *sled*
32. string — *spring*
33. back — *black*
34. sleep — *sweep*
35. *cat* — cap
36. tie — *pie*
37. *beads* — beans
38. *tail* — pail
39. *soup* — soap
40. ship — *chip*
41. *lamp* — lamb
42. nose — *toes*
43. thread — *spread*
44. *cone* — comb
45. *string* — ring
46. hat — *cat*
47. pipe — *pie*
48. beets — *beads*
49. *horse* — house
50. *cane* — can
51. gum — *gun*
52. train — *rain*
53. *bread* — thread
54. *ring* — rim
55. tree — *three*
56. swing — *string*
57. *cone* — coat
58. *bread* — spread
59. hand — *sand*

*The stimulus word in each pair is italicized

APPENDIX III. RULES FOLLOWED FOR CLASSIFICATION OF WORDS AND SENTENCES

A. RULES FOR COUNTING NUMBER OF WORDS*

1. Contractions of subject and predicate like "it's" and "we're" are counted as two words.
2. Contractions of the verb and the negative such as "can't" are counted as one word.
3. Each part of a verbal combination is counted as a separate word: thus "have been playing" is counted as three words.
4. Hyphenated and compound nouns are one word.
5. Expressions which function as a unit in the child's understanding were counted as one word. Thus "oh boy," "all right," etc. were counted as one word, while "Christmas tree" was counted as two words.

B. CLASSIFICATION OF SENTENCE STRUCTURE FROM DAVIS (5:82) AFTER McCARTHY

I. Complete sentences.
   - A. Functionally complete but structurally incomplete. This includes naming; answers in which omitted words are implied because they were expressed in the question; expletives; and other remarks, incomplete in themselves, which are clearly a continuation of the preceding remark.
   - B. Simple sentence without phrase.
   - C. Simple sentence containing (1) phrase used as adjective or adverb in apposition, (2) compound subject or predicate, (3) compound predicate.
   - D. Complex sentence (one main clause, one subordinate clause) with (1) noun clause used (a) as subject, (b) as object, (c) in apposition, (d) as predicate nominative, (e) as objective complement; (2) adjective clause (a) restrictive, (b) nonrestrictive; (3) adverbial clauses of (a) time, (b) place, (c) manner, (d) comparison, (e) condition, (f) concession, (g) cause, (h) purpose, (i) result; (4) infinitive.
   - E. Compound sentence (two independent clauses).
   - F. Elaborated sentence; (1) simple sentence with two or more phrases, or compound subject, or predicate and phrase; (2) complex sentence with more than one subordinate clause, or with a phrase or phrases; (3) compond sentence with more than two independent clauses, or with a subordinate clause or phrases.

II. Incomplete sentences.
   - A. Fragmentary or incomprehensible. Example: "Well – not this, but –."
   - B. (1)Verb omitted completely, (2) auxiliary omitted, verb or participle expressed, (3) verb or participle omitted, auxiliary expressed.
   - C. Subject omitted, either from main or subordinate clause.
   - D. Introducutory "there" omitted.
   - E. Pronoun other than subject of verb omitted.
   - F. Preposition (usually needed sign of infinitive) omitted.
   - G. Verb and subject omitted.

*Adapted by Davis (5:44) from McCarthy (27:36).

H. Main clause incomplete, subordinate clause or second clause of compound sentence complete.
I. Main clause complete, subordinate or second clause incomplete. Example: "I know why."
J. Omissions from both main and subordinate clauses.
K. Essential words present, but sentence loosely constructed because of (1) omission of conjunction, (2) insertion of parenthetical clause, (3) changes in form halfway in sentence. Example: "We have – my brother has a motorcycle."
L. (1) Definite, (2) indefinite article omitted.
M. Object omitted from either main clause or prepositional phrase.
N. Sentence left dangling.

APPENDIX IV. DATA ON ARTICULATION OF SPECIFIC SPEECH SOUNDS

APPENDIX TABLE 1. NUMBER OF SUBJECTS AT EACH AGE LEVEL CORRECTLY ARTICULATING THE SPECIFIC SPEECH SOUNDS

	CA							
Sound	3	3.5	4	4.5	5	6	7	8
				Consonant Elements				
m–	58	60	60	60	59	60	60	60
–m–	59	58	60	59	59	60	60	60
–m	57	60	60	60	60	60	60	60
n–	59	60	60	59	59	59	60	60
–n–	60	60	60	59	57	60	60	60
–n	57	57	60	60	59	58	60	60
–ng–	47	52	49	55	53	55	56	59
–ng	47	52	51	50	50	56	59	60
p–	55	59	58	57	58	60	60	60
–p–	55	58	58	58	59	60	60	60
–p	53	50	54	56	53	57	59	60
t–	60	60	60	60	60	60	60	60
–t–	16	16	20	17	19	53	50	50
–t	45	41	45	45	46	51	56	57
k–	54	58	58	56	56	59	59	60
–k–	55	60	58	59	60	58	60	60
–k	44	43	52	52	53	57	58	60
b–	58	60	59	59	60	60	60	60
–b–	59	60	60	60	60	60	58	60
–b	27	34	45	44	50	57	56	60
d–	59	60	60	59	58	60	60	60
–d–	46	52	60	55	55	58	59	60
–d	38	42	50	52	51	57	60	59
g–	53	57	58	56	59	58	60	60
–g–	60	60	60	60	60	60	59	60
–g	17	35	45	42	45	56	57	60
f–	53	54	56	58	55	60	60	60
–f–	49	53	54	60	56	59	60	60
–f	50	51	55	57	53	58	60	60
th–	16	17	29	36	40	51	54	58
–th–	17	24	35	39	40	55	57	59
–th	13	17	25	31	33	51	54	57
s–	42	51	46	48	47	46	55	58
–s–	39	49	46	45	47	43	53	57
–s	35	41	44	46	46	47	53	56
sh–	32	43	45	53	52	52	57	59
–sh–	24	32	37	47	44	52	57	57
–sh	24	38	45	52	52	52	57	58

APPENDIX IV, TABLE 1 *continued*

	CA							
Sound	3	3.5	4	4.5	5	6	7	8
v–	7	18	24	28	33	48	53	59
–v–	36	39	45	47	48	54	58	60
–v	13	14	23	23	30	45	49	58
~~th~~–	14	19	34	36	37	50	58	59
–~~th~~–	10	16	27	31	40	42	45	54
–~~th~~	12	7	14	18	24	40	47	55
z–	18	33	37	43	39	40	54	57
–z–	28	45	43	45	45	47	54	57
–z	15	21	25	30	32	29	47	45
–zh–	11	15	27	29	34	43	47	52
–zh	7	12	13	17	17	38	50	51
r–	35	39	45	47	51	52	55	58
–r–	34	42	52	50	51	56	57	59
–r	40	48	48	48	50	54	58	58
l–	40	44	53	51	52	57	60	60
–l–	44	43	49	52	50	59	59	58
–l	19	21	29	38	41	54	54	60
h–	56	59	60	60	60	60	60	60
–h–	52	55	56	58	59	59	60	60
w–	58	58	60	60	60	59	60	60
–w–	51	54	60	59	59	59	59	59
y–	42	49	55	55	52	58	60	60
–y–	44	48	56	46	53	56	59	57
hw–	6	11	15	11	6	9	5	5
–hw–	10	16	12	9	3	8	5	2
ch–	30	36	43	45	49	53	59	57
–ch–	28	38	44	52	51	53	57	58
–ch	26	35	42	53	52	50	56	58
j–	32	35	51	52	55	57	58	58
–j–	18	26	38	44	49	56	58	59
–j	13	13	36	34	41	43	49	52
				Vowels				
ē	60	60	60	60	60	60	60	60
ĭ	56	57	58	59	58	60	60	60
ĕ	60	60	60	60	60	60	60	60
ă	58	60	60	60	60	59	60	60
ŏ	60	60	60	60	60	60	60	60
ŭ	59	60	60	60	60	60	60	60
ŏŏ	59	59	60	59	60	60	60	60
ōō	59	60	60	60	60	60	60	60
ō	59	60	60	60	60	60	60	60
ô	42	39	45	47	50	60	60	60
ȧ	39	50	49	46	49	57	57	59
ûr	60	60	60	60	60	60	60	60
				Diphthongs				
ū	46	53	55	53	58	60	60	60
ā	60	60	60	60	60	60	60	60
ī	59	60	60	60	60	60	60	60
ou	59	60	60	60	60	60	60	60
oi	60	60	60	60	60	60	60	60

APPENDIX IV, TABLE 1 *continued*

Sound	CA 3	3.5	4	4.5	5	6	7	8
Double-Consonant Blends								
pl–	30	32	45	47	41	52	57	55
pr–	26	38	45	44	50	50	56	60
tr–	27	36	47	46	51	50	56	59
tw–	36	44	52	52	53	55	59	60
kl–	33	36	48	50	50	54	58	60
kr–	28	39	47	43	51	53	57	58
kw–	31	38	47	51	48	54	59	59
bl–	32	42	49	48	49	55	59	58
br–	31	40	47	44	52	52	56	60
dr–	30	38	46	46	50	55	57	59
gl–	34	37	47	47	49	52	58	60
gr–	27	37	43	46	49	56	57	59
fl–	24	30	43	43	45	55	60	60
fr–	25	33	40	46	46	52	58	57
thr–	4	13	22	29	31	44	55	53
shr–	13	23	24	26	36	37	48	52
sk–	27	40	45	42	44	45	51	56
sl–	27	35	41	41	43	38	54	52
sm–	29	36	45	41	45	46	52	58
sn–	30	38	45	45	43	44	53	57
sp	30	40	46	45	45	43	55	58
st–	25	39	47	45	45	45	55	55
sw–	27	35	40	39	39	42	53	55
–pl	8	20	25	35	41	50	57	59
–pr	40	49	51	50	54	55	59	58
–tr	9	20	15	19	23	40	41	47
–kl	5	14	19	34	37	53	58	59
–kr	38	45	49	44	51	54	57	58
–bl	7	16	24	33	38	52	58	60
–br	36	47	53	48	52	56	58	57
–dr	40	46	49	46	52	52	57	58
–gl	8	17	28	33	38	51	54	59
–gr	36	49	51	45	51	56	58	59
–fl	11	18	25	31	38	50	55	59
–fr	36	43	50	47	50	56	58	59
–shr	21	37	43	41	49	53	58	56
–sk	18	34	35	36	44	44	51	58
–sl	3	11	20	22	32	45	50	57
–sm	38	45	46	44	48	49	53	57
–sp	12	24	22	27	23	32	43	53
–st	18	23	29	28	32	43	51	55
–lp	25	32	49	55	52	57	59	60
–rp	30	40	43	44	47	54	57	58
–rt	38	42	45	43	49	49	49	57
–lk	11	24	33	42	44	55	55	59
–rk	32	45	48	45	51	54	56	59
–lb	20	26	40	40	49	55	56	60
–rb	21	26	35	31	41	47	54	55
–rd	17	31	37	30	48	52	58	58
–rg	22	29	35	30	41	52	51	55

APPENDIX IV, TABLE 1 *continued*

Sound	CA 3	3.5	4	4.5	5	6	7	8
–lf	26	33	44	47	47	55	59	60
–rf	30	34	43	42	46	47	53	58
–rth	13	20	28	34	38	52	56	55
–ks	37	45	47	48	46	48	54	59
–lz	16	27	29	35	28	41	52	58
–zm	28	36	42	39	43	43	54	57
–ngk	46	52	54	56	58	59	58	59
–mp	38	51	49	52	53	55	56	58
–nt	32	39	40	42	38	47	51	50
–nd	6	3	13	15	25	50	54	58
–kt	9	15	8	21	13	23	36	45
–pt	37	46	45	46	45	54	57	60
–ft	31	36	52	44	49	53	56	60
–lth	9	12	23	31	33	39	55	58
–tl	2	2	7	11	11	37	36	44
–lt	37	44	45	52	53	51	56	58
–rm	36	45	48	44	49	53	59	58
–rn	28	40	44	44	47	55	57	57
–mr	39	48	51	48	51	55	58	56
–nr	40	52	56	52	53	55	58	57
–thr	14	25	40	37	39	54	57	58
				Triple-Consonant Blends				
skr–	15	29	33	35	38	43	51	53
str–	15	29	39	38	45	46	51	57
skw–	18	32	37	33	34	47	55	57
spl–	21	26	39	35	40	42	50	56
spr–	16	32	37	34	43	42	47	54
–skr	20	33	34	35	43	44	52	55
–str	24	37	41	35	42	45	51	54
–rst	24	35	40	35	35	45	53	54
–ngkl	6	17	20	30	39	56	59	60
–nggl	6	13	21	34	39	50	57	60
–kst	18	28	31	34	35	40	54	57
–mpt	29	35	46	42	46	52	55	60
–mbr	29	39	44	43	49	55	57	58
–mps	33	43	47	48	46	47	56	57
–rch	21	31	41	41	41	52	56	55
–rj	10	23	32	33	38	47	54	56
–jd	3	12	20	22	25	43	52	54
–ntth	13	17	26	35	40	49	57	57
–lfth	0	3	5	7	7	17	28	34

APPENDIX TABLE 2. PERCENTAGE OF CORRECT ARTICULATION OF SPECIFIC SPEECH SOUNDS BY AGE WITH THE PERFORMANCE OF THE 8-YEAR-OLD SUBSAMPLE TAKEN AS A MEASURE OF TERMINAL STATUS

Sound	CA 3	3.5	4	4.5	5	6	7	8
				Consonant Elements				
m–	96.7	100.0	100.0	100.0	98.4	100.0	100.0	100.0
–m–	98.4	96.7	100.0	98.4	98.4	100.0	100.0	100.0
–m	95.0	100.0	100.0	100.0	100.0	100.0	100.0	100.0
n–	98.4	100.0	100.0	98.4	98.4	98.4	100.0	100.0
–n–	100.0	100.0	100.0	98.4	95.0	100.0	100.0	100.0
–n	95.0	95.0	100.0	100.0	98.4	96.7	100.0	100.0
–ng–	79.7	88.1	83.1	93.2	89.8	93.2	94.9	100.0
–ng	78.3	86.7	85.0	83.4	83.4	93.4	98.4	100.0
p–	91.7	98.4	96.7	95.0	96.7	100.0	100.0	100.0
–p–	91.7	96.7	96.7	96.7	98.4	100.0	100.0	100.0
–p	88.4	83.4	90.0	93.4	88.4	95.0	98.4	100.0
t–	100.0	100.0	100.0	100.0	100.0	100.0	100.0	100.0
–t–	78.9	71.9	78.9	78.9	80.7	89.5	98.2	100.0
–t	79.0	72.0	79.0	79.0	80.7	89.5	98.3	100.0
k–	90.0	96.7	96.7	93.4	93.4	98.4	98.4	100.0
–k–	91.7	100.0	96.7	98.4	100.0	96.7	100.0	100.0
–k	73.3	71.7	86.7	86.7	88.4	95.0	96.7	100.0
b–	96.7	100.0	98.4	98.4	100.0	100.0	100.0	100.0
–b–	98.4	100.0	100.0	100.0	100.0	100.0	96.7	100.0
–b	45.0	56.7	75.0	73.3	83.4	95.0	93.4	100.0
d–	98.4	100.0	100.0	98.4	96.7	100.0	100.0	100.0
–d–	76.7	86.7	100.0	91.7	91.7	96.7	98.4	100.0
–d	64.4	71.2	84.8	88.1	86.4	96.6	101.7	100.0
g–	88.4	95.0	96.7	93.4	98.4	96.7	100.0	100.0
–g–	100.0	100.0	100.0	100.0	100.0	100.0	98.4	100.0
–g	28.3	58.3	75.0	70.0	75.0	93.4	95.0	100.0
f–	88.4	90.0	93.4	96.7	91.7	100.0	100.0	100.0
–f–	81.7	88.4	90.0	100.0	93.4	98.4	100.0	100.0
–f	83.4	85.0	91.7	95.0	88.4	96.7	100.0	100.0
–th	27.6	29.3	50.0	62.1	69.0	87.9	93.1	100.0
–th–	28.8	40.7	59.3	66.1	67.8	93.2	96.6	100.0
–th	22.8	29.8	43.9	54.4	57.9	89.5	94.8	100.0
s–	72.4	87.9	79.3	82.8	81.0	79.3	94.8	100.0
–s–	68.4	86.0	80.7	79.0	82.5	75.5	93.0	100.0
–s	62.5	73.3	78.6	82.2	82.2	84.0	94.7	100.0
sh–	54.2	72.8	76.3	89.8	88.1	88.1	96.6	100.0
–sh–	42.1	56.2	64.9	82.5	77.2	91.3	100.0	100.0
–sh	41.4	65.5	77.6	89.7	89.7	89.7	98.3	100.0
v–	11.9	30.5	40.7	47.5	55.9	81.4	89.8	100.0
–v–	60.0	65.0	75.0	78.3	80.0	90.0	98.4	100.0
–v	22.4	24.1	39.7	39.7	51.7	77.6	84.5	100.0

Sound	CA 3	3.5	4	4.5	5	6	7	8
th–	23.7	32.3	57.6	61.0	62.7	84.8	98.3	100.0
–th–	18.5	29.6	50.0	57.4	74.1	77.8	83.4	100.0
–th	21.9	12.7	25.5	32.7	43.6	72.7	85.4	100.0
z–	31.6	57.9	64.9	75.5	68.4	70.2	94.8	100.0
–z–	49.1	79.0	75.5	79.0	79.0	82.5	94.8	100.0
–z	33.3	46.7	55.6	66.7	71.1	64.4	104.4	100.0
–zh–	21.2	28.8	51.9	55.8	65.4	82.7	90.4	100.0
–zh	13.7	23.5	25.5	33.3	33.3	74.5	98.1	100.0
r–	60.4	67.3	77.6	81.1	88.0	89.7	94.9	100.0
–r–	57.6	71.2	88.1	84.8	86.4	94.9	96.7	100.0
–r	69.0	82.8	82.8	82.8	86.2	93.1	100.0	100.0
l–	66.7	73.3	88.4	85.0	86.7	95.0	100.0	100.0
–l–	75.9	74.1	84.5	89.7	86.2	101.7	101.7	100.0
–l	31.7	35.0	48.3	63.3	68.3	90.0	90.0	100.0
h–	93.4	98.4	100.0	100.0	100.0	100.0	100.0	100.0
–h–	86.7	91.7	93.4	96.7	98.4	98.4	100.0	100.0
w–	96.7	96.7	100.0	100.0	100.0	98.4	100.0	100.0
–w–	86.4	91.5	101.7	100.0	100.0	100.0	100.0	100.0
y–	70.0	81.7	91.7	91.7	86.7	96.7	100.0	100.0
–y–	77.2	84.2	98.3	80.7	93.1	98.3	103.5	100.0
wh–	120.0	220.0	300.0	220.0	120.0	180.0	100.0	100.0
–wh–	500.0	800.0	600.0	450.0	150.0	400.0	250.0	100.0
ch–	52.7	63.2	75.5	79.0	86.0	93.0	103.5	100.0
–ch–	48.3	65.5	75.9	89.7	87.9	91.4	98.3	100.0
–ch	44.8	60.3	72.4	91.4	89.7	86.2	96.6	100.0
j–	55.2	60.3	87.9	89.7	94.8	98.3	100.0	100.0
–j–	30.5	44.1	64.4	74.6	83.1	94.9	98.3	100.0
–j	25.0	25.0	69.2	65.4	78.8	82.7	94.2	100.0
Vowels								
ē	100.0	100.0	100.0	100.0	100.0	100.0	100.0	100.0
ĭ	93.3	95.0	96.7	98.3	96.7	100.0	100.0	100.0
ĕ	100.0	100.0	100.0	100.0	100.0	100.0	100.0	100.0
ă	96.7	100.0	100.0	100.0	100.0	98.3	100.0	100.0
ŏ	100.0	100.0	100.0	100.0	100.0	100.0	100.0	100.0
ŭ	98.3	100.0	100.0	100.0	100.0	100.0	100.0	100.0
o͝o	98.3	98.3	100.0	98.3	100.0	100.0	100.0	100.0
o͞o	98.3	100.0	100.0	100.0	100.0	100.0	100.0	100.0
ō	98.3	100.0	100.0	100.0	100.0	100.0	100.0	100.0
ô	70.0	65.0	75.0	78.3	83.0	100.0	100.0	100.0
ȧ	66.1	84.8	83.1	78.0	83.1	96.6	96.6	100.0
ûr	100.0	100.0	100.0	100.0	100.0	100.0	100.0	100.0
Diphthongs								
ū	76.6	88.3	91.7	88.3	98.3	100.0	100.0	100.0
ā	100.0	100.0	100.0	100.0	100.0	100.0	100.0	100.0
ī	98.3	100.0	100.0	100.0	100.0	100.0	100.0	100.0
ou	98.3	100.0	100.0	100.0	100.0	100.0	100.0	100.0
oi	100.0	100.0	100.0	100.0	100.0	100.0	100.0	100.0
Double-Consonant Blends								
pl–	54.5	58.2	81.8	85.4	74.5	94.5	103.6	100.0

APPENDIX IV, TABLE 2 *continued*

Sound	CA 3	3.5	4	4.5	5	6	7	8
pr–	43.3	63.3	75.0	73.3	83.3	83.3	93.3	100.0
tr–	45.8	61.0	79.7	78.0	86.4	84.8	94.9	100.0
tw–	60.0	73.3	86.7	86.7	88.3	91.7	98.3	100.0
kl–	55.0	60.0	80.0	83.3	83.3	90.0	96.7	100.0
kr–	48.3	67.2	81.0	74.1	87.9	91.4	98.3	100.0
kw–	52.5	64.4	79.7	86.4	81.4	91.5	100.0	100.0
bl–	55.2	72.4	84.5	82.8	84.5	94.8	101.7	100.0
br–	51.7	66.7	78.3	73.3	86.7	86.7	93.3	100.0
dr–	50.9	64.4	78.0	78.0	84.8	93.2	96.6	100.0
gl–	56.7	61.7	78.3	78.3	81.7	86.7	96.7	100.0
gr–	45.8	62.7	72.9	78.0	83.1	94.9	96.9	100.0
fl–	40.0	50.0	71.7	71.7	75.0	91.7	100.0	100.0
fr–	43.9	57.9	70.2	80.7	80.7	91.3	101.8	100.0
thr–	7.5	24.5	41.5	54.7	58.5	83.0	103.8	100.0
shr–	25.0	44.2	46.2	50.0	69.2	71.2	92.3	100.0
sk–	48.3	71.5	80.4	75.0	78.6	80.4	91.1	100.0
sl–	51.9	67.3	78.8	78.8	82.7	73.1	103.8	100.0
sm–	50.0	62.1	77.6	70.7	77.6	79.3	89.7	100.0
sn–	52.7	66.7	79.0	79.0	75.5	77.2	93.0	100.0
sp–	51.7	69.0	79.3	77.6	77.6	74.1	94.8	100.0
st–	45.5	70.9	85.4	81.8	81.8	81.8	100.0	100.0
sw–	49.1	63.6	72.7	70.9	70.9	76.4	96.4	100.0
–pl	13.6	33.9	42.4	59.3	69.5	84.8	96.6	100.0
–pr	69.0	84.5	87.9	86.2	93.1	94.8	101.7	100.0
–tr	19.2	42.6	31.9	40.4	48.9	85.1	87.2	100.0
–kl	8.5	23.7	32.2	57.6	62.7	89.8	98.3	100.0
–kr	65.5	77.6	84.5	75.9	87.9	93.1	98.3	100.0
–bl	11.7	26.7	40.0	55.0	63.3	86.7	96.7	100.0
–br	63.2	82.5	93.0	84.2	91.3	98.3	101.8	100.0
–dr	69.0	82.8	84.5	82.8	89.7	89.7	98.3	100.0
–gl	13.6	28.8	47.5	55.9	64.4	86.4	91.5	100.0
–gr	61.0	83.0	86.4	76.3	86.4	94.9	98.3	100.0
–fl	18.6	30.5	42.4	52.5	64.4	84.8	93.2	100.0
–fr	61.0	72.9	84.8	79.7	84.8	94.9	98.3	100.0
–shr	37.5	66.1	76.8	73.3	87.6	94.7	103.6	100.0
–sk	31.0	58.6	60.3	62.1	75.9	75.9	87.9	100.0
–sl	5.3	19.3	35.1	38.6	56.2	79.0	87.8	100.0
–sm	66.7	79.0	80.7	77.2	84.2	86.0	93.0	100.0
–sp	22.6	45.3	41.5	50.9	43.4	60.4	81.1	100.0
–st	32.7	41.8	52.7	50.9	58.2	78.2	92.7	100.0
–lp	41.7	53.3	81.7	91.7	86.7	95.0	98.3	100.0
–rp	51.7	69.0	74.1	75.9	81.0	93.1	98.3	100.0
–rt	66.7	73.7	79.0	75.5	86.0	86.0	86.0	100.0
–lk	18.6	40.7	55.9	71.2	74.6	93.2	93.2	100.0
–rk	54.2	76.3	81.4	76.3	86.4	91.5	94.9	100.0
–lb	33.3	43.3	66.7	66.7	81.7	91.7	93.3	100.0
–rb	38.2	47.2	63.6	56.4	74.5	85.4	98.2	100.0
–rd	29.3	53.4	63.8	51.7	82.8	89.7	100.0	100.0
–rg	40.0	52.7	63.6	54.5	74.5	94.5	92.7	100.0
–lf	43.3	55.0	73.3	78.3	78.3	91.7	98.3	100.0

APPENDIX IV, TABLE 2 *continued*

Sound	CA 3	3.5	4	4.5	5	6	7	8
–rf	51.7	58.6	74.1	72.4	79.3	81.0	91.4	100.0
–rth	23.6	36.4	50.9	61.8	69.1	94.5	101.8	100.0
–ks	62.7	76.3	79.7	81.4	78.0	81.4	91.5	100.0
–lz	27.6	46.6	50.0	60.3	48.3	70.7	89.7	100.0
–zm	49.1	63.2	73.7	68.4	75.5	75.7	94.8	100.0
–ngk	78.0	88.1	91.5	94.9	98.3	100.0	98.3	100.0
–mp	65.5	87.9	84.5	89.7	91.4	94.8	96.6	100.0
–nt	64.0	78.0	80.0	84.0	76.0	94.0	102.0	100.0
–nd	10.3	5.2	22.4	25.9	43.1	86.2	93.1	100.0
–kt	20.0	33.3	17.8	47.7	28.9	51.1	80.0	100.0
–pt	61.7	76.7	75.0	76.7	75.0	90.0	95.0	100.0
–ft	51.7	60.0	86.7	73.3	81.7	88.3	93.3	100.0
–lth	15.5	20.7	39.7	53.4	56.9	67.2	94.8	100.0
–tl	4.5	4.5	15.9	25.0	25.0	84.1	81.8	100.0
–lt	63.8	75.9	77.6	89.7	91.4	87.9	96.6	100.0
–rm	62.1	77.6	82.8	75.9	84.5	91.4	101.7	100.0
–rn	49.1	70.2	77.2	77.2	82.5	96.5	100.0	100.0
–mr	69.7	85.8	91.1	85.8	91.1	98.3	103.6	100.0
–nr	70.2	91.3	98.3	91.3	93.0	96.5	101.8	100.0
–thr	24.1	43.1	69.0	63.8	67.2	93.1	98.3	100.0
Triple-Consonant Blends								
skr–	28.3	54.7	62.3	66.0	71.7	81.1	96.2	100.0
str–	26.3	50.9	68.4	66.7	79.0	80.7	89.5	100.0
skw–	31.6	57.9	64.9	57.9	60.0	82.5	96.5	100.0
spl–	37.5	46.5	70.0	62.5	71.5	75.1	89.4	100.0
spr–	29.6	59.3	68.5	63.0	80.0	77.8	87.0	100.0
–skr	20.0	60.0	61.8	63.6	78.2	80.0	94.5	100.0
–str	44.4	68.5	75.9	64.8	77.8	83.3	94.5	100.0
–rst	44.4	64.8	74.1	64.8	64.8	83.3	98.2	100.0
–ngkl	10.0	28.3	33.3	50.0	65.0	93.3	98.3	100.0
–nggl	10.0	21.7	35.0	56.7	65.0	83.3	95.0	100.0
–kst	31.6	49.1	54.4	60.0	61.4	70.2	94.8	100.0
–mpt	48.3	58.3	76.7	70.0	76.7	86.7	91.7	100.0
–mbr	50.0	67.2	75.9	74.1	84.5	94.8	98.3	100.0
–mps	57.9	75.5	82.5	84.2	80.7	82.5	98.3	100.0
–rch	38.2	56.4	74.5	74.5	74.5	94.5	101.8	100.0
–rj	17.9	41.1	57.2	59.0	67.9	84.0	96.5	100.0
–jd	5.6	22.2	37.0	40.7	46.3	79.6	96.3	100.0
–ntth	22.8	29.8	45.6	61.4	70.2	86.0	100.0	100.0
–lfth	00.0	8.8	14.7	20.6	20.6	50.0	82.3	100.0

APPENDIX V. MEDIAN OR MEAN SCORES ON MAJOR MEASURES NOT REPORTED IN TEXT

APPENDIX TABLE 3. MEDIAN TOTAL ARTICULATION SCORES FOR BOYS AND GIRLS, UPPER AND LOWER SOCIOECONOMIC STATUS GROUPS, AND TOTAL SUBSAMPLES, BY AGE

	Boys (N = 30)		Girls (N = 30)		USES (N = 18)		LSES (N = 42)		Total Subsamples (N = 60)	
CA	Mdn	Q	Mdn	Q	Mdn	Q	Mdn	Q	Mdn	Q
3	99.0	28.7	92.5	21.3	95.0	26.8	94.7	22.0	94.7	22.3
3.5	111.5	33.5	129.0	25.6	128.5	27.2	121.5	28.1	122.7	28.2
4	135.8	22.0	128.5	20.0	140.0	15.0	129.7	22.0	133.5	21.0
4.5	139.5	28.2	133.5	19.7	149.7	23.7	125.5	24.7	138.0	24.0
5	140.0	34.1	156.7	21.8	156.7	18.5	150.5	34.4	155.3	22.3
6	162.0	24.0	167.8	11.6	169.7	15.0	162.0	14.8	165.8	14.5
7	169.8	11.9	170.5	3.5	171.5	1.9	168.5	9.4	170.2	6.5
8	170.2	2.5	171.5	2.6	171.5	1.9	170.6	3.3	170.5	2.5

APPENDIX TABLE 4. MEDIAN SCORES ON CONSONANT ELEMENTS, CONSONANT BLENDS, VOWELS, AND DIPHTHONGS FOR TOTAL SUBSAMPLES (N = 60), BY AGE

	Consonant Elements (69) *		Double Blends (71) *		Triple Blends (19) *		Vowels (12) *		Diphthongs (5) *	
CA	Mdn	Q	Mdn	Q	Mdn	Q	Mdn	Q	Mdn	Q
3	44.9	7.7	30.5	12.0	4.7	3.5	11.8	0.6	5.0	0.3
3.5	49.5	7.5	44.5	15.7	10.6	5.6	12.0	0.6	5.0	0.2
4	54.5	4.1	51.8	12.0	10.5	4.0	12.0	0.4	5.0	0.3
4.5	57.3	5.2	53.0	14.9	12.8	5.0	12.0	0.5	5.0	0.3
5	59.5	7.0	62.7	12.9	15.2	5.1	12.0	0.5	5.0	0.3
6	64.5	3.6	66.8	6.7	17.8	4.5	12.0	0.2	5.0	0.2
7	66.2	2.4	68.8	2.5	18.5	1.3	12.0	0.2	5.0	0.2
8	66.3	1.5	69.5	1.6	18.9	1.0	12.0	0.3	5.0	0.3

* Number of this type of sound tested.

APPENDIX TABLE 5. MEDIAN SCORES ON CONSONANT ELEMENTS, BLENDS, VOWELS, AND DIPHTHONGS FOR BOYS AND GIRLS BY AGE

	Consonant Elements (69) *		Double Blends (71) *		Triple Blends (19) *		Vowels (12) *		Diphthongs (5) *	
CA	Mdn	Q	Mdn	Q	Mdn	Q	Mdn	Q	Mdn	Q
					Boys †					
3	46.0	8.0	32.5	15.5	5.5	3.8	12.0	0.5	5.0	0.3
3.5	47.5	9.9	39.5	19.3	8.5	5.0	12.0	0.6	5.0	0.3
4	55.5	3.6	51.5	12.6	13.3	4.4	12.0	0.5	5.0	0.3
4.5	55.7	7.6	53.5	16.7	13.5	5.2	12.0	0.4	5.0	0.3
5	58.0	10.3	53.5	15.0	13.0	6.4	12.0	0.6	5.0	0.3
6	63.5	6.1	63.5	8.3	17.5	5.5	12.0	0.2	5.0	0.2
7	66.2	4.3	68.5	6.5	18.1	2.7	12.0	0.3	5.0	0.2
8	65.5	0.7	69.4	2.0	18.8	0.8	12.0	0.3	5.0	0.3
					Girls †					
3	44.5	7.0	30.5	14.0	4.4	2.5	11.9	0.6	5.0	0.3
3.5	51.8	7.3	48.5	14.5	10.5	5.0	12.0	0.5	5.0	0.2
4	53.5	4.4	50.0	8.2	10.8	3.9	12.0	0.5	5.0	0.3
4.5	57.8	5.0	51.5	13.5	12.5	4.8	11.9	0.5	5.0	0.3
5	60.7	5.8	64.3	12.3	15.5	4.6	12.0	0.4	5.0	0.3
6	65.3	3.3	67.7	8.3	17.9	2.0	12.0	0.3	5.0	0.2
7	66.3	1.6	68.8	1.4	18.8	0.5	12.0	0.2	5.0	0.2
8	66.6	1.5	70.6	1.0	19.0	1.0	12.0	0.3	5.0	0.3

* Number of this type of sound tested. † N = 30 in each age group.

APPENDIX TABLE 6. MEDIAN SCORES ON CONSONANT ELEMENTS, BLENDS, VOWELS, AND DIPHTHONGS FOR UPPER AND LOWER SOCIOECONOMIC STATUS GROUPS BY AGE

	Consonant Elements (69) *		Double Blends (71) *		Triple Blends (19) *		Vowels (12) *		Diphthongs (5) *	
CA	Mdn	Q	Mdn	Q	Mdn	Q	Mdn	Q	Mdn	Q
					Upper Socioeconomic Status Groups (USES) †					
3	42.5	8.7	33.5	14.6	4.8	8.0	12.0	0.5	5.0	0.5
3.5	51.5	6.5	48.7	18.0	10.8	4.8	12.0	0.5	5.0	0.2
4	57.3	3.2	54.5	8.1	13.5	2.8	12.0	0.4	5.0	0.2
4.5	60.7	4.2	59.5	14.5	15.5	4.2	12.0	0.4	5.0	0.3
5	59.5	5.3	64.7	9.2	16.8	3.9	12.0	0.6	5.0	0.3
6	65.3	2.9	69.3	7.5	18.5	5.0	12.0	0.2	5.0	0.2
7	67.2	0.7	69.8	1.9	18.5	0.6	12.0	0.2	5.0	0.2
8	66.5	0.8	70.9	1.7	18.9	0.9	12.0	0.3	5.0	0.3
					Lower Socioeconomic Status Groups (LSES) ‡					
3	44.5	7.6	30.0	14.5	4.7	2.9	12.0	0.5	5.0	0.5
3.5	49.6	9.6	43.5	15.2	10.5	5.5	12.0	0.6	5.0	0.3
4	53.5	4.6	49.7	11.0	10.9	4.5	12.0	0.3	5.0	0.3
4.5	55.7	5.0	49.7	15.0	9.5	4.9	12.0	0.5	5.0	0.3
5	59.5	8.6	59.0	16.5	14.5	6.6	12.0	0.6	5.0	0.3
6	62.5	4.2	65.5	6.4	17.3	4.3	12.0	0.2	5.0	0.2
7	65.6	3.6	68.5	4.2	18.3	1.5	12.0	0.3	5.0	0.2
8	67.2	1.4	69.6	1.9	18.5	0.8	12.0	0.3	5.0	0.2

* Number of this type of sound tested. ‡ N = 42 in each age group.
† N = 18 in each age group.

APPENDIX TABLE 7. MEDIAN SCORES ON NASALS, PLOSIVES, FRICATIVES, COMBINATIONS, AND SEMIVOWELS FOR BOYS AND GIRLS, UPPER AND LOWER SOCIOECONOMIC STATUS GROUPS, AND TOTAL SUBSAMPLES, BY AGE

	Boys (N = 30)		Girls (N = 30)		USES (N = 18)		LSES (N = 42)		Total Subsamples (N = 60)	
CA	Mdn	Q	Mdn	Q	Mdn	Q	Mdn	Q	Mdn	Q
					Nasals (8) *					
3	8.0	0.5	8.0	1.0	8.0	1.0	8.0	0.5	8.0	0.4
3.5	8.0	0.5	8.0	0.6	8.0	0.4	8.0	0.4	8.0	0.4
4	8.0	0.5	8.0	0.3	8.0	0.5	8.0	0.4	8.0	0.3
4.5	8.0	0.4	8.0	0.3	8.0	0.3	8.0	0.4	8.0	0.5
5	8.0	0.5	8.0	0.4	8.0	0.6	8.0	0.5	8.0	0.4
6	8.0	0.4	8.0	0.3	8.0	0.3	8.0	0.5	8.0	0.3
7	8.0	0.2	8.0	0.3	8.0	0.3	8.0	0.3	8.0	0.3
8	8.0	0.3	8.0	0.3	8.0	0.3	8.0	0.3	8.0	0.3
					Plosives (18) *					
3	15.5	2.2	15.6	1.4	16.6	1.6	14.5	1.4	15.7	1.4
3.5	15.9	1.8	16.3	0.6	16.3	0.8	15.9	1.6	16.1	1.2
4	16.5	1.0	16.5	1.1	17.8	0.7	16.3	1.1	16.5	1.1
4.5	16.7	0.9	16.9	1.0	17.2	1.2	16.6	1.4	16.7	1.0
5	17.1	1.0	17.2	0.8	17.4	0.5	16.9	1.1	17.1	1.0
6	18.0	0.6	18.0	0.4	18.0	0.4	18.0	0.6	18.0	0.5
7	18.0	0.5	18.0	0.4	18.0	0.3	18.0	0.6	18.0	0.4
8	18.0	0.4	18.0	0.3	18.0	0.5	18.0	0.5	18.0	0.3
					Fricatives (23) *					
3	9.5	4.0	8.5	3.7	8.7	4.0	9.5	4.0	9.7	3.8
3.5	10.9	4.0	13.5	2.9	13.5	2.8	12.3	3.2	12.6	3.3
4	15.5	3.0	14.5	4.2	15.5	4.2	14.8	2.9	15.5	4.2
4.5	16.5	4.2	16.7	3.5	18.7	3.0	16.3	3.5	16.7	3.6
5	14.5	6.2	20.5	4.2	17.5	3.9	17.5	4.8	17.5	4.3
6	19.5	4.4	21.3	2.1	21.5	2.9	20.5	3.3	20.9	3.2
7	22.5	1.5	22.6	3.4	23.0	0.5	22.3	3.5	22.8	1.4
8	22.7	1.2	23.0	0.8	23.0	0.5	22.6	1.0	22.8	0.9
					Combinations (8) *					
3	4.5	4.2	4.6	2.3	5.5	3.4	4.6	3.0	4.8	2.5
3.5	4.3	2.0	3.5	2.0	4.8	2.1	3.9	1.9	4.2	2.1
4	5.7	1.2	6.4	1.5	6.6	0.9	5.6	1.5	6.1	1.6
4.5	5.8	1.2	5.9	1.1	6.8	1.5	5.6	1.0	5.8	1.1
5	6.3	0.7	6.5	0.6	6.1	0.6	6.3	0.7	6.3	0.6
6	6.3	0.6	6.3	0.4	6.5	0.6	6.2	0.5	6.3	0.5
7	6.5	0.3	6.4	0.4	6.6	0.2	6.4	0.4	6.5	0.3
8	6.4	0.3	6.4	0.4	6.5	0.3	6.4	0.3	6.4	0.3
					Semivowels (12) *					
3	7.5	3.0	7.4	3.0	7.7	3.6	7.9	2.8	7.7	3.0
3.5	10.2	1.5	11.4	2.3	10.8	2.2	10.6	2.2	10.6	1.7
4	10.5	2.3	10.5	2.7	11.7	2.3	10.5	2.6	10.5	2.4
4.5	11.2	1.4	11.7	1.4	12.0	1.5	10.9	1.3	11.3	1.4
5	11.5	1.6	12.0	0.9	12.0	0.5	11.5	2.0	12.0	1.5
6	12.0	0.6	12.0	0.5	12.0	0.5	12.0	0.5	12.0	0.4
7	12.0	0.5	12.0	0.3	12.0	0.2	12.0	0.5	12.0	0.3
8	12.0	0.3	12.0	0.3	12.0	0.5	12.0	0.3	12.0	0.3

* Number of each type of consonant sound tested.

APPENDIX TABLE 8. MEDIAN SCORES ON INITIAL, MEDIAL, AND FINAL CONSONANT ELEMENTS FOR BOYS AND GIRLS, UPPER AND LOWER SOCIO-ECONOMIC STATUS GROUPS, AND TOTAL SUBSAMPLES, BY AGE

	Boys (N = 30)		Girls (N = 30)		USES (N = 18)		LSES (N = 42)		Total Subsamples (N = 60)	
CA	Mdn	Q	Mdn	Q	Mdn	Q	Mdn	Q	Mdn	Q
					Initial (23) *					
3	16.8	3.0	15.8	3.1	15.8	2.8	16.5	2.8	16.8	2.8
3.5	17.7	2.5	18.5	2.6	17.5	1.9	18.4	3.0	18.3	2.4
4	20.2	1.4	19.3	1.5	20.3	1.0	19.5	1.5	19.7	1.4
4.5	20.1	2.1	20.5	1.0	20.5	1.5	20.2	1.9	20.4	1.3
5	20.3	2.7	21.8	1.3	21.3	1.3	20.9	2.5	20.5	1.8
6	20.5	1.8	22.3	0.6	21.8	1.1	22.1	1.4	22.0	1.5
7	22.2	0.6	22.4	0.4	22.5	0.3	22.2	0.6	22.3	0.4
8	22.4	0.3	22.4	0.4	22.5	0.3	22.4	0.3	22.4	0.3
					Medial (25) *					
3	17.5	3.5	16.8	2.8	16.5	2.5	16.5	3.3	16.5	3.0
3.5	18.6	3.5	19.5	1.9	19.5	2.0	18.6	2.9	18.5	2.9
4	20.7	1.1	20.5	1.6	21.6	1.1	20.1	2.0	20.5	1.2
4.5	21.5	3.6	21.7	2.6	22.5	2.1	21.2	2.6	21.7	2.7
5	21.5	3.0	22.3	1.6	21.8	2.0	21.5	2.9	21.9	2.0
6	23.2	1.3	23.6	1.3	23.7	1.5	23.3	1.2	23.4	1.2
7	23.7	1.5	23.9	0.9	24.2	0.6	23.4	1.5	23.7	1.0
8	23.9	0.6	24.3	0.4	24.2	0.4	24.1	0.7	24.1	0.6
					Final (21) *					
3	13.3	3.6	10.8	2.4	12.0	3.4	11.5	2.7	12.5	2.8
3.5	12.5	4.0	14.3	2.7	14.7	2.3	13.2	3.5	13.6	2.6
4	14.5	2.6	15.4	2.7	15.5	0.9	13.9	2.3	15.3	2.3
4.5	15.5	2.2	16.3	2.4	16.5	2.6	15.6	2.0	16.2	2.4
5	16.5	4.3	17.5	2.9	17.5	2.0	17.8	3.5	17.9	3.1
6	18.5	2.7	19.7	1.5	20.3	0.6	18.9	1.5	19.5	1.5
7	20.5	3.0	21.0	1.0	21.0	0.3	20.5	2.4	21.0	1.0
8	20.8	0.7	20.5	0.6	21.0	0.5	20.7	0.8	20.9	0.1

* Number of initial, medial and final consonants tested.

APPENDIX TABLE 9. MEDIAN TOTAL NUMBER OF WORDS USED IN 50 REMARKS BY BOYS AND GIRLS, UPPER AND LOWER SOCIOECONOMIC STATUS GROUPS, AND TOTAL SUBSAMPLES, BY AGE

	Boys (N = 30)		Girls (N = 30)		USES (N = 18)		LSES (N = 42)		Total Subsamples (N = 60)	
CA	Mdn	Q	Mdn	Q	Mdn	Q	Mdn	Q	Mdn	Q
3	214.5	28.7	193.5	33.0	229.0	35.7	193.5	33.0	206.5	27.4
3.5	228.5	35.0	235.5	28.5	264.5	23.0	220.7	29.0	232.5	30.5
4	245.5	53.0	285.5	39.0	280.0	53.3	248.7	39.3	254.5	45.3
4.5	277.5	34.5	272.0	33.1	292.5	19.0	252.0	38.7	274.0	35.0
5	261.0	39.3	299.5	44.5	285.0	50.3	273.0	42.0	277.0	40.8
6	318.0	48.7	320.0	47.2	353.5	48.7	328.0	48.6	332.5	49.7
7	363.5	28.7	349.5	34.5	359.0	29.5	358.0	26.0	355.5	32.0
8	375.0	34.5	371.0	47.7	385.5	34.0	360.5	41.7	375.0	42.0

APPENDIX TABLE 10. MEDIAN NUMBER OF DIFFERENT WORDS USED IN 50 REMARKS BY BOYS AND GIRLS, UPPER AND LOWER SOCIOECONOMIC STATUS GROUPS, AND TOTAL SUBSAMPLES, BY AGE

	Boys (N = 30)		Girls (N = 30)		USES (N = 18)		LSES (N = 42)		Total Subsamples (N = 60)	
CA	Mdn	Q	Mdn	Q	Mdn	Q	Mdn	Q	Mdn	Q
3	90.7	20.5	91.0	14.1	103.5	16.2	87.6	15.6	90.7	15.0
3.5	103.5	13.8	105.0	12.6	113.5	11.0	99.0	9.5	104.3	12.4
4	112.5	20.0	127.5	17.0	134.0	21.2	118.7	17.7	121.0	18.7
4.5	133.0	17.2	124.7	13.9	134.5	7.2	123.5	17.0	126.5	14.5
5	125.0	15.0	142.5	17.2	139.0	17.8	127.0	17.0	131.5	18.3
6	154.5	16.5	139.0	26.2	143.5	21.7	150.8	17.7	150.5	23.0
7	159.5	21.2	161.0	15.7	162.8	12.5	157.0	21.4	160.5	18.5
8	170.5	20.5	171.5	24.0	180.5	19.1	167.7	21.5	171.7	20.5

APPENDIX TABLE 11. MEAN NUMBER OF ONE-WORD REMARKS OUT OF 50 REMARKS MADE BY BOYS AND GIRLS, UPPER AND LOWER SOCIOECONOMIC STATUS GROUPS, AND TOTAL SUBSAMPLES, BY AGE

	Boys (N = 30)		Girls (N = 30)		USES (N = 18)		LSES (N = 42)		Total Subsamples (N = 60)	
CA	Mean	SD	Mean	SD	Mean	SD	Mean	SD	Mean	SD
3	4.96	5.1	7.23	9.9	5.61	9.0	6.31	6.0	6.09	7.5
3.5	4.53	4.8	3.36	3.0	2.28	2.4	4.67	4.4	3.95	3.9
4	4.67	4.8	3.17	4.6	3.89	5.2	3.93	4.5	3.92	4.2
4.5	4.17	6.6	2.87	3.0	1.55	1.8	4.36	3.8	3.52	4.8
5	2.97	3.1	2.30	2.3	2.83	3.0	2.55	2.7	2.64	2.7
6	0.90	2.9	1.23	1.8	1.11	1.5	1.05	2.7	1.07	2.3
7	0.20	0.4	0.27	0.7	0.22	0.4	0.24	0.6	0.24	0.5
8	0.37	1.0	0.33	0.8	0.17	0.4	0.43	1.0	0.35	0.9

BIBLIOGRAPHY

1. Ammons, R. B., and J. C. Holmes. The full-range picture vocabulary test: III. Results for a preschool population. Child Development, 20:5–14 (1949).
2. Anderson, J. E. The limitations of infant and preschool tests in the measurement of intelligence. Journal of Psychology, 8:351–79 (1937).
3. ———. An evaluation of various indices of linguistic development. Child Development, 8:62–68 (1937).
4. Annen, Sister Ida, O.S.B. The construction, analysis and evaluation of a vocabulary measure. Unpublished M.A. thesis, University of Oregon (1933).
5. Davis, Edith A. The development of linguistic skill in twins, singletons with siblings, and only children from age five to ten years. University of Minnesota Institute of Child Welfare Monograph, No. 14, University of Minnesota Press, Minneapolis, 1937.
6. ———. Mean sentence length compared with long and short sentences as a reliable measure of language development. Child Development, 8:69–79 (1937).
7. ———. Developmental changes in the distribution of parts of speech. Child Development, 9:309–17 (1938).
8. ———. Accuracy versus error as a criterion in children's speech. Journal of Educational Psychology, 30:365–71 (1939).
9. ———. The location of the subordinate clause in oral and written English. Child Development, 12:333–38 (1941).
10. Day, Ella J. The development of language in twins: I. A comparison of twins and single children. Child Development, 3:179–99 (1932).
11. Eckerson, Lois D. Estimation of individual differences in the total size of general English recognition vocabulary. Unpublished Ph.D. thesis, University of Southern California, 1938.
12. Haroian, Rose D. Preliminary validation of Mansur's speech sound discrimination test in the kindergarten and first grade. Unpublished M.Ed. thesis, Boston University, 1951.
13. Henderson, Florence. A study of the articulation of consonants by normal institutionalized children. Unpublished Ph.D. thesis, University of Wisconsin, 1935.
14. ———. Objectivity and constancy of judgment in articulation testing. Journal of Educational Research, 31:348–56 (1937).
15. Horn, E. The commonest words in the spoken vocabulary of children up to one and including six years of age. Twenty-fourth Yearbook of the National Society for the Study of Education, 24:186–98 (1925).
16. Institute of Child Welfare. The Minnesota scale for paternal occupations. Minneapolis, University of Minnesota Institute of Child Welfare, 1950.
17. Irwin, O. C. Research on speech sounds for the first six months of life. Psychological Bulletin, 38:277–85 (1941).
18. ———. The developmental status of speech sounds of ten feebleminded children. Child Development, 13:29–30 (1942).
19. ———. Reliability of infant speech sound data. Journal of Speech Disorders, 10:227–35 (1945).
20. ———. Infant speech sounds and intelligence. Journal of Speech Disorders, 10:293–95 (1945).

21. ———. Speech sound development of sibling and only infants. Journal of Experimental Psychology, 38:600–2 (1948).
22. ———. Infant speech: The effect of family occupational status and of age on sound frequency. Journal of Speech and Hearing Disorders, 13:320–23 (1948).
23. ———. Phonetic equipment of spastic and athetoid children. Journal of Speech and Hearing Disorders, 20:54–7 (1955).
24. LAWSHE, C. H. A nomograph for estimating the validity of test items. Journal of Applied Psychology, 26:846–49 (1942).
25. LITTLE, MARGUERITE, and H. M. WILLIAMS. An analytical scale of language achievement. University of Iowa Studies in Child Welfare, 13: No. 2, Part 4, 49–94 (1937).
26. LYNIP, A. W. The use of magnetic devices in the collection and analyses of the preverbal utterances of an infant. Genetic Psychology Monographs, 44:221–62 (1951).
27. MCCARTHY, DOROTHEA. The language development of the preschool child. University of Minnesota Institute of Child Welfare Monograph, No. 4, University of Minnesota Press, Minneapolis, 1930.
28. ———. Language development in children, Chapter 9 in Leonard Carmichael (editor) Manual of Child Psychology (2nd edition). Wiley, New York, 1954.
29. MANDALL, FLORENCE. The preliminary standardization and evaluation of a pictorial vocabulary test for young children. Unpublished M.A. thesis, Northwestern University, 1947.
30. MANSUR, W. The construction of a picture test for speech sound discrimination. Unpublished M.A. thesis, Boston University, 1950.
31. METRAUX, RUTH W. Speech profiles of the preschool child 18–54 months. Journal of Speech and Hearing Disorders, 15:37–53 (1950).
32. MILLER, G. A. Language and Communication. McGraw, New York, 1951.
33. ———. Speech and language, in S. S. Stevens (editor) Handbook of Experimental Psychology. Wiley, New York, 1951. Pp. 789–810.
34. MORAN, L. J. Vocabulary knowledge and usage among normal and schizophrenic subjects. Psychological Monographs, 67, No. 370 (1953).
35. POOLE, IRENE. Genetic development of articulation of consonant sounds in speech. Elementary English Review, 11:159–61 (1934).
36. ———. The genetic development of articulation of consonant sounds in children's speech. Unpublished Ph.D. thesis, University of Michigan, 1934.
37. PRONOVOST, W., and C. DUMBLETON. A picture-type speech sound discrimination test. Journal of Speech and Hearing Disorders, 18:258–66 (1953).
38. ROE, VIVIAN, and R. MILISEN. The effect of maturation upon defective articulation in elementary grades. Journal of Speech Disorders, 7:37–50 (1942).
39. SCHNEIDERMAN, NORMA. A study of the relationship between articulation ability and language ability. Journal of Speech and Hearing Disorders, 20:359–64 (1955).
40. SEASHORE, R. H. The measurement and analysis of extent of vocabulary. Psychological Bulletin, 30:709–10 (1933).
41. ———, and L. D. ECKERSON. The measurement of individual differences in general English vocabularies. Journal of Educational Psychology, 31:14–38 (1940).
42. SEGRE, R. H. The development and evaluation of a pictorial technique for measuring the vocabulary of younger children. Unpublished M.A. thesis, Northwestern University, 1942.
43. SMITH, F. A. The development and calibration of a pictorial vocabulary test for young children. Unpublished M.A. thesis, Northwestern University, 1946.
44. SMITH, MADORA E. An investigation of the development of the sentence and the extent of vocabulary in young children. University of Iowa Studies in Child Welfare, 3, No. 5 (1926).

45. ———. Grammatical errors in the speech of preschool children. Child Development, 4:182–90 (1933).

46. ———. A study of some factors influencing the development of the sentence in preschool children. Journal of Genetic Psychology, 46:182–212 (1935).

47. Smith, Mary K. Measurement of the size of general English vocabulary through the elementary grades and high school. Genetic Psychology Monographs, 24:311–45 (1941).

48. Templin, Mildred C. A study of sound discrimination ability of elementary school pupils. Journal of Speech Disorders, 8:127–32 (1943).

49. ———. Spontaneous versus imitated verbalization in testing articulation in preschool children. Journal of Speech Disorders, 12:293–300 (1947).

50. ———, and M. D. Steer. Studies of growth of speech in preschool children. Journal of Speech Disorders, 4:71–77 (1939).

51. Thorndike, E. L. The Teacher's Word Book of the Twenty Thousand Words Found Most Frequently and Widely in General Reading for Children and Young People. Bureau of Publications, Teacher's College, Columbia University, New York, 1932.

52. Travis, L. E. and Bessie J. Rasmus. The speech-sound discrimination ability of cases with functional disorders of articulation. Quarterly Journal of Speech, 17:217–26 (1931).

53. Wellman, Beth L., Ida M. Case, Ida G. Mengert, and Dorothy E. Bradbury. Speech sounds of young children. University of Iowa Studies in Child Welfare, 5: No. 2 (1936).

54. Williams, H. M. An analytical study of language achievement in preschool children. University of Iowa Studies in Child Welfare, 13: No. 2, Part 1, 9–18 (1937).

55. ———. A qualitative analysis of the erroneous speech sound substitutions of preschool children. University of Iowa Studies in Child Welfare, 13: No. 2, Part 2, 21–32 (1937).

56. ———, and Mary L. McFarland. A revision of the Smith Vocabulary Test for Preschool Children. University of Iowa Studies in Child Welfare, 13: No. 2, Part 3, 35–46 (1937).

57. Yedinack, Jeanette G. A study of the linguistic functioning of children with articulation and reading disabilities. Journal of Genetic Psychology, 74:23–59 (1949).

INDEX